Essential XML for Web Professionals

ISBN 0-13-066254-2

90000

9 780130 662545

The Prentice Hall Essential Web Professionals Series

Micah Brown, *Series Editor*

Essential XML
for Web
Professionals

Dan Livingston

Series Editor:
Micah Brown

Prentice Hall PTR
Upper Saddle River, NJ 07458
www.phptr.com

Library of Congress Cataloging-in-Publication Data

Livingston, Dan.
   Essential XML for Web professionals / Dan Livingston.
     p. cm. — (Prentice Hall essential Web professionals series)
   ISBN 0-13-066254-2
    1. XML (Document markup language) 2. Web sites—Design. 3. Internet
programming. I. Title. II. Series.

QA76.76.H94 L59 2001
005.7'2—dc21

2001036850

Editorial/Production Supervision: *Donna Cullen-Dolce*
Acquisitions Editor: *Karen McLean*
Manufacturing Buyer: *Alexis R. Heydt*
Cover Design: *Nina Scuderi*
Cover Design Director: *Jerry Votta*
Marketing Manager: *Jim Keogh*
Interior Design Manager: *Gail Cocker-Bogusz*
Interior Design: *Patti Guerrieri*

Prentice Hall books are widely used by corporations and government agencies for training, marketing, and resale.

The publisher offers discounts on this book when ordered in bulk quatities.

For more information, contact: Corporate Sales Department, Phone: 800-382-3419; Fax: 201-236-7141; E-mail: corpsales@prenhall.com; or write: Prentice Hall PTR, Corp. Sales Dept., One Lake Street, Upper Saddle River, NJ 07458.

Printed in the United States of America

ISBN 0-13-066254-2

Pearson Education LTD.
Pearson Education Australia PTY, Limited
Pearson Education Singapore, Pte. Ltd.
Pearson Education North Asia Ltd.
Pearson Education Canada, Ltd.
Pearson Educación de Mexico, S.A. de C.V.
Pearson Education—Japan
Pearson Education Malaysia, Pte. Ltd.

Contents

v

Foreword

XML is being ballyhooed as the Next Big Thing, and unlike B2B or push media (remember push?), it probably is. XML is the most exciting and significant thing to hit the Internet since HTML. The good news for you is it's fairly easy to learn (easier than HTML). Microsoft and many others are adopting and developing in XML. XML has the promise to make life a good bit easier for many programmers, so learning XML is a guaranteed marketable skill for the foreseeable future. In other words, learn XML and you'll make more money and your life will be easier. I'm not kidding—I'm seeing it happen to most of the people I know.

◆ Who This Book Is For

This book is aimed directly at Web developers, which includes both Web page authors and software developers whose applications run over the Web. You don't have to know HTML to learn XML, but it will help if you do. You don't have to know C, Java, PHP, Perl, JavaScript, or any other language. XML is a markup language, not a programming language.

◆ What You Will Learn

This book's purpose in life is to teach you XML so that you can go out into the world and start creating working, valid XML documents. This book is designed to take a novice and turn him or her into a professional XML developer within a few days.

XML comes in many flavors, and the most popular ones are covered here, such as DTDs, XML Schema, XHTML, XSLT, XLink, XPath, SMIL, and others. Sound like alphabet soup? Don't worry—at the end of this book you'll be able to dazzle clients and supervisors alike with your intimate knowledge of such things.

The examples in the book are also available on the Web at *www.wire-man.com/xml* and at *www.phptr.com/essential*. If you have any questions, complaints, comments or feedback, I welcome them at xmldan@wire-man.com. I'd love to hear from you.

◆ What You Will Not Learn

This book does not cover SAX, SOAP, XML-RPC, RSS, RDF, TREX, RELAX, and so on (Well, I cheated a little and covered DOM in the last chapter.)

This book is also not exhaustive—the world of XML is growing exponentially, and instead of overwhelming you with a million-page tome containing every possible form of XML, my goal is to take you from being a novice to being a professional. This book is a tutorial. There's certainly some good reference material in here, but my goal is to teach you XML, first and foremost.

Acknowledgments

I'd like to thank Karen McLean at Prentice Hall for giving me the chance to write this book. I had a great time doing it. Karen's been my editor for a few years now, and I'm always grateful for her insight. I'd also like to thank Bart Blanken for helping make this book become real.

Leon Atkinson gets my thanks for being my reality check and making sure everything in here is actually true.

Major thanks to my wife Tanya for all the support and encouragement, as always.

No thanks at all to my stupid cats, who kept knocking my notes off the desk and stepping on the keyboard. It's time for a dog.

This book was written to the music of the Beastie Boys, Eminem, and Metallica. The research for the XLink chapter was done in Maui. I want to do more research there.

About the Author

Coming from a background in marine zoology, Dan Livingston was drawn to Web design and development in early 1996. His Web sites, which have included high-profile clients such as Apple, Pacific Bell, Charles Schwab, and Landor, have won numerous awards, been praised by human interface expert Donald A. Norman, and been featured in design books and on CNN. His DHTML site Palette Man has received international recognition. Dan worked at the design firm Clear Ink before starting his own Web design and development company, Wire Man Productions. He continues to produce titles for Prentice Hall's Essential and Advanced series.

1 Introduction to XML

Welcome to the world of XML! The good news is that one of the reasons everyone's excited about XML is that it's easy to learn and to use. If you've had any exposure to HTML, you're ready to jump into XML with no worries. XML is also incredibly powerful—it's a simple tool that lets you create documents as complex as you need them to be, so you can use XML for simple little jobs or massive enterprise applications. Not only that, but Microsoft is getting behind XML in a big, big way—it's an integral part of .NET and HailStorm. So even if everyone else in the world abandons the promise of XML, anyone knowing it will still have a job.

◆ What XML Is

So what is this XML thing, really? XML stands for Extensible Markup Language (yes, it should be called EML, but everyone agreed XML was much cooler). To understand what an "Extensible Markup Language" can do, let's look first at what a "markup language" is, and then we'll look at the "extensible" part.

What's a Markup Language?

A markup language is a way of describing a document by placing tags in the document. HTML is an example of a simple markup language: you use bold tags and table tags to describe certain sections of words and numbers, and image tags to place the content of another file in the main file (that is, placing an image into a Web page). It's up to a Web browser to look at your HTML and decide what to do with it. When you create a document using XML, it looks a lot like HTML (see Example 1–1):

EXAMPLE 1–1 A SIMPLE XML DOCUMENT

```
<?xml version="1.0" ?>
<customers>
    <customer number="040">
        <name>Tony Basil</name>
        <customer_since year="1994" />
    </customer>
    <customer number="041">
        <name>Steve Perry</name>
        <customer_since year="2000" />
    </customer>
</customers>
```

Don't worry what this means or how to read it—I'm just giving you a little taste. See how there are beginning and ending tags, and how some tags are nested inside each other? It's just like HTML. This sort of marking up in a document is the sign of a markup language.

Markup languages differ from many other programming languages in that markup languages can't contain functions, conditional logic, or loops.

What's "Extensible?"

The "Extensible" part is important, because XML isn't really a markup language—it's a metamarkup language. That is, you'll use XML to create your very own markup language. In fact, when you use XML, you *have* to create your own markup language. Technically speaking, there's no such thing as a document written in XML, since they're all documents that use XML to create their own markup languages. This custom markup language is called an *XML-based language*. Think of XML as blue Play-Doh—a shapeless mass just waiting to be molded into something specific by your capable hands. When you create something out of this blue mass, you've created a *Play-Doh–based thing.* It's still Play-Doh, but you've made your own thing out of it. And instead of a blue sculpture, you've created a text document full of your custom markup language.

XML's functionality is also known as "providing arbitrary structure."

I'm going to do something that's technically inaccurate but will make both of our lives much easier: Let's agree that when we encounter a document that was written in XML, we'll call it an "XML document," even though it's technically an "XML application." If you find this offensive, you may flame me at danxml@wire-man.com.

Summary

So XML is a metamarkup language, which means it's a way for you to create any markup language you can dream up in plain old text. Doesn't sound too awe-inspiring, does it? Just wait— XML can do amazing stuff.

◆ What XML Is Good For

XML allows anybody to create their own information, mark it up in the way that makes the most sense to them, and send it to anyone else absolutely free. XML is an open standard, so you don't have to pay to use XML any more than you have to pay to use the alphabet.

XML was created so that richly structured documents could be used over the Web. That is, documents that have a very predictable and possibly complex structure can be shared over the Web. Documents that are richly structured can contain complex data—the kind of data used by big corporations.

Send Anything Anywhere to Anybody

The promise of XML is that it's an easy way for different applications to talk to each other. If an application can parse, or understand, XML, then it can send or receive any kind of information to any other application that understands XML. A handheld computer can talk to your refrigerator, which could talk to a customer database that talks to an enterprise CRM (customer relationship management) system, which contacts the handheld computer. Or, for a more down to earth example, imagine switching email clients without having to worry about which emails are associated with which client—if everything was in XML, all email clients could understand everything from all the other email clients. Right now, most of this information flow occurs through proprietary, expensive systems that only a few applications are allowed to understand. As an example of why this is important: the last language that offered this ease of use was HTML. HTML certainly has become wildly popular, and only Web servers and browsers can handle HTML.

Everyone Can Understand Everything

Some of you may already be asking, "But how can anyone else understand this custom language I just created out of thin air?" The short answer is that when you send someone an XML document, you also send the dictionary to your custom language. If an application knows XML, then it can use that dictionary to read any document in your markup language.

XML is the computer equivalent of the Babel fish from the book *The Hitchhiker's Guide to the Galaxy* by Douglas Adams. If you haven't read this book, the Babel fish is a fictional little beast that looks likes a goldfish but lives in one's ear. This fish can translate anything it hears into the language of its host. So, if you have a Babel fish in your ear, you can understand anything anyone says to you. XML works the same way. If an application can parse XML, then it can understand any XML document that gets sent its way (as long as the dictionary file comes along with it).

Write Once, Display Everywhere

Imagine this: you write a brilliant column describing how using clusters of nanosatellites instead one large satellite can generally reduce development costs by 50% and production time by 30%. It turns out to be wildly popular and your publisher wants it in their magazine, on the Web site in HTML, on a CD, and in Word and PDF format for download.

Usually, this would mean many different copies of an original article—one in Word format, one in HTML, one in Quark, one in PDF, etc. If something needs to be changed in the article, it has to be changed in all of those versions, which can be difficult and time-consuming to do. However, if your article was in XML and stored in a central place, all of those applications could look at the information in that single XML document and display it in that application's own special way. If the article has to be altered, you make the change to the one XML file, and all of the applications can look at the same place to update the version they have.

Free and Clear

XML is free from any intellectual property restrictions. There are no patents, trademarks, copyrights, or trade secrets that you will ever have to worry about. This is because XML is a specification created by the World Wide Web Consortium (W3C), the same folks that brought you HTML. As a result, XML is free to the world and well documented to boot. For a little easy reading, the specification can be found at *www.w3.org/XML* and in Appendix A.

Save the Data

Odd as it may seem, the onset of computers and digital media may result in the long-term loss of much more data than if the data was written on paper. For example, if you have a VisiCalc spreadsheet on a 5 1/4" disk, it won't be easy to get that information back without spending a lot of time and energy. If the file is in something crazy like Lotus Jazz, it may be lost to the world forever. There are some data formats out there that no one knows how to read because they were never documented.

XML solves this problem by being a very simple data format—it's just text, and text is pretty darn resistant to corruption. You can corrupt parts of a text document without much affecting the other parts.

◆ A Brief History of XML

XML's granddaddy is SGML, Standard Generalized Markup Language. SGML is powerful, and often used by the defense industry and anyone else who deals with large quantities of structured data. Unfortunately, SGML is mind-bendingly complex and almost as mind-bendingly expensive: On the low end, Adobe's Framemaker + SGML 6.0 retails for $1449. If you need to use SGML, you already know about it, and either someone else would be paying for it or you'd be using Jade, a complex, open-source SGML parser.

Technically, XML is a direct descendent of SGML. XML essentially simplifies SGML by throwing out a lot of mostly useless stuff.

XML's closest sibling is HTML, which is a super-simplified version of SGML that even you and I can understand. HTML's purpose in life is to describe hypertext documents. While HTML is wonderfully simple to learn, it's quite limited: It only understands a handful of tags whose main purpose is to format text.

HTML isn't very good at describing what data means, only what it should look like. In other words, HTML is just a picture of information.

Some folks at the W3C decided to create a language that combines the power of SGML with the simplicity of HTML, and XML is what they came up with. As it turns out, they did a really good job—there isn't much that SGML can do that XML can't, and in some ways it's easier to learn than HTML.

When the W3C put together XML, they had some very specific goals in mind:

1. *XML shall be straightforwardly usable over the Internet.* Ideally, users will be able to view XML documents as easily as HTML documents. This is only true for a few browsers right now, but XML support is expected to grow.

2. *XML shall support a wide variety of applications.* That is, XML should be useful to a number of applications, not just Web browsers. Applications that allow authoring, content analysis, image creation, and so on should benefit from incorporating XML.

3. *XML shall be compatible with SGML.* Most of the folks who worked on defining XML are intimately familiar with the sometimes mind-blowing amount of data in SGML that many large corporations have. If XML is to have a chance of being really useful, the SGML → XML translation must be a simple one.

4. *It shall be easy to write programs that process XML documents.* The word "easy" here means that it should take two weeks for a computer science graduate student to write a program that can process an XML document. At least, that's the informal guideline that was used.

5. *The number of optional features in XML is to be kept to the absolute minimum, ideally zero.* Optional features often cause compatibility problems, since one application may understand the optional feature, while the other may not. Two examples are Netscape's `<layer>` tag and Internet Explorer's `<iframe>` tag. Both are great features, but useless in any other browser.

6. *XML documents should be human-legible and reasonably clear.* You should be able to look at raw XML and pretty much figure out what the content means.

7. *The XML design should be prepared quickly.* This is a message to the group that created XML from themselves. Standards efforts are usually as zippy as a lazy glacier, and the need for XML was immediate.

8. *The design of XML shall be formal and concise.* Essentially, XML should be easy for machines to understand, not just humans. Machines are very good at understanding documents that are built according to a small set of rules that are absolutely followed.

9. *XML documents shall be easy to create.* While there are some very fancy (and useful) XML editors on the market, you don't need anything fancier than a basic text editor (for example, NotePad or SimpleText) to create an XML document.

10. *Terseness in XML markup is of minimal importance.* Or, "no shortcuts." SGML has several features that minimize key-strokes, and while this decreases typing time, it makes the document harder to read and understand for both people and machines. Thus, XML does not include these features.

Did the W3C succeed in meeting their goals? Most people think they did, and admirably. But who cares what people think? After you're done with this book, you'll be able to decide for yourself.

◆ Recap

We've looked at the big picture in this chapter—what this XML thing really is, what it looks like, what it can do, where it came from, and why it's here. This is all important to know, but too much big-picture stuff makes my head hurt. In the next chapter, we'll get into some real XML!

2 Your First XML

IN THIS CHAPTER

- Overview
- Elements & Nodes
- Structure & Syntax
- Attributes
- Viewing XML
- Comments and the Five Special Symbols
- Recap

We'll start writing our first real XML by creating documents for a fictional company called Stitch, *an online fashion magazine. In the process, we'll look at all of the parts of an XML document and what they're called, and we'll look all of the rules for creating a perfect XML document (there aren't that many).*

◆ Overview

Stitch is a company with an online store that sells shirts, sweatshirts, and some other stuff. When a customer places an order for a number of items in different sizes and colors, they will want to know whether all of those items in the ordered amounts are in stock. Imagine that in order to get this information, the Web site sends an XML document describing the order to a program that compares the order to the warehouse's database, and answers with, "Yes, those items are in stock," or "No, we don't have all of those right now."

That means our XML document has to list all the items in the order, including the color, size, and how many of each item. We'll look at an example of this document, and then examine it in detail.

The *Stitch* Store looks like Figure 2–1. The user can choose from shirts, sweatshirts, hats, mugs, and martini glasses, and drag that item to their shopping cart.

The user drags one or more items to the shopping cart and determines the size and quantity. When they hit the "Buy! Now!" button, our program creates an XML document that represents the order and sends it to the program at the warehouse. Such a document could look something like Example 2–1.

FIGURE 2–1 The *Stitch* Store

EXAMPLE 2–1 SAMPLE ORDER IN XML

```
<?xml version="1.0" ?>
<order>

    <shirts>
        <shirt quantity="4">
            <size>XXL</size>
            <color>purple</color>
        </shirt>
        <shirt quantity="1">
            <size>M</size>
            <color>red</color>
        </shirt>
    </shirts>

    <sweatshirts>
        <sweatshirt quantity="1">
            <size>XL</size>
            <color>blue</color>
        </sweatshirt>
        <sweatshirt quantity="2">
            <size>XL</size>
            <color>red</color>
        </sweatshirt>
    </sweatshirts>

    <hats>
        <hat color="gray" quantity="1" />
        <hat color="bronze" quantity="342" />
    </hats>

    <mug quantity="1" />

    <martiniGlasses quantity="0" />

</order>
```

Now let's start taking this thing apart.

◆ Elements & Nodes

In XML, tags are known as *elements* or *nodes*. The terms are more or less interchangeable. In the above example, the `<hat>` tag is both an element and a node, as are `<sweatshirts>` and `<martiniGlasses>`. Depending on where they are, some elements/nodes have special names.

Types of Elements

For example, the tag that encompasses all other tags is called the *root element*. In this example, the <order> tag is the root element.

When an element (or tag or node) is nested inside another, the element on the inside is called a *child* of the outer element. In this case, the term "node" is used more often than "element." For example, <size> is a *child node* of <shirt>. The <shirt> node is a child node of <shirts>.

Nodes that are on the same level are called *sister nodes*. For example, <size> and <color> are sister nodes. The five different products you can buy are also sister nodes: <shirts>, <sweatshirts>, <hats>, <mugs>, and <martiniGlasses>.

Technically, even the text between the opening and closing tags of an element is a special kind of node called a *text node*. For example, in <size>XXL</size>, "XXL" is a text node.

Empty Elements

You've probably noticed that some elements have closing tags and some don't. The rule in XML is that every tag has to be closed in some way. However if there isn't anything inside an element—no text or other tags—then you can simply place a forward slash as the last character in the tag. For example, we can use <mugs quantity="1" /> instead of <mugs quantity="1"></mugs>.

Naming Elements

XML is pretty lenient when is comes to the names of your elements. Element names can begin with a letter, an underscore (_), or a colon (:), though I recommend sticking with letters except in special cases we'll examine later. The rest of the element's name can consist of any number of letters, numbers, underscores, hyphens, colons, and periods.

You should also know that element names are case sensitive. For example, <CAT> is a completely different element than <Cat> or <cat>.

◆ Structure & Syntax

There are some structural rules that have to be followed in any XML document. Within those rules, you can be as flexible and inventive as you want. If your document follows all of these rules, then your XML is called *well-formed*. XML that isn't well-formed will be rejected and ignored by almost every XML parser.

You should note that HTML does not work this way. The XML people thought it would be good to force applications to read only proper XML to prevent software companies from changing the language arbitrarily, such as with the <BLINK> tag. Yep, this is a good correction.

Root Element

Every XML document must have a root element. The root element is a tag that encloses all of the other tags except the intital <?xml ?> line (see Example 2–2).

EXAMPLE 2–2 BASIC STRUCTURE OF AN XML DOCUMENT

```
<?xml version="1.0" ?>
<root_element>
    ... everything else ...
</root_element>
```

In Example 2–1, the root element is <order>.

Closing Tags

Unlike HTML, XML tags must be closed. In HTML, you can get away with using <p> without the corresponding </p>. Not so in XML. In those cases when the tag to be used doesn't warrant a closing tag, end the tag with a forward slash (see Example 2–3).

EXAMPLE 2–3 EXAMPLES OF CLOSING TAGS

```
<?xml version="1.0" ?>
<root_element>
    <tag1>La la la</tag1>
    <tag2 name="Space Station" />
</root_element>
```

Notice that root_element and tag1 need closing tags, but tag2 simply ends with a />, which is a shortcut for </tag2>.

Proper Nesting

Unlike HTML, XML tags must be properly nested. In HTML, you can get away with zap!, but not in XML. If tag2 is started inside tag1, tag2 must be closed before </tag1>.

Values Must Be in Quotation Marks

XML allows for attributes, like the `name="Space Station"` in `tag2` of Example 2–3. Unlike HTML, where you can get away without using quotation marks, like `<table border=0>`, XML requires attribute values to be enclosed in quotation marks.

XML Version Declaration

The first line of any XML document should spell out which version is being used (1.0 is the only version available right now). This declaration is inside a special kind of tag called a *processing instruction*. All processing instructions start with `<?` and end with `?>`. This is a special kind of tag, so it doesn't need a closing tag.

This version declaration is optional, but if you include it, it has to be on the first line of your document. Later in this book we'll look at other processing instructions that can be included in the version declaration.

◆ Attributes

Hopefully, the concepts of attributes are familiar to you from HTML. For example, in `<img src="dog.gif">`, the attribute is `src="dog.gif"`. In Example 2–3, the `tag2` element has an attribute: `name="Space Station"`. Elements in XML can have an unlimited number of attributes.

Attributes have two parts: the name and the value. For the image tag above, the name is `src` and the value is `dog.gif`. Nope, the value doesn't include the quotation marks. In the `tag2` example, the name is `name` and the value is `Space Station`.

Rules about Attributes

As mentioned earlier, the values of attributes must be enclosed in quotation marks. You can't get away with anything like `border=0` in XML. If the value of your attribute has a double quote inside of it, you can enclose the whole value in single quotes (just like JavaScript). For example, `attName='"this is my value," she said'` is perfectly valid.

The rules for naming attributes are the same for naming elements: names can begin with a letter, an underscore (_), or a colon (:), and the rest of the name can consist of letters, numbers, underscores, hyphens, colons, and periods. Names can be as long as you want them to be.

Use of Attributes vs. Text Nodes

It may seem like attributes and text nodes could serve the same purpose. For example, look at the two snippets below.

```
<shirt>
    <size>XXL</size>
</shirt>
```

and

```
<shirt size="XXL" />
```

They encapsulate the same information, just in different ways. Which one is better—text node or attribute? Well, that's really a judgement call—it's up to you to decide. Generally, the information in attributes is considered less significant than the information in elements. The role of an attribute is to describe the content that follows it.

◆ Viewing XML

At this writing, the only reliable way to view XML in a browser is to use Internet Explorer (IE). This may be fine, since by the time this book hits the shelves, Netscape may be nothing more than a melancholy memory. Figure 2–2 shows what Example 2–1 looks like in IE5.

It's not really fancy, but IE has a nifty little feature. Did you notice the little dashes that were in front of some of the tags? IE put those dashes there. If you're following along at home, click on those dashes. The tags are collapsed and the dashes turn to pluses, as in Figure 2–3.

In the next chapter, we'll need a more powerful parsing tool than Internet Explorer provides, but it's good enough for this chapter.

◆ Comments and the Five Special Symbols

It's usually helpful to add some documentation and annotation to your documents. Fortunately, XML comments look like HMTL comments: they start with `<!--` and end with `-->`. The only difference is that XML doesn't allow you to place double hyphens inside comments.

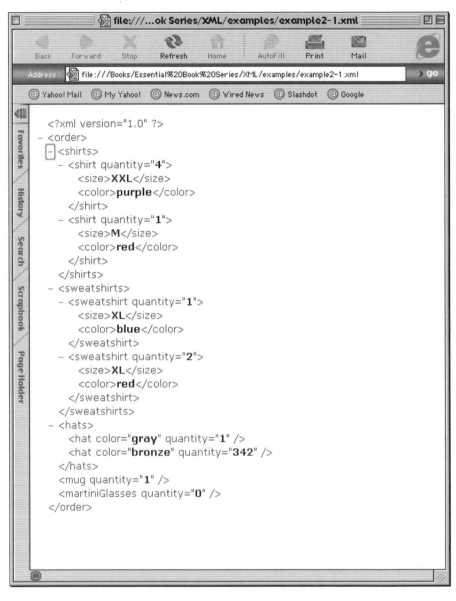

```
<?xml version="1.0" ?>
- <order>
  - <shirts>
    - <shirt quantity="4">
        <size>XXL</size>
        <color>purple</color>
      </shirt>
    - <shirt quantity="1">
        <size>M</size>
        <color>red</color>
      </shirt>
    </shirts>
  - <sweatshirts>
    - <sweatshirt quantity="1">
        <size>XL</size>
        <color>blue</color>
      </sweatshirt>
    - <sweatshirt quantity="2">
        <size>XL</size>
        <color>red</color>
      </sweatshirt>
    </sweatshirts>
  - <hats>
      <hat color="gray" quantity="1" />
      <hat color="bronze" quantity="342" />
    </hats>
    <mug quantity="1" />
    <martiniGlasses quantity="0" />
  </order>
```

FIGURE 2–2 Displaying Example 2–1

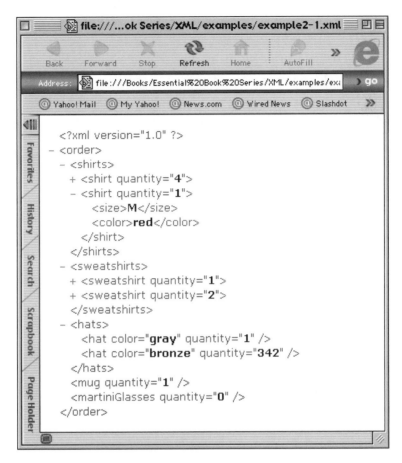

FIGURE 2–3 Some collapsed tags

Another similarity to HTML is XML's five special symbols, which look a lot like HTML entities. The five symbols are

- `&amp;`—this displays an ampersand (&)
- `&lt;`—this displays a less than sign (<)
- `&gt;`—this displays a greater than sign (>)
- `&quot;`—this displays a double quote (")
- `&apos;`—this displays a single quote (')

Unlike HTML, these are the only symbols/entities that you can use without pre-defining them in your DTD (we'll cover that in the next chapter). Here's an example of their use:

```
<needALoan>If value of home &lt; 200,000, no loan for
you!</needALoan>
```

◆ Recap

We've started writing a little more XML, and we've looked at all of the really important rules for creating an XML document. Not too bad, was it? Most languages take a lot longer to learn, but since XML is a metamarkup language, it's just a set of rules that allow you to create your own language (that's what the "extensible" part of its name means). It might be helpful to imagine that XML is an alphabet, and it's up to you to decide what your language's words are.

3 Defining XML: DTDs

You've heard that XML is metamarkup language—that is, it allows you to create your very own markup language. However, you can't go creating this new language willy-nilly. XML does have a few rules that absolutely have to be followed. When you create this custom markup language of yours, you also have to provide a dictionary for that language. One way to do that is to provide a DTD.

◆ What Is a DTD?

DTD stands for document type definition. A document type definition is a text document that defines all the parts of your XML document: all the elements, attributes, lists, entities, their properties, and their relationships to each other. Let's look at Example 3–1, which is slightly tweaked from last chapter.

EXAMPLE 3–1 AN ORDER FROM THE *STITCH* STORE

```
<?xml version="1.0" ?>
<order>

    <shirt_list>
        <shirt quantity="4">
            <size>XXL</size>
            <color>purple</color>
        </shirt>
        <shirt quantity="1">
            <size>M</size>
            <color>red</color>
        </shirt>
    </shirt_list>

    <sweatshirt_list>
        <sweatshirt quantity="1">
            <size>XL</size>
            <color>blue</color>
        </sweatshirt>
        <sweatshirt quantity="2">
            <size>XL</size>
            <color>red</color>
        </sweatshirt>
    </sweatshirt_list>

    <hat_list>
        <hat color="gray" quantity="1" />
        <hat color="bronze" quantity="342" />
    </hat_list>

    <mugs quantity="1" />

    <martiniGlasses quantity="0" />

</order>
```

Without writing a DTD, we can figure out what it will say; there's such a thing as an <order> and within that order there are `<shirts>`, `<sweatshirts>`, `<hats>`, and so on. Certain items come in sizes and colors, while others don't vary at all.

A DTD can live inside of an XML document, so the document can come with its own dictionary, or the DTD can be in a separate file. When a DTD is in a separate file, it's called an external DTD. External DTDs can be much more useful that internal ones. Let's see why.

◆ Why DTDs Are Good

If every programmer on earth created his or her own markup language, XML wouldn't be too useful. The thing that gives XML a serious punch is that multiple documents can use the same DTD. That probably doesn't sound earth-shattering, so let's look at it a little closer.

Imagine that all the chemists out there want their computers to communicate with all the other chemists. Chemical notation can be a tricky thing to create in different programs. The Russian scientist using WordPerfect 2 can't readily share formulas with the San Diegan using Office XP. There isn't any sort of standard. Now, if some central body of chemists, like the American Chemical Society, comes forth with a DTD that defines a special Chemical Notation XML, suddenly all of those scientists have a standard way to communicate with each other. They can create XML documents that conform to a single standard DTD. It doesn't matter which word processor they're using—they can send each other XML files and no one is forced to have a certain word processor. All of their documents link to the same DTD that lives somewhere on the Internet.

Many organizations have already done this: Chemical Markup Language already exists, as do MathML, HRXML (for job descriptions and resumes), and many others. We'll be examining a few Web-related ones later on in Chapter 13.

Testing Your DTD

How can you tell if the DTD you're writing actually works? Unfortunately, Internet Explorer won't help us here. IE checks your XML to see if it's *well-formed* (that is, follows proper XML syntax), but it doesn't check if your XML is *valid*, that is, if your XML follows the rules set in the DTD.

The program I've found to be most useful in writing XML is called XML Spy. It's a Windows-only program, and you can download a 30-day trial version at *http://www.xmlspy.com*. Once

you have it installed and running, make sure you choose View →
Text View. Otherwise, your document will be displayed in a
fancy, collapsible system that doesn't look anything like the code
in this book.

Calling an External DTD

So how do you link one of these DTDs to your XML document?
All you have to do is add a single line to your code.

```
<?xml version="1.0" standalone="no" ?>

<!DOCTYPE order SYSTEM "stitchStore.dtd">

<order>
    …
</order>
```

Yep, it's the DOCTYPE line that calls the DTD. We're referenc-
ing a DTD and immediately stating the name of the root element
(in this case, order). It's a SYSTEM DTD, which means that it's
just some DTD we wrote and that's it's in an external file—it's
not a serious, accepted standard. Then, we state where this DTD
actually is: in this case, it's in a nearby file called stitch-
Store.dtd. Except for a few cases, we'll be spending our time in
this book calling an external DTD.

Did you notice the <?xml ?> line? We added a new attribute:
standalone="no". This tells the XML parser that there's a DTD
to be retrieved. This attribute isn't necessary, but it increases the
document's readability.

Calling a Public DTD

Much of the time, you'll want to access a DTD that's a standard
(i.e., that some industry has given their official stamp of approval to). Accessing these DTDs is a little different than accessing a local DTD. Here's the syntax:

```
<!DOCTYPE root_element PUBLIC dtd_name "url">
```

Naming a public DTD is surprisingly complex, because DTD
names have their own syntax. Here's an example:

```
-//Irving Archibite//DTD Stitch_store//EN//
```

The minus sign in front can also be a plus sign: use minus if
the DTD hasn't been approved by a standards body (like the In-

ternational Standards Organization, or ISO) and use the plus sign if it has been approved by such an organization.

After either the plus or the minus sign, type two slashes and the owner of the DTD. Then, two more slashes, the letters DTD, and the label of the DTD. This label is often a very short description of the DTD. To finish it off, type two more slashes, a two-letter code for the language (EN stands for English), and top it off with another pair of slashes.

◆ Defining Elements

To build this DTD, we'll be starting out simple and getting more complicated. So Example 3–2 is the first XML document that we're going to write a DTD for:

EXAMPLE 3–2 SIMPLE XML AND DTD

```
<?xml version="1.0" standalone="no" ?>

<!DOCTYPE order  SYSTEM "example3-2.dtd">

<order>9 shirts</order>
```

and here's the DTD:

```
<!--
    This is the DTD for example 3-2
-->

<!ELEMENT order (#PCDATA)>
```

HOW THE CODE WORKS

Clearly, the only important line in the DTD is the `<!ELEMENT>` line. This line defines an element called `order`, and determines that any kind of text can be inside of that element. The `#PCDATA` stands for *parsed character data*, which are letters, numbers, and just about everything else except other tags.

The above DTD allows for any XML document that looks like this:

```
<order>
    any kind of text in here
</order>
```

This DTD does not allow for the presence of other elements in `<order>`. The example below would not be allowed by our DTD because of the presence of the `<shirts>` element:

```
<order>
    <shirts>17 purple XXL</shirts>
</order>
```

Nor would the example below be allowed—elements cannot nest inside themselves.

```
<order>
    <order>42 martini glasses</order>
</order>
```

However, we actually want other elements to live inside the `<order>` element, so we need to modify this DTD. Let's look at the XML document we want to create a DTD for (Example 3–3), and then we'll check out the new DTD.

EXAMPLE 3–3 NESTED ELEMENTS AND DTD

```
<?xml version="1.0" standalone="no" ?>

<!DOCTYPE order   SYSTEM "example3-3.dtd">

<order>
    <shirt_list>
        <shirt>
            <size>XXL</size>
            <color>purple</color>
        </shirt>
    </shirt_list>
</order>
```

And here's the DTD:

```
<!--
    This is the DTD for example 3-3
-->
```

1. `<!ELEMENT order (shirt_list)>`
2. `<!ELEMENT shirt_list (shirt)>`
`<!ELEMENT shirt (size,color)>`

3. `<!ELEMENT size (#PCDATA)>`
`<!ELEMENT color (#PCDATA)>`

HOW THE CODE WORKS

1. Let's start with `<order>`. Notice that inside of the parentheses (which you always have to use), we have the name of another element called `shirt_list` instead of `#PCDATA`. This means that a `<shirt_list>` element can appear inside the `<order>` element. You should know that an element can contain other elements or text, but not both.

2. We then define two more elements, `shirt_list` and `shirt`, each of which have elements that appear inside of them: A single `shirt` element can be inside `shirt_list`, and the elements `size` and `color` can appear inside `shirt`. Note that we used commas to separate the different elements that can appear inside `shirt`.

3. Finally, we create two elements that just contain text: `size` and `color`.

◆ Advanced Element Definition (or Making Children Behave)

So far, we aren't able to do much with elements. We can define them and determine whether they contain a single instance of one or more other elements, or whether they just contain character data. We don't have a way to say, "This element can occur more than once," or "This element may or may not exist." In short, we do not yet have any decent tools to control the behavior of children elements. The good news is that the purpose of this section is to give you those tools. The bad news is… well, we'll discuss it later—it isn't so bad.

One or More Children

In the example above, there can be only a single order of shirts. That is, only a single `<shirt>` element can exist inside `<shirt_list>`. Not much of a list, is it? Fortunately, we can introduce a little flexibility. In the line that defines the `shirt_list` element, we add a plus sign that will allow for any number of shirt elements, as long as there is at least one.

```
<!ELEMENT shirt_list (shirt+)>
```

With this method, we can assure that `shirt_list` will have at least a single `shirt` listed, and has no upper boundary. We don't have to change any other line in the DTD—not even the line that defines the `shirt` element.

Zero or More Children

If this was a real order from a real online store, we couldn't guarantee that someone is going to buy a shirt. It's possible that a customer may order zero shirts, or they may buy 100 of them. To allow for zero or more elements, we use an asterisk instead of a plus sign.

```
<!ELEMENT shirt_list (shirt*)>
```

So a plus sign means one or more elements can appear, and an asterisk means that zero or more elements can appear. We're not done yet—you can also determine that only zero or one element appears.

Zero or One Children

Let's expand our document to include mugs (see Example 3–4).

EXAMPLE 3–4 AN ORDER WITH MUGS

```
<?xml version="1.0" standalone="no"?>

<!DOCTYPE order SYSTEM "example3-4.dtd">
<order>
    <shirt_list>
        <shirt>
            <size>XXL</size>
            <color>purple</color>
        </shirt>
    </shirt_list>
    <mugs>90</mugs>
</order>
```

In this order, a customer is asking for both shirts and a bunch of mugs. There's only one list of shirts and only one kind of mug. Thus, the `shirt_list` and `mugs` elements might occur once or not at all (by the way, we're assuming there's only one kind of mug). To allow an element to occur once or never, use a question mark. In this case:

```
<!--
    This is the DTD for example 3-4
```

```
-->
<!ELEMENT order (shirt_list?, mugs?)>

<!ELEMENT shirt_list (shirt*)>
<!ELEMENT shirt (size, color)>
<!ELEMENT size (#PCDATA)>
<!ELEMENT color (#PCDATA)>

<!ELEMENT mugs (#PCDATA)>
```

HOW THE CODE WORKS

The question mark method is used on the `order` definition. Notice that both elements inside `order` can occur either zero or one times. That is, `shirt_list` may be present and `mugs` may be present, but neither will show up more than once, and it's possible that neither will be there (in which case we have a very short order).

Specific Number of Children

Let's say that the *Stitch* store is running a special offer: If a customer buys at least three different kinds of shirts, he or she gets a discount. How do we specify that our XML order form must have at least three shirt elements? There isn't a clean way to specify how many times an element may appear inside another, but there is a relatively simple workaround. If the customer must buy at least three different kinds of shirts, then this code would work:

```
<!ELEMENT shirt_list (shirt, shirt, shirt+)>
```

Hopefully, the rule isn't that the customer has to buy a thousand different shirt styles (this is the bad news I was talking about earlier—not so terrible, is it?).

Choosing Among Children

Now suppose that we're adding martini glasses to the *Stitch* store. However, a customer may only choose to buy some martini glasses or buy some mugs, but not both, because the expense of shipping glass and porcelain is too much when there are both mugs and martini glasses in the same shipment. In other words, in the `order` element, users may choose shirts, and either mugs or martini glasses. How do we do this?

```
<!ELEMENT order (shirt_list?, (mugs | martiniGlasses)?) >
```

HOW THE CODE WORKS

We're doing a couple different things in this line. First, we're allowing either `mugs` or `martiniGlasses` to be an element in `order`, but not both. The vertical line (|) means "or." We're also grouping `mugs` and `martiniGlasses` together with parentheses, because we want that pair to be treated differently than `shirt_list`. So what's allowed in the XML that's based on this DTD? There are all the possible combinations:

1. `shirt_list`
2. `shirt_list, mugs`
3. `shirt_list, martiniGlasses`
4. `mugs`
5. `martiniGlasses`
6. `[nothing]`

If we wanted the customer's order to contain only a single kind of item, either shirts or mugs or martini glasses, then the code would look like this:

```
<!ELEMENT order (shirt_list | mugs | martiniGlasses)?>
```

Twins

If we wanted to go nuts, we could demand that if the customer buys any mugs, then they *have* to order some martini glasses as well. How do we code for this kind of mandatory pairing? Simple!

```
<!ELEMENT order (shirt_list?, (mugs, martiniGlasses)?)>
```

Maybe Children, Maybe Not

As specific as DTDs can get, they can also get equally vague, with the most ambiguous code you can write is:

```
<!ELEMENT order ANY>
```

This means that anything can go in the order element. The contents still have to be either other elements or character data, but there are no rules as to which elements, how many of them, or what order they have to be in. Try to stay away from ANY—the whole idea of XML is to build structured data, and if you're using ANY, there's a chance you haven't thought through your structure well enough.

◆ Element Definition Summary

We've gone over a lot of rules: let's review them in Table 3–1.

TABLE 3–1 Summary of Element Definition Rules

Code	Description
`<!ELEMENT foo (bar)>`	`bar` may appear inside `foo` once
`<!ELEMENT foo (bar, bar)>`	`bar` may appear twice and only twice inside `foo`
`<!ELEMENT foo (bar, zip)>`	`bar` and `zip` may appear once inside `foo`
`<!ELEMENT foo (bar?)>`	`bar` may appear once or not at all inside `foo`
`<!ELEMENT foo (bar+)>`	`bar` can appear any number of times inside `foo`, with a minimum of at least one appearance
`<!ELEMENT foo (bar*)>`	`bar` can appear any number of times inside `foo`, whether zero or 3000
`<!ELEMENT foo (bar | zip)>`	Either `bar` or `zip` can appear once inside foo, but not both
`<!ELEMENT foo ANY>`	Anything can go inside the element
`<!ELEMENT foo EMPTY>`	Nothing can go inside the element (except attributes)

Also, your element definitions can be in any order in your DTD. That is, you don't have to start by defining your root element and working your way down. You can define any element at any time.

◆ Defining Attributes

Any element in XML can have an unlimited number of attributes. Here are two elements with attributes:

```
<shirt quantity="1">
<hat color="gray" quantity="7" />
```

The `shirt` element has a `quantity` attribute with a value of 1. The `hat` element has two attributes: `color` and `quantity`, with values of "gray" and "7," respectively. To allow for an attribute in a DTD, use this format:

```
<!ATTLIST elementName attributeName type default>
```

Creating an attribute actually involves more choices on your part as a programmer than creating an element. Here are some of the questions you *must* answer to create your attribute:

1. Is the attribute optional?
2. Does the attribute have a default value?
3. Can the attribute's value be anything, or are there restrictions?

We'll start by examining all the possibilities for setting a default value in your attribute.

◆ Setting Default Values

Let's look at an example. If an attribute is optional and its value can be anything, then this will work:

```
<!ATTLIST shirt quantity CDATA #IMPLIED>
```

In this case, the type is CDATA, which stands for "character data." It's similar to the #PCDATA we saw earlier, but without the P and the #. The value of a CDATA attribute can be anything you can type (except other elements, of course).

We've also described the default state of this attribute as #IMPLIED, which means that the attribute is optional. If an attribute is not optional and must be present, then we use #REQUIRED:

```
<!ATTLIST shirt quantity CDATA #REQUIRED>
```

When either #IMPLIED or #REQUIRED are used, you cannot set a default value for your attribute. All you're saying is, "This attribute must exist," or "This attribute is optional." To set a default value, you have two choices. Let's look at the easy one first:

```
<!ATTLIST shirt quantity CDATA "1">
```

We forego using #IMPLIED or #REQUIRED in favor of simply stating what the default value is. This means that if the attribute is not set in the XML document, the parser is instructed to insert that attribute and its value. For example, if your XML document may include:

```
<shirt>
    <size>XXL</size>
    <color>blue</color>
</shirt>
```

If an XML parser saw this XML combined with the `ATTLIST` above, it would insert the `quantity` attribute, as if had already existed in the XML document. However, if the XML document already has a `quantity` attribute, say `<shirt quantity="9">`, then the value of 9 overrides the default value of 1.

Here's the final way to define the default state of your attribute:

```
<!ATTLIST shirt quantity CDATA #FIXED "1">
```

By inserting a `#FIXED` before the default value, you say that the attribute's value can only be 1. If the XML document does not include the attribute, the XML parser inserts it. If the attribute is in the XML document, it has to have the same value as the default value. For example, `<shirt quantity="5">` would result in an error, because `quantity` is fixed: it must to be equal to 1.

This can be a little confusing, so let's look at all four states, as well as a few examples of invalid code (see Table 3–2).

TABLE 3–2 Attribute Default States and Syntax

Code	Description
`<!ATTLIST foo bar CDATA "default">`	If this attribute is not in the XML document, the parser automatically includes it, and the attribute's value is default. If the attribute is included in the XML document, then that value overrides the default value.
`<!ATTLIST foo bar CDATA #FIXED "default">`	If this attribute is not in the XML document, the parser automatically includes it, and the attribute's value is default. If the attribute is included in the XML document, then that value must equal the default value.
`<!ATTLIST foo bar CDATA #REQUIRED>`	This attribute must exist an XML document that references the DTD.
`<!ATTLIST foo bar CDATA #IMPLIED>`	This attribute may or may not exist in the XML document.
`<!ATTLIST foo bar CDATA #FIXED "default" #REQUIRED>`	INVALID. Default states cannot be combined.
`<!ATTLIST foo bar CDATA "default" #IMPLIED>`	INVALID. Default states cannot be combined.

Think you have default states down? Great! Let's move on to all the different types of attributes.

◆ Setting and Choosing Attribute Types

The attribute type of CDATA is the only one we've looked at so far, and it's the most permissive—just about anything can go in a CDATA attribute. However, there are many others, and we'll be looking at each one.

Enumerated

The next most common type after CDATA is called "Enumerated," which really means a list of acceptable values. For example:

```
<!ATTLIST hats color (red | blue | green) #REQUIRED>
```

This means that there are only three allowed values for the color attribute: red, blue, or green. Any other value, like "yellow" or "bordeaux," will result in invalid XML. Notice that you don't have to enclose the characters in quotes. Also, you don't actually type the word "Enumerated" anywhere. You just create a list of possible values and voila! Your attribute has a type of Enumerated. Make sure your list is enclosed by parentheses and a vertical bar separates each entry.

SIDE NOTE

You may be asking yourself how to create an attribute value that has a quote in it. Don't worry—that's handled via *entities,* which we'll examine later in this chapter.

Also, the vertical bar is actually optional. You can just separate the attribute value options with a single space and your DTD will still be valid. However, your code will be easier to read if you include the vertical bar, and I recommend you always use it.

It is possible to create a list with only a single thing in it. For example,

```
<!ATTLIST hats color (red) #REQUIRED>
```

Here's a brain-teaser: What's the difference, if any, between the previous line and the following one:

```
<!ATTLIST hats color CDATA #FIXED "red">
```

Think about it . . . There is a difference, but it's subtle.

Figured it out? The only difference is that with the first line, the XML document *must* have the attribute present. In the second, the attribute doesn't have to be present because the parser will insert it if it's missing.

Let's look at one more.

```
<!ATTLIST hats color (red) #FIXED "blue">
```

What would happen here? Well, if you tried to run a DTD with this line, the XML parser would reject it, because you're giving the parser conflicting instructions. The only allowable value should be "red" or "blue", but it definitely can't be both. So this line of code is invalid.

That's it for Enumerated. The next types in line are ID, IDREF, IDREFS, NMTOKEN, and NMTOKENS. There are also some types called ENTITY, ENTITIES, and NOTATION, but we'll deal with those separately later in this chapter.

ID

The goal of an ID attribute is to create a unique element in an XML document. The value of an ID attribute must be unique and nonrepeating in the document—no other ID attribute may have the same value. ID attributes are great for product codes, customer IDs, SKUs, or anything else that requires a unique value.

The value of an ID attribute must be a valid XML element name. That is, it can start with a letter or an underscore, which can be followed by letters, numbers, underscores, periods, and hyphens. This can be annoying, because it means that you can't use a value that has all numbers (which many ID codes are). Let's imagine this line is in your XML's DTD.

```
<!ATTLIST shirt product_code ID #REQUIRED>
```

In which case, the XML could be

```
<shirt product_code = "sh_2398">
```

If this line of code existed, then no other element could have an attribute value of "sh_2398", even if it's a different element with a different attribute.

IDREF

The IDREF type allows an attribute to refer to an ID attribute elsewhere in the document. The value of an IDREF attribute must be equal to the value of an ID attribute in the XML document. For example, let's imagine we want to send the URLs of images of the shirts that the customer ordered.

```
<!ATTLIST shirt product_code ID #REQUIRED>

<!ELEMENT image EMPTY>
<!ATTLIST image product_ref IDREF #REQUIRED>
```

Let's look at Example 3–5:

EXAMPLE 3–5 USING ID AND IDREF

```
<?xml version="1.0" standalone="no"?>
<!DOCTYPE order SYSTEM "example3-5.dtd">
<order>
    <shirt_list>
        <shirt product_code="sh_2398">
            <size>XXL</size>
            <color>purple</color>
        </shirt>
        <shirt product_code="sh_2402">
            <size>XXL</size>
            <color>purple</color>
        </shirt>
    </shirt_list>
    <mugs>90</mugs>

    <image product_ref="sh_2398" />
    <image product_ref="sh_2402" />
</order>
```

and the DTD:

```
<!--
    This is the DTD for example 3-5
-->
<!ELEMENT order (shirt_list?, mugs?, image*)>
<!ELEMENT shirt_list (shirt*)>
<!ELEMENT shirt (size, color)>
<!ATTLIST shirt product_code ID #REQUIRED>
```

```
<!ELEMENT size (#PCDATA)>
<!ELEMENT color (#PCDATA)>
<!ELEMENT mugs (#PCDATA)>

<!ELEMENT image EMPTY>
<!ATTLIST image product_ref IDREF #REQUIRED>
```

You should note that IDREFs don't need to be unique—that is, you can have several IDREF attributes that point to the same ID.

IDREFS

The only difference between IDREF and IDREFS is that the value of an IDREFS attribute has a list of IDs, instead of just one. Let's tweak the product_ref attribute:

```
<!ATTLIST image product_ref IDREFS #REQUIRED>
```

What does this mean for the XML? It means that the product codes can be listed in a single attribute value, separated by white space:

```
<image product_ref="sh_2398 sh_2402" />
```

Oddly enough, you're allowed to repeat an ID value in this list without producing an error:

```
<image product_ref="sh_2398 sh_2398 sh_2398" />
```

I'm not sure why you'd want to do such a thing, but the ability's there if you need it.

NMTOKEN & NMTOKENS

NMTOKEN is short for "name token." The only restriction on an NMTOKEN attribute is that the value has to be a valid XML name, just like the value of an ID attribute. The difference is that the value of an NMTOKEN attribute can occur multiple times in your XML document, while the ID attribute only allows a single instance of each value.

Why use NMTOKEN? If you're using a programming language to manipulate XML, it's helpful for the data to be easily handled by your language. For example, white space can often complicate things. It's not accidental that the rules for XML naming are the same for many programming languages, such as Java and JavaScript.

If you want your attribute's value to be a list of acceptable values, then use NMTOKENS. It's rarely used, but nice to have when you need it.

These attribute types are different beasts than the others, so we'll treat them separately in the next section.

◆ Defining Entities and Notation

The purpose of entities is to hold content. This content can be some text, an image, or another DTD. Instead of typing a bunch of text or copying and pasting from another DTD, you can just refer to that entity's name as a shortcut. If you're going to create an entity that's an image (or some other form of binary data that isn't text), it's called an *unparsed entity*. An entity that holds text, or something that you can type in with a keyboard, is called a *parsed entity*.

Predefined Entities

XML comes with several predefined entities; everything else you'll have to create yourself. Here are the predefined entities (they'll look familiar):

- < stands for (<)
- > stands for (>)
- & stands for (&)
- " stands for (")
- &apost; stands for (')

Here's how you'd implement it in an XML document:

```
<twins names="John &amp; Jim" />
```

or

```
<equation>x &lt; 2/y</equation>
```

Otherwise, the XML parser would interpret the < as the beginning of a new tag. Use these predefined entities in your XML document.

Shortcuts for Text

The simplest kind of entity is a shortcut for text. This shortcut is defined in the DTD, and the entity is placed in the XML. Let's say we want to add contact information to the order just in case there's a problem and someone at the clothing warehouse has to call someone at *Stitch* headquarters.

First, create this contact element

```
<!ELEMENT contact (#PCDATA)>
```

Then, create the shortcut for text (the entity)

```
<!ENTITY irv "Irving Archibite (415) 555-3278">
```

And in the XML:

```
<contact>&irv;</contact>
```

The syntax for this kind of entity is:

```
<!ENTITY entity_name "entity_content">
```

To call that entity, add an ampersand to the beginning of the entity's name and a semicolon to the end:

```
&entity_name;
```

Entity Jargon

Now that you've seen an entity, you're ready for some jargon. All entities can be described using three different categories. It takes a little while to absorb these descriptions, and it's confusing at first. But once you have it down, it's much easier to create entities. (Don't worry—we'll still be looking at examples of everything.)

Parsed or Unparsed

We mentioned this one earlier. Parsed entities are composed of text, like the `irv` entity example above. Unparsed entities are usually pointers to other files that contain nontext data, like images or even applications. Most of the entities we'll be looking at will be parsed.

General or Parameter

Entities are created to be used either in an XML document (as in the example of above) or in a DTD (we haven't seen one of these yet). If an entity is slated to be used in an XML document, it's called a general entity. If it's to be used in a DTD, it's called a parameter entity. There are a few exceptions, but we'll ignore those until later.

Internal or External

An entity's purpose is to hold content, and that content can be spelled out inside the DTD (as in the example above), or it can be stored in a separate file. That separate file can be just about anything, be it text or a PowerPoint presentation. When an entity's content is spelled out in the DTD, it's an *internal entity*. If the content is in another file, it's an *external entity*.

Parameter Entities

A parameter entity is an entity used in the DTD and not in the XML document. The way you can tell a parameter entity from a general entity (those used in XML documents) is the presence of a percentage sign (%).

Example 3–6 shows a parameter entity called pc.

EXAMPLE 3–6 PARAMETER ENTITIES

```
<!ELEMENT order (shirt_list?, mugs?, image*)>
<!ELEMENT shirt_list (shirt*)>
<!ELEMENT shirt (size, color)>
<!ATTLIST shirt product_code ID #REQUIRED>

<!ENTITY % pc "(#PCDATA)">
<!ELEMENT size %pc;>
<!ELEMENT color %pc;>
<!ELEMENT mugs %pc;>

<!ELEMENT image EMPTY>
<!ATTLIST image product_ref IDREF #REQUIRED>
```

HOW THE CODE WORKS

This is pretty similar to the general entity. Notice that in the ENTITY line of code, there's a percent sign and a space before the entity's name. That sign and space are your only real clues that this entity is destined for use in the DTD and not the XML document.

Technically, pc is a parsed parameter internal entity: It's plain ol' text, destined for use in the DTD, and its content is spelled out inside the document itself.

Internal parameter entities are used extensively in more complex DTDs, and these entities are often nested.

External Entities

External entities are those that point to different files, instead of a quick blurb inside the document, and they can be useful in case you have a large entity or need an entity that a number of documents can share.

External General Entities (for the XML)

Let's start by looking at the simplest example: reading a file that holds some XML. This will involve three files: the external text file, the DTD, and the XML document. We'll start by looking at the DTD in Example 3–7, since that's the file that defines the external entity.

EXAMPLE 3–7 CALLING AN EXTERNAL ENTITY

```
<!--
    This is the DTD for example 3-7
-->
<!ELEMENT order (shirt_list?, mugs?)>
<!ELEMENT shirt_list (shirt*)>
<!ELEMENT shirt (size, color)>
<!ATTLIST shirt product_code ID #REQUIRED>

<!ELEMENT size (#PCDATA)>
<!ELEMENT color (#PCDATA)>
<!ELEMENT mugs (#PCDATA)>

<!ENTITY shirts SYSTEM "entity3-7.txt">
```

HOW THE CODE WORKS

Only concern yourself with the last line of this DTD. We're creating an entity called `shirts`. The DTD knows to look elsewhere for the content of the entity because we included the word SYSTEM. Once the parser sees SYSTEM, it knows it'll have to look for a different file. Therefore we follow SYSTEM with the location of the file, which can also be a URL. Here's what this file looks like:

EXAMPLE 3–7 EXTERNAL ENTITY

```
<!--
    Text for example 3-7.xml
-->
<shirt_list>
    <shirt product_code="sh_2398">
        <size>XXL</size>
        <color>purple</color>
    </shirt>
    <shirt product_code="sh_2402">
        <size>XXL</size>
        <color>purple</color>
    </shirt>
</shirt_list>
```

HOW THE CODE WORKS

This is just a simple chunk of content that we'll be pulling into the real XML document. This text doesn't have to be XML—it could easily be a long description of a single shirt, calling it "pleasantly textured with rustic charm" (or something).

And here's the actual XML that uses this entity:

EXAMPLE 3–7 XML

```
<?xml version="1.0" standalone="no"?>
<!DOCTYPE order SYSTEM "example3-7.dtd">
<order>
      &shirts;
    <mugs>90</mugs>
</order>
```

HOW THE CODE WORKS

The XML doesn't care if the entity is external or internal. The XML just places an entity, no matter where it comes from. It's up to the DTD to create the entity, and once it's created, it looks the same to the XML, no matter where it came from.

Now let's look at how to pull in other pieces of a DTD.

External Parameter Entities (for the DTD)

External parameter entities are pretty powerful because they allow you to create a DTD that's composed of other DTDs. For example, you could create an entity that contains the DTD for VoiceXML, and add your own elements to that public DTD.

We'll create a simple example by splitting the DTD we've been using into two pieces and then combining them by using an entity. The part we'll split off is the section that defines the image element and its attribute. Here's the bit that we'll split off:

EXAMPLE 3–8 EXTERNAL DTD ENTITY (IMAGE_DTD.TXT)

```
<!ELEMENT image EMPTY>
<!ATTLIST image product_ref IDREF #REQUIRED>
```

And here's the DTD that creates the entity:

```
<!--
      DTD for example 3-8
-->

<!ELEMENT order (shirt_list?, mugs?, image*)>
<!ELEMENT shirt_list (shirt*)>
<!ELEMENT shirt (size, color)>
<!ATTLIST shirt product_code ID #REQUIRED>

<!ELEMENT size (#PCDATA)>
<!ELEMENT color (#PCDATA)>
<!ELEMENT mugs (#PCDATA)>

<!ENTITY % img SYSTEM "example3-8_2.dtd">

%img;
```

HOW THE CODE WORKS

The code to create an external parameter entity looks like that for an external general entity: all we did was add that percent sign. Then, we included the entity. That's it! Using this method, you can include any number of DTDs in your own DTD (make sure you ask the owner of the other DTD first, though).

Well, that's it for the parsed entities. Table 3–3 has a brief summary.

Unparsed Entities and Notations

Entities aren't limited to just text—just about anything made of zeros and ones can be an entity: images, applications, bytecode,

TABLE 3–3 Parsed Entity Type Summary

Type	Description	Example
Internal general	Entity content spelled out in DTD; entity to be used in XML document	`<!ENTITY wm "Wire Man">`
External general	Entity content is in a different file; entity to be used in XML document	`<!ENTITY wm SYSTEM "wm.txt">`
Internal parameter	Entity content spelled out in DTD; entity to be used in the DTD	`<!ENTITY % purp "(purple)">`
External parameter	Entity content is in a different file; entity to be used in DTD	`<!ENTITY % purp SYSTEM "purp.dtd">`

video games, anything. There's no official way to describe what an unparsed entity contains. That is, there's no standard notation for describing nontext data. For example, let's say you want to create an entity that contains a GIF image. The first thing you have to do is create a description of what kind of data the entity will contain. To do this, use notations. For example, we could describe a GIF image like this:

```
<!NOTATION gif SYSTEM "image/gif">
```

The syntax of these notations is this:

```
<!NOTATION notation_name SYSTEM "data_description">
```

The name of the notation is similar to the name of an entity—it's the way you refer to the notation elsewhere in the DTD. The description can be anything you want—this is the part that has no official standard. The example above is as valid as this:

```
<!NOTATION gif SYSTEM "image/dog.food">
```

This means that any XML parser you use must understand the data description you provide.

Now that we've looked at notations, let's see how to use those notations when we create an unparsed entity.

```
<!ENTITY shirt_pict SYSTEM "shirt.gif" NDATA gif>
```

This looks just like a parsed external general entity, with a couple of things added on at the end: an NDATA and a notation name. We now have an unparsed entity called shirt_pict. Now what? How do we embed this entity in our document?

Embedding Unparsed Entities

It turns out we have to use attributes to include unparsed entities in your XML document—you can't include unparsed entities with a percent or an ampersand with the entity's name the way you can with parsed ones. You have to create a special type of attribute. Remember attribute types? There's CDATA, Enumerated, ID, IDREF, NMTOKEN, etc. Is it coming back now? There were three types we didn't look at: ENTITY, ENTITIES, and NOTATION.

Here's how an ENTITY attribute works. First, we establish the unparsed data's notation and entity that will hold that data.

```
<!NOTATION gif SYSTEM "image/gif">
<!ENTITY shirt_pict SYSTEM "shirt.gif" NDATA gif>
```

Elsewhere in the DTD, we set up an element and an attribute that will hold the unparsed entity in the XML document. Note that the attribute type is ENTITY.

```
<!ELEMENT graphic EMPTY>
<!ATTLIST graphic source ENTITY #REQUIRED>
```

And in the XML, we actually call the entity. Notice that there's no ampersand or percent sign, nor does it end with a semicolon:

```
<graphic source="shirt_pict" />
```

Provided that your XML browser is capable of displayed unparsed entities (as of this writing neither Netscape nor IE can do this), you would see a picture of a shirt amidst the XML.

A rarely used attribute type is ENTITIES. If you choose this, then a number of entities can be listed in the attribute.

```
<!NOTATION gif SYSTEM "image/gif">
<!ENTITY shirt_pict SYSTEM "shirt.gif" NDATA gif>
<!ENTITY mug_pict SYSTEM "mug.gif" NDATA gif>
<!ENTITY hat_pict SYSTEM "hat.gif" NDATA gif>
```

```
<!ELEMENT graphic EMPTY>
<!ATTLIST graphic source ENTITIES #REQUIRED>
```

and in the XML:

```
<graphic source="shirt_pict mug_pict hat_pict" />
```

As a side note, we should now look at the NOTATION attribute type. This type allows an attribute to have the name of a notation as its value. For example:

```
<!NOTATION gif SYSTEM "image/gif">
<!NOTATION jpg SYSTEM "image/jpg">
<!NOTATION png SYSTEM "image/png">
<!ATTLIST graphic type NOTATION (jpg | gif | png)>
```

and in the XML:

```
<graphic source="shirt_pict" type="jpg" />
```

◆ Recap

Now this was a dense chapter. It contains all you really need to know about DTDs, and a lot of information was just crammed down your throat. You've made it this far—well done! You certainly deserve a break. Next, we'll be looking at another way to structure your XML, an alternative to the DTD. This alternative is called XML Schema, and it's gaining in popularity. After you're properly recovered, turn the page and check it out!

4 Defining XML: XML Schema

IN THIS CHAPTER

- Introduction to Namespaces
- Introduction to XML Schema
- Simple Types
- Recap

DTDs aren't the only way to spell out the structure of an XML document. Instead of using a DTD, you can use something called an XML Schema. Using an XML Schema has several advantages over a DTD, as it allows you to more exactly define what kind of data can be in your XML document, like phone numbers, zip codes, or email addresses. XML Schema is a language created by the W3C to address some of the limitations of DTDs. An XML Schema is written in XML. It can act to define a regular XML document because it is parsed differently than regular XML. One of the ways to achieve this is by using something called a namespace.

◆ Introduction to Namespaces

In XML, you can gather together elements like `<order>` and `<shirt_list>` into groups and give those groups a special name. Let's say we want to name our group of elements "Irving." In order to refer to any of Irving's elements, we'd use this: `<Irving: elementName>`. For example, `<Irving:shirt>` and `<Irving: order>`. These elements are a part of the Irving namespace.

Namespaces can be useful if you want to use elements from two different sources and some of those elements have the same name. In that case, you'd want to give the elements in each source a special name, so that the elements from each group can be distinguished from each other. If you have two groups (or namespaces) called Irving and Fuji, and an element called shirt in each group, you'd refer to them as `<Irving:shirt>` and `<Fuji:shirt>`. XML parsers will understand that they're dealing with two different elements, even though they have the same name.

How do you set up a namespace in XML? It looks like this:

```
<order xmlns:Irving="http://www.wire-man.com/ns/irving">
```

What we've done here is to create a namespace called "Irving." Presently, there is nothing in this namespace—it's an empty container. Strangely, namespaces actually have two names: a real name and a nickname. A namespace's real name should be unique—no other namespace in the world should have the same real name. So the W3C decided that the real name of a namespace should look exactly like a URL. The odd thing is that while it looks like a URL, it isn't. Namespace names don't point to actual files—they're just names. Imagine if your real name was your full address, as if your nickname was "Shane" and your real name was "37828 Robina Avenue Palmdale, CA". That address may or may not exist—its only purpose is to give a name that's unique in the whole world. In this case, "Irving" is the namespace's nickname and "http://www.wire-man.com/ns/irving" is its real name.

The rest of the XML could look like this:

```
<order xmlns:irving="http://www.wire-man.com/ns/irving">
    <shirt>9 purple</shirt>
    <irving:shirt>5 orange</irving:shirt>
</order>
```

Another reason to use namespaces is to have certain elements treated differently than others. There are XML parsers that look for certain namespaces and treat elements in that namespace differently than normal, nonnamespace elements. XML Schema is one of these special namespaces. You probably have many questions about namespaces, but don't worry—we'll cover them in Chapter 6. For now, you now know as much as you need to understand XML Schema.

◆ Introduction to XML Schema

XML Schema is written in XML, and it's just a namespace—a collection of elements that gets special treatment from XML parsers. The W3C created the XML Schema language to overcome several limitations of DTDs:

- All DTD elements are global. That is, DTD elements are not context-sensitive—it doesn't matter where an element is defined. This means that all elements must have different names.
- DTDs aren't written in XML, which means that XML parsers can't read them; a special subparser is required.
- DTDs can't specify exactly what kinds of information, like dates, zip codes, or email addresses, go inside an element.

Should you use a DTD or XML Schema? It doesn't really matter. DTDs are more popular right now.

Enough preparation! Let's look at the world's simplest XML Schema document (see Example 4–1).

EXAMPLE 4–1 A SHORT XML SCHEMA

```
<?xml version="1.0" ?>
<xsd:schema
    xmlns:xsd="http://www.w3.org/2000/10/XMLSchema">
</xsd:schema>
```

HOW THE CODE WORKS

As you can see, this is just an XML document, albeit different than anything we've seen before. In the next line we're defining a namespace call xsd. This is where we say, "This is an XML Schema document!" It may look a little odd because we're using the namespace before we define it. See how the <xsd:schema> appears in the same line as the xmlns:xsd? It may look odd, but it works. Note that this is technically an invalid document, because there's nothing inside the xsd:schema elements yet (there needs to be something that serves as the root element of the XML document). We'll fix that shortly.

Let's look at some simple XML, and then at the corresponding XML Schema.

```
<order>9 shirts</order>
```

Now's let's look at the XML Schema required to create this XML (see Example 4–2).

EXAMPLE 4–2 AN XML SCHEMA WITH AN ELEMENT

```
<?xml version="1.0" ?>
<xsd:schema
    xmlns:xsd="http://www.w3.org/2000/10/XMLSchema">
    <xsd:element name="order" type="xsd:string" />
</xsd:schema>
```

HOW THE CODE WORKS

We introduced another line of code and used an XML Schema element called xsd:element to create an element with a name of order and a type of xsd:string. In the XML Schema view of the world, all XML elements are one of two types: *simple type* or *complex type*. Simple type elements have no attributes and contain no other elements—they only hold text or are empty. Complex type elements are everything else: elements that contain some combination of other elements, attributes, and text. Our order element is a simple type element: It only contains some text. Let's look more closely at simple types.

SIDE NOTE

Since XML Schema is really just a form of XML, it can be confusing to refer to "elements." After all, what kind of elements am I referring to? The ones in the XML document, like order, or the elements in the XML Schema document, like xsd:scheme and xsd:element? Unless noted otherwise, "element" will refer to an XML element, just like we've been using it. If I'm talking about an XML Schema element (that is, anything that starts with xsd:), I'll call it an "XML Schema element." Hopefully, that should make things clear.

In the example above, I cheated a little bit—the XML with the <order> line isn't 100% correct. You'll notice that we haven't covered how to link an XML document to its XML Schema. When using DTDs, we used DOCTYPE. When we want to link to XML Schema, though, we use the root element of the XML to call the XML Schema document (which normally have a file extension of .xsd) document, and a couple of unexpected attributes. Example 4–3 shows what it would look like:

EXAMPLE 4–3 MORE ATTRIBUTES

```
<?xml version="1.0" encoding="UTF-8"?>

<order
```

```
    xmlns:xsi="http://www.w3.org/2000/10/XMLSchema-instance"
    xsi:noNamespaceSchemaLocation="example4-2.xsd">
    9 shirts
</order>
```

HOW THE CODE WORKS

Weird, huh? For now, just trust me on this one. We'll cover what this means in the next chapter, when we cover namespaces in more detail. All you need to know right now is to place the file-name of your XML Schema document in the xsi:noName-spaceSchemaLocation attribute.

Now that we've seen the basics of an XML Schema and can build a simple one, let's dig a little deeper into elements that are simple types. We'll cover complex types later in this chapter.

◆ Simple Types

All simple type elements are alike in that they contain only text and no attributes. There isn't just a single simple type element, there are many and you can even create your own. For example, string (from xsd:string above) is a simple type that allows its element to contain any kind of text at all, like the #PCDATA of the DTD. Thus, the order element above could contain just about anything. However, there are a lot more simple types than just string.

For example, let's say we wanted to use a price element in our XML document, like this:

```
<priceUSDollars>24.50</priceUSDollars>
```

It'd be nice to set it up so that only numbers could be in this element. There is a way:

```
<xsd:element name="priceUSDollars" type="xsd:decimal" />
```

HOW THE CODE WORKS

The decimal type restricts the text inside the priceUSDollars element to contain only numbers (positive or negative). Anything else will result in invalid XML. Here's some examples of invalid XML using our XML Schema:

```
<priceUSDollars>totally expensive</priceUSDollars>
```

and

```
<priceUSDollars>24.50 - 10% off</priceUSDollars>
```

Both of these elements contain more than a single number, and are thus outside of the decimal type ken.

SIDE NOTE

If you haven't noticed yet, XML Schema elements always start with xsd: and yes, you will get tired of typing those four characters. If you know how to build a keyboard shortcut, do it.

Other Number-Based Simple Types

There are other ways for your elements to be restricted to numbers other than simple decimal. Here's a list of all the possibilities, along with descriptions and examples.

xsd:integer	
Description	An element with a simple type of integer can be any whole number that's positive, negative, or 0.
Example	`<xsd:element name="price" type="xsd:integer" />` `<price>31</price>`

xsd:positiveInteger	
Description	An element with a simple type of positiveInteger can be any whole number that's positive, but not negative or 0.
Example	`<xsd:element name="price" type="xsd:positiveInteger" />` `<price>1</price>`

xsd:negativeInteger	
Description	An element with a simple type of negativeInteger can be any whole number that's negative, but not positive or 0.
Example	`<xsd:element name="temperature" type="xsd:negativeInteger" />` `<temperature>-20</temperature>`

xsd:nonPositiveInteger	
Description	An element with a simple type of nonPositive Integer can be any whole number that's negative or 0, but not positive.
Example	`<xsd:element name="temperature" type="xsd: nonPositiveInteger " />` `<temperature>0</temperature>`

xsd:nonNegativeInteger	
Description	An element with a simple type of nonNegativeInteger can be any whole number that's positive or 0, but not negative.
Example	`<xsd:element name="population" type="xsd:nonNegativeInteger" />` `<population>17</population>`

xsd:float	
Description	An element with a simple type of float can be a single-precision 32-bit floating-point number, like 3.5 or 4.5e+8. Also includes positive infinity (INF), negative infinity (-INF), and not a number (NaN).
Example	`<xsd:element name="magnification" type="xsd:float" />` `<magnification>8e-5</ magnification >`

xsd:double	
Description	An element with a simple type of double can be a 64-bit double-precision floating-point number (see xsd:float above).
Example	`<xsd:element name="magnification" type="xsd:double" />` `<magnification >6e+14</ magnification >`

We'll start looking at integrating some of these simple types into larger XML Schemas later in the chapter. Right now, it's enough that you're exposed to them.

Another popular set of simple types are those that restrict values to date and time values.

Date- and Time-Based Simple Types

You can also specify your element to contain just time and date information. The formatting of this information is predetermined, though. For example, dates are in the format *YYYY-MM-DD*, so "1999-07-07" is acceptable for a date, but "August 7, 1999" is not.

Let's look at all of the time and date simple types, like we did numbers. Also, as with numbers, we'll look at these simple types in larger XML Schemas so you can see how it all fits together.

xsd:date	
Description	A date element must be in the format *YYYY-MM-DD*.

Example	`<xsd:element name="birthday"`
	`type="xsd:date" />`
	`<birthday >1970-01-28</birthday >`

xsd:time	
Description	A time element must be in the form *hh:mm:ss.sss*. You can also add an optional z, *+hh:mm* or *-hh:mm* at the end to indicate a time zone difference. Use z if the time is in UTC (Coordinated Universal Time, or Greenwich Mean Time), or use the additional hours and minutes to indicate difference from the UTC. The hours use the 24-hour clock.

Example	`<xsd:element name="alarm"`
	`type="xsd:time" />`
	`<alarm>05:45:00</alarm>`

xsd:timeInstant	
Description	This type allows you to combine date and time into a single string. The formats are the same except that there's a T between the date and the time: *YYYY-MM-DDThh:mm:ss.sss* along with the optional time zone information described above.

Example	`<xsd:element name="death"`
	`type="xsd:timeInstant" />`
	`<death>2000-09-12T17:21:35</death>`

xsd:timeDuration

Description	This type is a little odd. The format is *PnYnMnDnTHnMnSn*. P = Period is mandatory. The other letters stand for what you're used to, except the T.

Example	`<xsd:element name="timeAloft"`
	`type="xsd:timeDuration" />`
	`<timeAloft>P2Y3M6D14TH4M12S34</timeAloft>`

xsd:month

Description	This type specifies a certain month and year. Format is *YYYY-MM*.

Example	`<xsd:element name="deadline"`
	`type="xsd:month" />`
	`<deadline >2001-06</deadline >`

xsd:year

Description	This type specifies a year. Format is *YYYY*.

Example	`<xsd:element name="moveToNY"`
	`type="xsd:year" />`
	`<moveToNY >1944</moveToNY >`

xsd:century

Description	This type specifies a century—it's just the first two digits of a four-digit year. For example, the century of 1969 is "19."

Example	`<xsd:element name="columbus"`
	`type="xsd:century" />`
	`<columbus >14</columbus >`

xsd:recurringDate

Description	This type specifies a day and a month, but no year. The format is *--MM-DD*. Note the double hyphen in front.

Example	`<xsd:element name="birthday"`
	`type="xsd:recurringDate" />`
	`<birthday >--11-28</birthday >`

xsd:recurringDay	
Description	This type specifies a certain day of the month. The format is ---*DD*. Note the triple hyphen in front.
Example	`<xsd:element name="balanceCheckbook"` `type="xsd:recurringDay" />` `<balanceCheckbook>14</balanceCheckbook>`

Miscellaneous Simple Types

There's more out there than just numbers, times, and dates. Here are the rest of the simple types.

xsd:boolean	
Description	This type specifies true or false (0 or 1 can also be used).
Example	`<xsd:element name="married"` `type="xsd:boolean" />` `<married>true</married>`

xsd:language	
Description	This type specifies a language, formatted according to the two-character abbrieviations in the ISO639. For example, English is EN.
Example	`<xsd:element name="spoken"` `type="xsd:language" />` `<spoken>EN</spoken>`

xsd:uri-reference	
Description	Even though it's uri, not url, this type specifies a URL.
Example	`<xsd:element name="home"` `type="xsd:uri-reference" />` `<home>http://www.wire-man.com</home>`

xsd:NMTOKEN	
Description	This type forces the text to be a valid XML name.
Example	`<xsd:element name="name"` `type="xsd:NMTOKEN" />` `<name>Irving</name >`

That's it for the basic simple types. This is a lot more than a DTD offers, certainly. For XML Schema, though, it's just a springboard. Using these simple types and a few restrictions, you can create your own simple type. Let's check it out.

Creating Custom Simple Types

If you have exacting standards for the kind of data you need, like nine-digit zip codes or a date like "March 4, 1987," you can create your own custom simple type.

For example, let's say that we want a simple type element called `color`, and that element can contain any one of four colors. That is, any of the following is acceptable:

```
<color>purple</color>
<color>orange</color>
<color>blue</color>
<color>bordeaux</color>
```

However, these are the only colors that are acceptable. Remember, we can't specify this in a DTD. The best a DTD could provide us with is this:

```
<!ELEMENT color (#PCDATA)>
```

Defining attributes in a DTD allow us to specify a list of acceptable values.

```
<!ATTLIST hats color (red | blue | green) #REQUIRED>
```

This is better than nothing, but still pretty limited.

XML Schema does provide us a way to specify acceptable text in a simple type element (see Example 4–4):

EXAMPLE 4–4 LIMITING ACCEPTABLE VALUES

```
<?xml version="1.0" ?>
<xsd:schema
xmlns:xsd="http://www.w3.org/2000/10/XMLSchema">
1.<xsd:element name="color">
  2.<xsd:simpleType>
      3.<xsd:restriction base="xsd:string">
          4.<xsd:enumeration value="purple" />
          <xsd:enumeration value="orange" />
          <xsd:enumeration value="blue" />
          <xsd:enumeration value="bordeaux" />
      5.</xsd:restriction>
```

```
      </xsd:simpleType>
    </xsd:element>
</xsd:schema>
```

HOW THE CODE WORKS

1. In this schema, we're creating an element called `color`. There isn't any `order` in this schema, as in the previous examples, just the simple element of `color`. Notice that we haven't defined any kind of `type` for this element in this line.

2. We're going to need several lines of code to specify this element's type, so we start by saying, "Here comes a description of a custom simple type!" by coding `<xsd:simpleType>`.

3. We then start by spelling out some details. The simple type for the `color` element will be based on the `xsd:string` type (all custom simple types have to be based on one of the predefined types that are listed in the previous sections). Since we're going to start with `xsd:string` and to start restricting it, we'll use the XML Schema element `xsd:restriction`.

4. Here's where we finally spell out exactly what our color element can contain. We use `xsd:enumeration` to create a list of acceptable values. In the XML document, any one, but only one, of these values is acceptable.

5. Remember to close all the tags.

There are many other ways to create your own simple type. Let's check some of them out.

Forcing Text to Fit a Pattern

Sometimes you'll want your data to adhere to a certain pattern, like a zip code, a long date, or an email address. To create this pattern, you can use a special language called regular expression to determine what sort of characters can appear where. Regular expressions may be familiar to you already if you've used Perl. If you haven't used regular expressions before, it may be a little confusing, and the subject is complex enough to warrant a long chapter by itself. A thorough look at regular expressions is beyond the scope of this book, but I can refer you to a great book that covers regular expressions: *Essential Perl for Web Professionals* by Micah Brown, Chris Bellew, and yours truly.

We won't look at regular expressions in a lot of detail, but I'll cover the basics. First, let's look at Example 4–5, which has XML Schema that defines a phone number with area code in this format: (123) 456-7890:

EXAMPLE 4–5 USING A PATTERN

```
<xsd:element name="phone_number">
<xsd:simpleType>
    <xsd:restriction base="xsd:string">
        <xsd:pattern value="(\d{3})\s\d{3}-\d{4}" />
    </xsd:restriction>
</xsd:simpleType>
</xsd:element>
```

HOW THE CODE WORKS

The only new thing here is the XML Schema element xsd:pattern. This XML Schema element's only attribute is value, which holds the regular expression statement. What does all that stuff mean?

\d	any digit
\D	any nondigit
\s	white space, carriage return, new line, or return
\S	any non–white space character
(ab)*	anything in parentheses may appear zero or more times
(ab)+	anything in parentheses may appear one or more times
(ab)?	Anything in parentheses may appear zero or one time
a{n}	"a" must appear n times in a row

So the regular expression we used means the text (in order)

- Must start with an open paren (
- Followed by three digits
- Followed by a close paren) and a space
- Followed by three more digits
- Followed by a hyphen
- And ends with four digits

There's a lot more you can do with regular expressions, and if you have any need for xsd:pattern, I recommend you learn all you can—regular expressions can be darn powerful.

Limiting Numerical Values

Imagine that in your online store, people get a discount if they order 500 or more shirts. However, the warehouse only holds so many shirts, and it can't handle orders for more than 2000 shirts. There are four ways to limit these numbers: `maxInclusive`, `minInclusive`, `maxExclusive`, and `minExlcusive` (see Example 4–6).

EXAMPLE 4–6 IMPOSING MAXIMUM AND MINIMUM VALUES

```
<xsd:element name="numShirtsDiscountOrder">
    <xsd:simpleType>
        1.<xsd:restriction base="xsd:integer">
            2.<xsd:maxInclusive value="2000" />
            3.<xsd:minInclusive value="500" />
        </xsd:restriction>
    </xsd:simpleType>
</xsd:element>
```

HOW THE CODE WORKS

1. Note that the foundation of our simple type is `xsd:integer` instead of `xsd:string`, as in earlier examples.
2. To set an upper limit, you can use `xsd:maxInclusive`, which in this case is set to 2000. That means the text inside the `numShortsDiscountOrder` can be a number less than or equal to 2000. If we had used `xsd:max-Exclusive`, the text could be a number less than but not equal to 2000.
3. To set a lower limit, we used `xsd:minInclusive`, so that the number in the `numShortDiscountOrder` element must be equal to or greater than 500. If we used `xsd:minExclusive`, the number in the element would have to be greater then 500.

There are a few more ways to constrain number values in your XML. These ways involve limiting the number of digits in the number—we can limit the total number of digits in a number and the maximum number of digits to the right of the decimal point (see Example 4–7).

EXAMPLE 4–7 FORCING PRECISION ON YOUR NUMBERS

```
<xsd:element name="scienceNum">
    <xsd:simpleType>
        <xsd:restriction base="xsd:decimal">
            <xsd:precision value="6" />
```

```
            <xsd:scale value="3"/>
         </xsd:restriction>
      </xsd:simpleType>
</xsd:element>
```

HOW THE CODE WORKS

There are two new XML Schema elements here: `xsd:precision` and `xsd:scale`. `xsd:precision` places an upper limit on the total number of digits a number can have, while `xsd:scale` controls the maximum number of digits to the right of the decimal point. The XML lines below are both valid.

```
<scienceNum>123.453</scienceNum>
<scienceNum>7</scienceNum>
```

Limiting Length of Strings

Now imagine that we're taking an order from a customer, and part of that order is which state the customer lives in. We want to limit that state field to a two-character abbreviation. To do this, we'll use an XML Schema element called `xsd:length` (see Example 4–8).

EXAMPLE 4–8 LIMITING STRING LENGTH

```
<xsd:element name="state">
    <xsd:simpleType>
        <xsd:restriction base="xsd:string">
            <xsd:length value="2"/>
        </xsd:restriction>
    </xsd:simpleType>
</xsd:element>
```

HOW THE CODE WORKS

This one is pretty simple—it allows only two characters in the `state` element.

We can also place upper and lower limits on a text string. Let's say that we want to allow abbreviations as well as the state's full name. That means we want a minimum of two characters and a maximum of 13 characters. Here's how we do that (see Example 4–9):

EXAMPLE 4–9 SETTING MAXIMUM AND MINIMUM STRING LENGTHS

```
<xsd:element name="state">
    <xsd:simpleType>
        <xsd:restriction base="xsd:string">
```

```
      <xsd:minLength value="2" />
      <xsd:maxLength value="13" />
   </xsd:restriction>
   </xsd:simpleType>
</xsd:element>
```

HOW THE CODE WORKS

There are two new XML Schema elements here: `xsd:minLength` and `xsd:maxLength`. They're pretty self-explanatory: they set the minimum and maximum lengths of a text string.

Creating Lists

All of the simple types we've looked at so far contain just one item per element: that is, a single date, number, or string. If, for some reason, you want your element to contain a list of items separated by white space, XML Schema has the type for you: `xsd:list` (see Example 4–10).

EXAMPLE 4–10 MAKING A LIST

```
<xsd:element name="sizes">
    <xsd:simpleType>
        <xsd:list itemType="xsd:string" />
    </xsd:simpleType>
</xsd:element>
```

HOW THE CODE WORKS

Notice that instead of `xsd:restriction`, we used `xsd:list`, which allows us to create a list of items separated by a single white space. Here's an example of XML that would adhere to the above schema:

```
<sizes>XL XXL S XS M</sizes>
```

You can also limit the size of the list by adding some parameters inside of it.

```
<xsd:list itemType="xsd:string">
    <xsd:length value="5" />
</xsd:list>
```

This code would set the size of our list to five items, no more and no less. We also could've used:

```
<xsd:list itemType="xsd:string">
    <xsd:minLength value="2" />
```

```
    <xsd:maxLength value="7" />
</xsd:list>
```

In this case, your space-delimited list could contain any-where from two to seven items. The other limitations you can use in a list are xsd:pattern, xsd:enumeration, and xsd:whiteSpace.

SIDE NOTE

xsd:whiteSpace
The syntax for this XML Schema element is

```
<xsd:whiteSpace value="preserve | replace |
collapse">
```

- preserve doesn't affect any white space, line feeds, or car-riage returns in the text item.
- replace replaces all tabs, line feeds, and carriage returns with white spaces.
- collapse performs a replace on the text, and then col-lapses all contiguous white space into a single white space, as well as deleting any trailing white space.

Combining Simple Types

Not only do you have impressive freedom to determine the type of data in your XML, you can also combine various simple types into a single, larger simple type. For example, there could be two ways to describe when a customer ordered from your store: either the actual date or one of the values "today," "tomorrow," or "yes-terday" (not that I would recommend this). To combine these two types, we introduce a new XML Schema element: xsd:union (see Example 4–11).

EXAMPLE 4–11 COMBINING SIMPLE TYPES WITH XSD:UNION

```
<xsd:element name="orderDate">
<xsd:simpleType>
    <xsd:union>
        <xsd:simpleType>
            <xsd:restriction base="xsd:string">
                <xsd:enumeration value="yesterday" />
                <xsd:enumeration value="today" />
                <xsd:enumeration value="tomorrow" />
            </xsd:restriction>
        </xsd:simpleType>
```

```
<xsd:simpleType>
        <xsd:restriction base="xsd:date" />
    </xsd:simpleType>
  </xsd:union>
</xsd:simpleType>
</xsd:element>
```

HOW THE CODE WORKS

With all the nested XML Schema elements, this is pretty hard to read, but the general structure is pretty simple. Within the `xsd:union` element, simply list all of the simple types you'd like to use, one after the other. For this example, here's some valid XML:

```
<orderDate>yesterday</orderDate>
<orderDate>2001-04-19</orderDate>
```

Both of these lines are valid XML, because they contain either a date or one of the allowed strings.

Determining an Element's Content

You can also exert complete control over an element's content and set it explicitly. Or, if you're feeling more flexible, you can simply give your element a default value. Example 4–12 shows both.

EXAMPLE 4–12 PREDETERMINING CONTENT

```
<xsd:element name="color" type="xsd:string" fixed="blue" />
<xsd:element name="size" type="xsd:string" default="M" />
```

HOW THE CODE WORKS

For the `color` element, the only XML possible is `<color>blue</color>`. There's no other option. For size, though, any string is possible, and if the element is omitted in the XML, the parser will automatically place `<size>M</size>` into the appropriate spot.

Reusable Custom Simple Types

Sometimes it's useful to create a custom simple type that can be used for more than one element. For example, let's say that we need several phone numbers from a corporate customer: main, cell, and fax. It'd be a pain to have to recreate the `<xsd:simple-Type>` elements for each main element. Fortunately, there's an easy way to define a simple type and reuse it over and over again. All you have to do is create a simple type that isn't inside a xsd:element, and you give the simple type a name, as in Example 4–13.

EXAMPLE 4–13 REUSING A CUSTOM SIMPLE TYPE

```
<xsd:simpleType name="phoneNumber">
<xsd:restriction base="xsd:string">
     <xsd:pattern value="(\d{3})\s\d{3}-\d{4}" />
</xsd:restriction>
</xsd:simpleType>

<xsd:element name="mainPhone" type="phoneNumber" />
<xsd:element name="cellPhone" type="phoneNumber" />
<xsd:element name="faxPhone" type="phoneNumber" />
```

HOW THE CODE WORKS

This code is pretty similar to what you've seen before, except that the xsd:simpleType doesn't occur inside a xsd:element, and it has its own name. That name can be used to set the type of other elements in your XML Schema.

◆ Recap

Whew! That's a lot of material to learn quickly. We've looked at what an XML Schema is, and some of the advantages it has over a DTD, as well as the myriad of simple types out these. There are gazillions of simple types out there, and I covered the most commonly used ones. However, XML Schema changes from time to time, so check *www.w3.org/TR/xmlschema-2/* to see the latest.

If you haven't already, I strongly recommend typing these examples into an XML editor like XML Spy—it's the best way to learn.

Complex types are, well, complex enough to warrant a separate chapter, and that's coming up next.

5 XML Schema: Complex Types

Any XML element that contains an attribute or has other elements inside of it is known as a complex type element. Complex type elements can contain any combination of text, attributes, and elements.

◆ Elements Containing Other Elements

Let's say we have some simple XML:

```
<shirt>
    <color>purple</color>
    <size>XL</size>
</shirt>
```

We need to define the element shirt, and place the elements color and size inside of it. Since shirt is a complex type element, we use the code in Example 5–1.

EXAMPLE 5–1 NESTED ELEMENTS

```
1.<xsd:element name="shirt">
   2.<xsd:complexType>
      3.<xsd:sequence>
         4.<xsd:element name="color" type="xsd:
            string"/>
            <xsd:element name="size" type="xsd:string"/>
         </xsd:sequence>
      </xsd:complexType>
</xsd:element>
```

HOW THE CODE WORKS

1. As with simple type elements, we start with xsd:element and don't use the type attribute.
2. We start the definition of this element's type with xsd: complexType.
3. Since there is a sequence of elements inside the shirt element, which contains color and size, we use xsd: sequence. This means that both the size and color elements must appear exactly once and in the order provided (in this case, color comes first).
4. We declare the color and size elements as simple types.

But what happens when you want elements to show up more than once, or at least to have that option?

Cardinality

In XML Schema, we can define the cardinality of an element (that is, the number of possible occurrences). Let's check out the XML Schema that produces the following XML.

```
<completeOrder>
    <shirt>9 purple XL</shirt>
    <shirt>3 blue S</shirt>
    <shirt>11 orange XXL</shirt>
    <sweatshirt>19 green</sweatshirt>
    <mugs>8 porcelain</mugs>
</completeOrder>
```

We set the cardinality of an element using two new attributes in xsd:element - minOccurs and maxOccurs. We use both of these attributes in Example 5–2.

EXAMPLE 5–2 NEST ELEMENTS WITH CARDINALITY

```
<xsd:element name="completeOrder">
    <xsd:complexType>
        <xsd:sequence>
        1.<xsd:element name="shirt" minOccurs="0"
maxOccurs="unbounded" type="xsd:string" />
            <xsd:element name="sweatshirt" minOccurs="0"
maxOccurs="unbounded" type="xsd:string" />
        2.<xsd:element name="mugs" minOccurs="0"
maxOccurs="100" type="xsd:string" />
            <xsd:element name="hats" minOccurs="0"
maxOccurs="50" type="xsd:string" />
        </xsd:sequence>
    </xsd:complexType>
</xsd:element>
```

HOW THE CODE WORKS

1. For the `shirt` and `sweatshirt` elements, they can either not appear at all (`minOccurs="0"`) or they can appear an infinite number of times (`maxOccurs="unbounded"`). In the XML above, the `shirt` element only appears three times, but it could appear any number of times.

2. The `mugs` and `hats` elements can appear or not, but they're limited to a maximum appearance of 100 and 50 times, respectively.

Either `minOccurs` or `maxOccurs` can be attributes in an element—both don't have to be there (although `maxOccurs` had better be equal to or more than `minOccurs`). These two attributes have default values: they're both set to 1 unless you say otherwise (see Table 5–1).

TABLE 5–1 XML Schema and DTD Differences

XML Schema	DTD Equivalent
minOccurs=0 maxOccurs="unbounded"	element*
minOccurs="0" maxOccurs="1"	element?
minOccurs="1" maxOccurs="unbounded"	element+
Default: minOccurs="1" maxOccurs="1"	element

You may have noticed that `xsd:sequence` is pretty strict. Fortunately, XML Schema gives us a few more options: `xsd:choice` and `xsd:all`.

xsd:choice

This option is good if you have a list of elements (or groups of elements), and the XML can choose from this list (see Example 5–3).

EXAMPLE 5–3 CHOICE FROM A LIST OF ELEMENTS

```
<xsd:element name="singleItemOrder">
<xsd:complexType>
   <xsd:choice>
        <xsd:element name="shirt" type="xsd:string" />
        <xsd:element name="sweatshirt" type="xsd:string"/>
        <xsd:element name="mugs" type="xsd:integer"/>
   </xsd:choice>
</xsd:complexType>
</xsd:element>
```

HOW THE CODE WORKS

The syntax for using `xsd:sequence` and `xsd:choice` is exactly the same. In this example, the XML could have one of three elements inside `<singleItemOrder>`: `<shirt>`, `<sweatshirt>`, or `<mugs>`, but not all three.

Element groups that are choices or sequences can be nested within each other, as in Example 5–4.

EXAMPLE 5–4 NESTED GROUPS OF ELEMENTS

```
<xsd:element name="multipleItemOrder">
<xsd:complexType>
   <xsd:choice>
        <xsd:sequence>
            <xsd:element name="shirt" type="xsd:string" />
            <xsd:element name="sweatshirt"
type="xsd:string"/>
        </xsd:sequence>
        <xsd:choice>
            <xsd:element name="mugs" type="xsd:string" />
            <xsd:element name="martiniGlasses"
type="xsd:string"/>
        </xsd:choice>
        <xsd:element name="hats" type="xsd:integer"/>
   </xsd:choice>
```

```
</xsd:complexType>
</xsd:element>
```

HOW THE CODE WORKS

There are a few things going on here. The `multipleItemOrder` element can contain one of a few different things:

1. The sequence of `<shirt>` and `<sweatshirt>`,
2. A choice between `<mugs>` and `<martiniGlasses>`, or
3. The single element `<hats>`.

Only one of these options is valid.

xsd:all

`xsd:all` behaves exactly the same as `xsd:sequence`, except that the elements don't have to appear in any predetermined order. Example 5–5 shows how.

EXAMPLE 5–5 IGNORING ORDER IN A SEQUENCE

```
<xsd:element name="completeOrder">
<xsd:complexType>
    <xsd:all>
        <xsd:element name="shirt" type="xsd:string" minOc-
curs="0" maxOccurs="unbounded"/>
        <xsd:element name="sweatshirt" type="xsd:string"
minOccurs="0" maxOccurs="unbounded"/>
        <xsd:element name="mugs" type="xsd:string" minOc-
curs="0" maxOccurs="100"/>
        <xsd:element name="hats" type="xsd:string" minOc-
curs="0" maxOccurs="50"/>
    </xsd:all>
</xsd:complexType>
</xsd:element>
```

HOW THE CODE WORKS

This example is exactly the same as Example 5–2—the grouping type has only changed from `xsd:sequence` to `xsd:all`. The XML spawned by the code above could have the four elements (`shirt`, `sweatshirt`, `mugs`, and `hats`) appear in any order.

We've covered how to nest elements, and that's vital, but that's only part of the story—we need attributes in there as well.

◆ Defining Attributes

Adding an attribute to an element is pretty simple. Let's say we want this empty element with three attributes:

```
<order shirts="9" mugs="3" hats="45" />
```

No sweat. Example 5–6 points the way.

EXAMPLE 5–6 DEFINING ATTRIBUTES

```
<xsd:element name="order">
    <xsd:complexType>
        <xsd:attribute name="shirts" type="xsd:integer"/>
        <xsd:attribute name="mugs" type="xsd:integer"/>
        <xsd:attribute name="hats" type="xsd:integer"/>
    </xsd:complexType>
</xsd:element>
```

HOW THE CODE WORKS

Attributes are added to the structure of an element in the same way other elements are: Their declarations are nested inside an `xsd:complexType`.

Attributes must have a simple type, such as `xsd:integer` or `xsd:string`. The simple type can even be a custom one, but it cannot be a complex type. Would you even want to your attributes to contain nested elements? I shudder to think of it.

Attribute Uses

When you define an attribute, you can also decide how it is to be used. Is it required or optional, and does it have a default value? You can determine these things with the `use` attribute in the `xsd:attribute` XML Schema element:

```
<xsd:attribute name="hat" type="xsd:string" use="required">
```

This requires the use of the `hat` attribute. Table 5–2 lists the other values.

Attributes and Elements

To incorporate attributes into an element that contains nested elements, the attribute declarations must come last, after all the element declarations. There's no real reason for this, other

TABLE 5-2 Defining How Attributes Are to Be Used

Item	Description
use="required"	Attribute must be present.
use="optional"	Attribute may or may not be present. This is the default value, so you don't need to use this one.
use="prohibited"	Attribute is forbidden from being present in the XML.
use="fixed" value="*mandatoryValue*"	If the attribute is present in the XML document, it must have the value of *mandatoryValue*. If the attribute is not present, then no value is set.
use="default" value="*defaultValue*"	If the attribute is not present in the XML document, the parser in instructed to insert it and give it a value of *defaultValue*. If the attribute is present, then its value overrides *defaultValue*.

than that it forces some organization on your code (see Example 5–7).

EXAMPLE 5-7 ATTRIBUTES AND NESTED ELEMENTS

```
<xsd:element name="order">
<xsd:complexType>
    <xsd:sequence>
        <xsd:element name="shirts" type="xsd:string"/>
        <xsd:element name="sweatshirts"
type="xsd:string"/>
        <xsd:element name="mugs" type="xsd:string"/>
        <xsd:element name="hats" type="xsd:string"/>
    </xsd:sequence>
    <xsd:attribute name="orderDate" type="xsd:date"/>
    <xsd:attribute name="source" type="xsd:string"/>
</xsd:complexType>
</xsd:element>
```

HOW THE CODE WORKS

All we did was tack on a couple `xsd:attribute` tags to the end of the complex type definition. Here's what the resulting XML could look like:

```
<order orderDate="2001-04-18" source="cellPhone">
    <shirts>9 purple</shirts>
    <sweatshirts>7 blue</sweatshirts>
    <mugs>4 travel</mugs>
    <hats>20 baseball</hats>
</order>
```

Attributes and Text

Say that instead of combining attributes and nested elements, you'd like to combine attributes and simple text, like this:

```
<shirt quantity="4">XL purple</shirt>
```

This looks like a simple type element with an attribute. That's all it is, but the addition of that attribute automatically makes shirt a complex type element.

The code to accomplish this is surprisingly complicated. Have a look at Example 5–8.

EXAMPLE 5–8 COMBINING ATTRIBUTES AND TEXT

```
<xsd:element name="shirt">
    <xsd:complexType>
        1.<xsd:simpleContent>
            2.<xsd:restriction base="xsd:string">
                3.<xsd:maxLength value="30" />
                4.<xsd:attribute name="quantity"
type="xsd:integer"/>
            </xsd:restriction>
        </xsd:simpleContent>
    </xsd:complexType>
</xsd:element>
```

HOW THE CODE WORKS

1. Here's something new. (Notice this is xsd:simple-Content, not xsd:simpleType.) In order to allow this element to contain text, we must wrap the simple type restrictions and attribute declarations with a xsd:simpleContent. This XML Schema element is only necessary when your element contains attributes and text, but no other elements.

2. We can use xsd:restriction the same as if we were inside a xsd:simpleType. That means you can restrict the text inside this element in the ways you could if it was a simple type element.

3. Here we constrain the number of characters in the text to 30. This is the same `xsd:maxLength` we saw in the last chapter.

4. Finally, inside the `xsd:restriction`, we have the attribute declaration. This isn't really a restriction on the text, but this is where the statement goes. It's a little counterintuitive, but it works.

What happens when you don't want to restrict the text? If that's the case, then you don't need to use `xsd:restriction`, right? In this case, we use a new XML Schema element called `xsd:extension`, which is the theoretical opposite of `xsd:restriction`: It adds to the element instead of subtracts. Example 5–9 shows the code you'd use if you didn't want to restrict the text in any way.

EXAMPLE 5–9 USING `XSD:EXTENSION`

```
<xsd:element name="shirt">
    <xsd:complexType>
        <xsd:simpleContent>
            <xsd:extension base="xsd:string">
                <xsd:attribute name="quantity"
type="xsd:integer"/>
            </xsd:extension>
        </xsd:simpleContent>
    </xsd:complexType>
</xsd:element>
```

That's right, we added an attribute using both `xsd:restriction` and `xsd:extension`. It's odd, but take a deep breath and make peace with it.

Attributes, Text, and Nested Elements

Combining attributes, text, and nested elements is pretty simple. Let's say you want to produce this XML:

```
<order orderDate="2001-04-18">To ship overnight: <shirt>9
purple XL</shirt> and <mugs>7 Roadrunner style</mugs> to
Fairfax, CA</order>
```

Example 5–10 shows XML Schema that would spawn such a thing:

EXAMPLE 5–10 ATTRIBUTES, TEXT, AND ELEMENTS

```
<xsd:element name="order">
<xsd:complexType mixed="true">
```

```
<xsd:sequence>
      <xsd:element name="shirts" type="xsd:string"/>
      <xsd:element name="mugs" type="xsd:string"/>
</xsd:sequence>
<xsd:attribute name="orderDate" type="xsd:date"/>
</xsd:complexType>
</xsd:element>
```

HOW THE CODE WORKS

Did you notice the `mixed="true"` attribute in `xsd:complexType`? It means that the complex type contains text, attributes, and nested elements. That's all you need to include text, along with the attributes and elements. Makes more sense than the `xsd:simple-Content` thing you had to deal with earlier, doesn't it?

◆ Creating Custom Complex Types

Much like simple types, you can create your own custom complex types and use them later in your code. Example 5–11 defines both simple and complex types.

EXAMPLE 5–11 CUSTOM COMPLEX TYPES

```
<!-- define simple types -->
<xsd:simpleType name="colorType">
    <xsd:restriction base="xsd:string">
          <xsd:enumeration value="purple" />
          <xsd:enumeration value="orange" />
          <xsd:enumeration value="blue" />
          <xsd:enumeration value="grey" />
    </xsd:restriction>
</xsd:simpleType>

<xsd:simpleType name="sizeType">
    <xsd:restriction base="xsd:string">
          <xsd:enumeration value="M" />
          <xsd:enumeration value="L" />
          <xsd:enumeration value="XL" />
    </xsd:restriction>
</xsd:simpleType>


<!-- define complex type -->
1.<xsd:complexType name="sizeColorType">
    <xsd:sequence>
          <xsd:element name="size" type="sizeType" />
          <xsd:element name="color" type="colorType" />
    </xsd:sequence>
```

```
        <xsd:attribute name="quantity" type="xsd:integer" />
</xsd:complexType>


<!-- define elements -->
```
2.`<xsd:element name="shirt" type="sizeColorType" />`
```
<xsd:element name="sweatshirt" type="sizeColorType" />
```

HOW THE CODE WORKS

1. To create a custom complex type, simply add a name attribute, and don't place the `xsd:complexType` inside any other XML Schema element.
2. Here's where we call our custom complex type and apply it to both the `shirt` and `sweatshirt` elements.

Here's an example of some XML based on the XML Schema above:

```
<shirt>
    <size>M</size>
    <color>blue</color>
</shirt>
<sweatshirt>
    <size>XL</size>
    <color>orange</color>
</sweatshirt>
```

◆ Referencing Elements and Attributes

You've probably noticed that XML Schema code isn't as readable as a DTD. The more you add to an XML Schema, the harder it gets to read, as elements and types are nested deeper and deeper into each other. A sufficiently complex document is especially difficult to read and almost impossible to debug. Luckily, XML Schema provides a way for you to modularize your code so it's easier to read, understand, and debug.

XML Schema allows you to define an element or attribute and then refer to it later. We do this to an element in Example 5–12.

EXAMPLE 5–12 REFERRING TO AN ELEMENT

1.`<xsd:element name="shirt" type="xsd:string" />`

```
<xsd:element name="shirt_list">
    <xsd:complexType>
```

```
        <xsd:sequence>
            2.<xsd:element ref="shirt" maxOccurs="un-
bounded" />
        </xsd:sequence>
    </xsd:complexType>
</xsd:element>
```

HOW THE CODE WORKS

1. Here's where we define the simple type element of `shirt`.
2. We now place this element inside the `shirt_list` element by referring to it using the `ref` attribute. Imagine that we're making a clone of the `shirt` element and moving it in another place.

You can make as many clones of elements as you want, and each clone has its own cardinality (that is, its own `minOccurs` and `maxOccurs`).

Attributes have the same flexibility, and the syntax is the same (see Example 5–13).

EXAMPLE 5–13 REFERRING TO AN ATTRIBUTE

```
<xsd:attribute name="quantity"
type="xsd:nonNegativeInteger"/>

<xsd:complexType name="quantityAttrType">
    <xsd:attribute ref="quantity"/>
</xsd:complexType>

<xsd:element name="mugs" type="quantityAttrType"/>
<xsd:element name="hats" type="quantityAttrType"/>
```

HOW THE CODE WORKS

In this chunk of code, we create an attribute called `quantity`. When we create a custom complex type called `quantityAttr-Type`, we call (or clone) `quantity` and then attach that complex type to two elements. In this way, we can easily and quickly attach attributes to elements.

◆ New Complex Types Based on Existing Types

It's possible to create a new custom complex type by using an existing complex type as a template (see Example 5–14). This can be useful if you have many related complex types to deal with in your data. I know the complexity of this is getting a little crazy, but hang in there—if you've made it this far, you can handle this last bit.

EXAMPLE 5–14 CREATING A NEW CUSTOM TYPE

```
<!-- define simple types -->
<xsd:simpleType name="colorType">
  <xsd:restriction base="xsd:string">
      <xsd:enumeration value="purple"/>
      <xsd:enumeration value="orange"/>
      <xsd:enumeration value="blue"/>
      <xsd:enumeration value="grey"/>
  </xsd:restriction>
</xsd:simpleType>

<xsd:simpleType name="sizeType">
  <xsd:restriction base="xsd:string">
      <xsd:enumeration value="M"/>
      <xsd:enumeration value="L"/>
      <xsd:enumeration value="XL"/>
  </xsd:restriction>
</xsd:simpleType>


    <!-- define complex types -->
1.<xsd:complexType name="sizeColorType">
  <xsd:sequence>
      <xsd:element name="size" type="sizeType"/>
      <xsd:element name="color" type="colorType"/>
  </xsd:sequence>
  <xsd:attribute ref="quantity"/>
</xsd:complexType>

2.<xsd:complexType name="shirtDescType">
  3.<xsd:complexContent>
      4.<xsd:extension base="sizeColorType">
          <xsd:sequence>
          <xsd:element name="material" type="xsd:string" />
          <xsd:element name="collar" type="xsd:string" />
          <xsd:element name="sleeve" type="xsd:string" />
          </xsd:sequence>
      </xsd:extension>
  </xsd:complexContent>
</xsd:complexType>

<!--define attribute -->
<xsd:attribute name="quantity" type="xsd:nonNegative
Integer"/>

<!-- define element -->
<xsd:element name="shirt" type="shirtDescType"/>
```

HOW THE CODE WORKS

1. `sizeColorType` is the complex type that we'll be using as a template later on. It contains two elements: `size` and `color`.
2. This is the complex type that we'll build on top of `size-ColorType`.
3. This is a new XML Schema element: `xsd:complex-Content`. Remember how `xsd:simpleContent` was used to combine text and attributes? Here's its older brother.
4. To bring the template complex type into the one we're building, we use `xsd:extension` and call the template type as the base to build from. Since we're building on top of the complex type template (we're adding to it, extending it), we use `xsd:extension`. If we were creating a complex type that had elements that were more restricted than the complex type we're bringing in, we'd use `xsd:restriction` instead of `xsd:extension`.

This is a great way to both expand and modularize your code. It may seem a little odd, but try it and play around with it for awhile and it'll become more intuitive.

◆ Miscellaneous

There are a few more things to look at in XML Schema: named groups of elements and attributes, documenting your code (beyond comments), and including external files.

◆ Named Groups of Elements and Attributes

Another way for you to control the readability and infrastructure of your XML Schema document is to create reusable groups of elements and attributes. These groups are named by you, which allows you to refer to them elsewhere in the document. As with elements and attributes, calling these groups of elements or attributes is like cloning them and placing that clone wherever the reference is.

Groups of Elements

You can create a group of elements at the root level of your XML Schema document and then refer to that group any number of times in that same document. Inside of that group, the list of elements must be a `sequence`, `choice`, or `all`. Example 5–15 shows it in action.

EXAMPLE 5–15 NAMED GROUP OF ELEMENTS

```
<!-- define simple types -->
<xsd:simpleType name="colorType">
    <xsd:restriction base="xsd:string">
        <xsd:enumeration value="purple"/>
        <xsd:enumeration value="orange"/>
        <xsd:enumeration value="blue"/>
        <xsd:enumeration value="grey"/>
    </xsd:restriction>
</xsd:simpleType>
<xsd:simpleType name="sizeType">
    <xsd:restriction base="xsd:string">
        <xsd:enumeration value="M"/>
        <xsd:enumeration value="L"/>
        <xsd:enumeration value="XL"/>
    </xsd:restriction>
</xsd:simpleType>


<!-- define group -->
1.<xsd:group name="sizeColorGroup">
    <xsd:sequence>
        <xsd:element name="size" type="sizeType"/>
        <xsd:element name="color" type="colorType"/>
    </xsd:sequence>
</xsd:group>


<!-- define elements -->
<xsd:element name="shirt">
    <xsd:complexType>
        2.<xsd:group ref="sizeColorGroup" />
    </xsd:complexType>
</xsd:element>

<xsd:element name="sweatshirt">
    <xsd:complexType>
        3.<xsd:group ref="sizeColorGroup" />
    </xsd:complexType>
</xsd:element>
```

HOW THE CODE WORKS

1. Creating a group is pretty simple. Inside the `xsd:group` element, place `xsd:sequence`, `xsd:choice`, or `xsd:all`. Then include your list of elements (you can even include another `xsd:group` if you want). You can't place an attribute inside of a group, though.

2. Here, we clone the `sizeColorGroup` and place that clone inside the `shirt` element.

3. We do the same thing to the `sweatshirt` element: clone the group `sizeColorGroup` and place it in `sweatshirt`.

We can also create groups of attributes in a similar way using the `xsd:attributeGroup` element.

Groups of Attributes

If we want to tweak our XML so that all the information about shirts and sweatshirts is contained within attributes, it might look like this:

```
<shirt quantity="2" color="purple" size="XL" material=
"cotton" />
<sweatshirt quantity="1" color="orange" size="M"
material="cotton" />
```

Since these elements contain the same set of attributes, we can create a group of attributes and place that group into both the `shirt` and `sweatshirt` elements, as in Example 5–16.

EXAMPLE 5–16 GROUP OF ATTRIBUTES

```
<!-- define simple types -->
<xsd:simpleType name="colorType">
    <xsd:restriction base="xsd:string">
        <xsd:enumeration value="purple"/>
        <xsd:enumeration value="orange"/>
        <xsd:enumeration value="blue"/>
        <xsd:enumeration value="grey"/>
    </xsd:restriction>
</xsd:simpleType>
<xsd:simpleType name="sizeType">
    <xsd:restriction base="xsd:string">
        <xsd:enumeration value="M"/>
        <xsd:enumeration value="L"/>
        <xsd:enumeration value="XL"/>
    </xsd:restriction>
</xsd:simpleType>
```

```
      <!-- define attribute group -->
1.<xsd:attributeGroup name="clothesAttrGroup">
    <xsd:attribute name="quantity"
type="xsd:nonNegativeInteger" />
    <xsd:attribute name="color" type="colorType" />
    <xsd:attribute name="size" type="sizeType" />
    <xsd:attribute name="material" type="xsd:string" />
</xsd:attributeGroup>


<!-- define elements -->
<xsd:element name="shirt">
    <xsd:complexType>
        2.<xsd:attributeGroup ref="clothesAttrGroup" />
    </xsd:complexType>
</xsd:element>

<xsd:element name="sweatshirt">
    <xsd:complexType>
        3.<xsd:attributeGroup ref="clothesAttrGroup" />
    </xsd:complexType>
</xsd:element>
```

HOW THE CODE WORKS

1. To define a group of attributes, use the `xsd:attribute-Group` element. Then simply list as many attributes (and only attributes) as you want.
2. Here's the first reference, much like other references you've seen, an `xsd:attributeGroup` element with a `ref` attribute.
3. Here's the reference for the `sweatshirt` element.

Annotation and Documentation

To officially add documentation to your XML Schema and it make more readable and decipherable, you embed an `xsd:documentation` element inside `xsd:annotation`, like this:

```
<xsd:annotation>
    <xsd:documentation>
    This schema is designed to validate any XML document
that contains order information from the Stitch Store
    </xsd:documentation>
</xsd:annotation>
```

You can place these elements anywhere in your document—anywhere it'd be helpful for you or another programmer to understand what's going on.

Including External Files

You can create your schema from several different documents if you like by using a couple of simple tags. To include an entire external schema, use the `xsd:include` element like so:

```
<xsd:include schemaLocation="filename.xsd" />
```

Using this XML Schema element is just like copying and pasting the code from an external file into your file—it's a complete inclusion. However, you aren't allowed to redefine anything that's in the external file.

There is a way around this, though. If you call an external file using `xsd:redefine`, the external file is included, but you're given an opportunity to redefine any of the elements, attributes, types, or groups in that external file. Here's an example:

```
<xsd:redefine schemaLocation="shirts.xsd">
    <xsd:element name="shirt" type="newShirtType" />
    <xsd:simpleType name="newColorType">
        <xsd:restriction base="xsd:string">
            <xsd:maxLength value="20" />
        </xsd:restriction>
    </xsd:simpleType>
</xsd:redefine>
```

HOW THE CODE WORKS

All of your redefinitions have to be placed inside the `xsd:redefine` element, and they override anything that's inside the `shirts.xsd` file.

◆ Recap

Congratulations! You've now seen the vast majority of what's possible in an XML Schema, and you can see the differences between XML Schema and DTDs. If you're interested in learning more, definitely check out *www.w3.org/XML/Schema* for the latest updates.

There's also an alternative to XML Schema out there called TREX that's easier to read than XML Schema. I don't know how popular it will be, but check it out at *www.thaiopensource.com/trex/tutorial.html*.

Take a break! When you're fully rested, come on back and we'll dive into namespaces.

6 Namespaces

IN THIS CHAPTER

Nothing in XML combines simplicity and confusion quite like namespaces. Many people start by thinking that namespaces are pretty simple, try to look deeper for extra significance, get seriously confused, realize that there isn't a whole lot to namespaces after all, and finally understand that they already know all they need to. I'll try to short-circuit this cycle and keep it simple.

◆ Purpose

Imagine you need to merge two (or more) XML documents into a single large one. Unfortunately, some of the elements in the various files have the same name. For example, `<order>` may appear in two of the XML documents. Programmers needed a way

83

to have all of these elements in a single document, even though in XML, elements must have different names. Their answer was to create something called a namespace, which is really just a naming scheme. What does a namespace look like?

```
<prefix:elementName />
```

The prefix is the name of the namespace (actually, just part of the name, but we'll cover that later). That's all a namespace is: just a different way to name elements so elements with duplicate names can be differentiated from each other. Namespaces can also be markers to an application to treat certain elements differently than normal XML. From what I've seen, this is the most common use of namespaces—XML Schema is an example, as well as XSLT and XLink, both of which we'll look at later.

◆ Syntax

In order to use a namespace prefix on an element, you have to declare a namespace, which is just a way of telling your XML "I'm going to start using a prefix now." Here's how you declare a namespace:

```
<anyElement xmlns:localName="URI">
```

So what's going on here, exactly? Well, a namespace has two names, really: a nickname (or more officially, a local name) and a real name (the URI). The local name is used in the XML document (that's what the prefix is: a namespace local name). The real name of a namespace is the URI. Notice that we're calling this a URI instead of a URL—URI is essentially the new name for URL. URI stands for Universal Resource Identifier, whereas URL is Universal Resource Locator. A URL should point to something on the Internet, while a URI is just a text string that looks like a URL—it may or may not actually point to something. A namespace's real name must be unique—no other namespace in the whole world should have the same real name as yours. For example:

```
<order xmlns:stitch="http://www.wire-man.com/ns/stitch" />
```

The idea is that when you create a namespace name (a URI), you use a domain name that's under your control or that you have permission to use. Thus, you can assure that your URI is indeed unique.

It's important that this is clear to you, or you'll get confused pretty quickly: A URI does not point to anything. If you type in a namespace name in a browser, you will probably get a "File Not Found" error. A URI is just a name, not necessarily a thing.

SIDE NOTE

URIs can be relative, but that use is deprecated, so don't use it. Besides, if you use a URI that looks like a relative URL, you're losing the required uniqueness of your namespace name.

Default Namespaces

Technically, you don't have to create a local name when you declare a namespace:

```
<anyElement xmlns:="URI">
```

This is perfectly valid and is called a *default namespace*. The element that declared the namespace and all of its descendents are considered part of this default namespace, even though there's no prefix, and elements all look like normal XML.

◆ What Namespaces Are

Namespaces are containers for names of elements and attributes. Namespaces do not contain the elements themselves, just their names. Imagine a list of all the kids in a class. Only the names of the kids are on the list, not the kids themselves. That's all namespaces are—a bunch of names.

Namespaces are also a two-part naming system, since all namespace have both a local name and a namespace name (URI).

Namespaces don't really exist as either physical or conceptual entities. They don't do anything except rename some elements. The term "namespace" implies that there's some kind of physical "space" where the names are. There is no space or entity, just some two-part names.

◆ What Namespaces Are Not

Most of the confusion surrounding namespaces has to do with thinking namespaces are something more than they are. Namespaces are not a way to combine XML documents. They are not a technology. It's possible for namespaces to be used in such an XML-merging technology, but namespaces themselves can't do it.

A namespace's URI doesn't point to anything. URIs are identifiers, not Web pages or files. Don't try to resolve the URIs— chances are good that nothing will happen.

SIDE NOTE

Some people have recently started to store files at their namespace URIs in a language called RDDL that spells out the expected names in a namespace. However, this is 100% voluntary—it can provide helpful info, but you don't need to do it yourself.

XML namespaces are not the same as traditional namespaces. A traditional namespace is a set of zero or more single names. Each name is unique and each name follows rules (if there are any) that govern what the names look like. Examples of traditional namespaces include the following:

- All the allowable element names in an XML document
- All the U.S. Postal Codes
- Phone numbers
- Names of tables in a relational database
- Scientific names of all the plant and animal species

Namespaces are often used in computer science as a way to contain a group of identifiers.

Namespaces do not have a structure. They're just a bunch of names. Even though a namespace is defined over a bunch of XML elements, and that group of elements definitely has a structure, the namespace itself doesn't even see the structure. It knows its scope (defined below), but it doesn't see the structure of the defining element's descendents.

Namespaces don't apply to entities, notations, or processing instructions.

Elements are not automatically placed in a namespace. If you do not define a namespace, elements do not belong to one.

Some programs/technologies consider the xmlns attribute a "namespace declaration," while others just see it as an attribute. For example, DTDs don't see namespaces, so xmlns is just another attribute. XML Schema documents, though, recognize xmlns as a namespace declaration. We'll cover DTD and XML Schema validation of namespaces later in this chapter.

◆ Using Namespaces

As you've seen, namespaces are declared by the `xmlns` attribute.

Anyone can create a namespace—no standards body is required. You should use only URIs that you can control, though, or there's a potential for serious bugs in the future. Even though it probably doesn't really matter if you use a random domain name that isn't yours, why take the chance? There's no reason not to choose a proper URI, so you might as well do it. If you don't have your own domain name, ask a friend who does (I'm assuming that if you made it to Chapter 6 in an XML book, you or one of your friends has at least one domain name).

Scope

The scope is all of the elements that are affected by the namespace declaration. The scope is the name of the element containing the declaration, and the names of all of the descendents (including attributes).

When a namespace is declared, the namespace covers the element that defines it and all descendent elements. In this case, `store` and `shirt` are in the `wire` namespace. To add a complicating factor, the `wire` namespace does not include the `mugs` element. So what's going on? Well, there is no `mugs` element—there's an element called `wiremugs` that happens to have a colon in the middle of it: `wire:mugs`. The namespace is in scope for the defining element and all of its descendents.

```
<wire:store xmlns:wire="http://www.wire-man.com/ns/1">
    <wire:shirt>9 purple XXL</wire:shirt>
</wire:store>
<wire:mugs>10 "WTF?" black</wire:mugs>
```

The `wire` namespace covers the `store` element and everything inside the `store` element, which in this case is only the `shirt` element. Though `wire:mugs` looks like it's part of the namespace, it's not, because it's out of scope.

Overriding a Namespace

You can also override a namespace by reassigning a local name to a new namespace, as in Example 6–1.

EXAMPLE 6–1 REDEFINING A NAMESPACE

```
<wire:order xmlns:wire="http://www.wire-man.com/ns/1">
    <wire:store>
        <wire:shirt xmlns:wire="http:/www.wire-
man.com/ns/shirts">
            <wire:color>purple</wire:color>
        </wire:shirt>
    </wire:store>
</wire:order>
```

You cannot "undeclare" a namespace if there's a local name involved. You can only reassign it. That is, you cannot disconnect a prefix like `wire` from its namespace of "http://www.wire-man.com/ns/1"—you can only reassign a prefix (i.e., a local name) to another namespace name (i.e., a URI).

You can, however, "undeclare" a default namespace with an `xmlns=""`.

```
<wire:order xmlns="">
```

Multiple Namespaces

Multiple namespaces can be in the scope at the same time, as in Example 6–2.

EXAMPLE 6–2 CO-EXISTING NAMESPACES

```
<wire:order xmlns:wire="http://www.wire-man.com/ns/1">
    <wire:store>
        <wire:shirt xmlns:stitch="http:/www.wire-
man.com/ns/stitch">
            <wire:color>
                <stitch:shade>lavender</stitch:shade>
            </wire:color>
        </wire:shirt>
    </wire:store>
</wire:order>
```

Namespaces and Attributes

When element names become part of a namespace, all of the attribute names that are part of those elements become part of the namespace automatically. You don't need to prefix the attribute names with the local name (though you can)—only the element needs a prefix.

◆ Namespaces and DTDs

If you want to validate your namespace-filled XML against a DTD, you have to declare each prefixed element separately in the DTD. DTDs don't know anything about namespaces. To the DTD, the xmlns is just another attribute and prefixed elements are just elements whose names happen to contain a colon. Example 6–3 shows how this is done.

EXAMPLE 6–3 SPECIFYING NAMESPACES IN A DTD

```
<?xml version="1.0" encoding="UTF-8"?>
<!DOCTYPE  wire:order [
    <!ELEMENT wire:order (wire:store)>
    <!ATTLIST wire:order xmlns CDATA #FIXED
"http://www.wire-man.com/ns/1">

    <!ELEMENT wire:store (#PCDATA)>
]>

<wire:order xmlns="http://www.wire-man.com/ns/1">
    <wire:store>Stitch Store</wire:store>
</wire:order>
```

The lack of direct support for namespaces in DTDs is one of the reasons some people are migrating to XML Schema.

◆ Namespaces and Validity

DTDs can do nothing when it comes to validating namespaces. A DTD cannot validate whether a namespace is truly unique. Thus, there's no such thing as validation based on namespaces, as one might expect.

It's important that you're clear on this point: Namespaces do not assist in any way to validate a document. It can be confusing because it looks like the namespace name is a URL that leads to some kind document and that this document is a namespace reference of some kind. This has confused a lot of people, and continues to. Don't be confused! The URI is just an identifier, like the PIN number for your ATM card.

Validity is defined in the XML 1.0 specification. Namespaces are not technically part of the XML 1.0 spec—they're layered on top of it. Thus, namespaces have nothing to do with the validity of an XML document.

◆ Namespaces and XML Schema

XML Schema handles namespaces a little more directly and elegantly than DTDs. In a DTD, you must declare each element with its prefix. When using namespaces with XML Schema, it's best to create a separate XML Schema document for each namespace that you'll be using. The good news is that you only need to specify the namespace name (URI) in the XML Schema document. The opposite was true in the DTD: We defined elements with the local name. This means that when a namespace's elements are defined in an XML Schema document, you can use any prefix you want to in the actual XML.

How do you create an XML Schema document that understands the use of namespaces in an XML document? All you have to do is add a few attributes to xsd:schema, as in Example 6-4.

Let's say this is your XML:

EXAMPLE 6–4 SOME XML AND ITS XML SCHEMA

```
<?xml version="1.0" encoding="UTF-8"?>

<pants:order
  xmlns:xsi="http://www.w3.org/2000/10/XMLSchema-instance"
  xsi:noNamespaceSchemaLocation="namespace2.xsd"
  xmlns:pants="http://www.wire-man.com/ns/1">
    <store>30 paisley capri</store>
</pants:order>
```

Here's the way to code the XML Schema for it.

```
<?xml version="1.0" encoding="UTF-8"?>
1.<xsd:schema
        2.xmlns:xsd="http://www.w3.org/2000/10/XMLSchema"
        3.targetNamespace="http://www.wire-man.com/ns/1"
        4.xmlns:wire="http://www.wire-man.com/ns/1">

<xsd:element name="order">
<xsd:complexType>
   <xsd:sequence>
        <xsd:element name="store" type="xsd:string" />
   </xsd:sequence>
</xsd:complexType>
</xsd:element>

</xsd:schema>
```

HOW THE CODE WORKS

1. Everything that defines a namespace goes in the xsd:schema element.
2. This is the line that defines this XML document as an XML Schema.
3. targetNamespace determines what namespace name (URI) the XML can use. In the XML above, notice that we're declaring a namespace called "pants" and "http://www.wire-man.com/ns/1."
4. To make the targetNamespace valid, we have to declare a namespace in the XML Schema document using the same URI as targetNamespace. I don't really know why this is true—it's just part of the XML Schema setup. Notice that the local name used in the XML Schema document ("wire") does not have to be the same as the local name in the XML document ("pants").

Notice that a total of three attributes have the same value: targetNamespace, xmlns:wire, and xmlns:pants.

The above method only pulls the global elements into the namespace. Did you notice that order was not prefixed with pants? We need yet another attribute:

```
<xsd:schema
xmlns:xsd="http://www.w3.org/2000/10/XMLSchema"
targetNamespace="http://www.wire-man.com/ns/1"
xmlns:wire="http://www.wire-man.com/ns/1"
elementFormDefault="qualified">
```

HOW THE CODE WORKS

The attribute that assigns the namespace to all elements is elementFormDefault="qualified". Once we do this, then store element must be prefixed into pants:store in the XML document.

If you want to include some elements in the namespace and not others, you can skip elementFormDefault in xsd:schema and add form="qualified" to the individual element. For example:

```
<xsd:schema
    xmlns:xsd="http://www.w3.org/2000/10/XMLSchema"
    targetNamespace="http://www.wire-man.com/ns/1"
    xmlns:wire="http://www.wire-man.com/ns/1">
```

```
<xsd:element name="order">
<xsd:complexType>
    <xsd:sequence>
        <xsd:element name="store" type="xsd:string"
form="qualified"/>
    </xsd:sequence>
</xsd:complexType>
</xsd:element>

</xsd:schema>
```

If the situation is reversed, and you want to exclude an element from the namespace, simply add the attribute `form="unqualified"`.

◆ Recap

That's it for namespaces. We'll be using them in a few other places in this book, namely the chapters on XSLT and XLink. Remember that namespaces are containers for names. It's as if a namespace is a bucket that you toss a name into. The only function of a namespace is the two-part naming of elements. That's all a namespace is, and that's all it does. It's a good tool to have, but it's not as complicated as many people think it is.

7 XLink: Creating Links in XML

The folks that created XML wanted a way to create powerful links in XML, something much more sophisticated that the simple <a> tag from HTML.

They accomplished this by adding a layer on top of XML, and they called that layer XML Linking Language *(XLink for short), much in the same way XML Schema was layered on top of an XML document. XLink is simpler than XML Schema, though, so this chapter isn't quite as technically challenging as some of the earlier ones.*

◆ Introduction to XLink

XLink is a standardized way to create links in XML. You could always code your own custom links and stay away from XLink, but it's quite well thought-out and useful, so I'd recommend using it. As of this writing, XLink is a "Proposed Recommendation," which means that it isn't quite final yet. Be sure to check out *www.w3.org/TR/xlink* to see what the latest state of the recommendation is.

XLink is essentially a set of attributes that you attach to your own XML elements. XLink works by allowing you to create elements that represent links between various resources, as well as elements that describe those links.

XLink requires an *XLink application*, which is a software module that can parse the XLink language. An XLink application is usually part of a larger XML parser.

XLink lives in a namespace—it's just a bunch of attributes that begin with `xlink:`.

What XLink Can Do

XLink can create simple links, similar to the familiar `<a>` tag from HTML. The starting point of an HTML link is surrounded by the `<a>` tag, and the ending point of the link is an external file (or a named anchor in the same file). XLink can do more, though—it can allow a link to connect to multiple resources at once and can more precisely specify the link's behavior.

XLink allows XML to

- Create linking relationships between more than two resources.

- Associate metadata with links (similar to the oft-neglected `title` attribute of the `<a>` tag.

- Create a link that exists in a place separate from the resources it connects.

How XLink Is Implemented

Let's look at a quick example.

```
<myLinks xmlns:xlink="http://www.w3.org/1999/xlink">
    <!-- your links and such -->
</myLinks>
```

Yes, this is a namespace. But instead of affecting elements, like we saw in the last chapter, this namespace is only to be used on attributes. You could use the `xlink` prefix before elements, but it would confuse the XML application, so keep the prefix connected only to the attributes.

Let's look at what a simple link looks like:

```
<contactLink xlink:type="simple" xlink:href="contact.xml">
    Contact us!
</contactLink>
```

We'll be going over this structure in more detail later. I just wanted you to see what a simple link looked like.

◆ Concepts and Terminology

XLink uses some pretty specific terminology based on a certain worldview. Let's see how XLink views the world. We'll start by looking at a familiar link using XLink's worldview, define some terms, and cover some concepts.

Let's analyze the `<a href="`*xx*`">` tag from an XLink point of view. This tag:

- Uses a URI as a locator technology.
- Expresses the hyperlink at the starting point of the link.
- Identifies the ending point of the link (via the `href` attribute).
- Enables users to initiate traversal of the link from one end to the other end (that is, users click on link A to go to page B, not the other way around).

◆ Definitions

Let's look at XLink's vocabulary.

resource

A resource, technically, is any addressable chunk of information or services. Examples are Web pages, images, sounds, and named portions of a document. Resources come in two flavors: remote and local. A remote resource is one that can be addressed using a URI—it's usually a resource that exists in an external file. A local resource is a resource that is part of the document that contains the link. In an `<a>` tag, the local resource is the content that the user can click on, whether it's text or an image.

link

A link is an explicit relationship between resources or portions of resources.

XLink element

An XLink element is an XML element whose attributes conform to XLink specifications and assert the existence of a link.

traverse

To traverse a link is to follow or use the link for any reason. A traversal occurs between two resources. A link can contain any number of traversals, since links can contain multiple connections among multiple resources.

arc

An arc is information about how to move across a traversal, including its direction, and its starting and ending point See Figure 7–1.

inbound traversal

An inbound traversal leads from a remote resource to a local resource.

outbound traversal

An outbound traversal leads from a local resource to a remote resource.

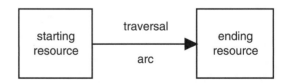

FIGURE 7–1 An arc

third-party traversal

A third-party traversal leads from a remote resource to another remote resource. In this case, the link is in a separate place than either of the participating resources.

XLink application

An XLink application is a software module that parses `xlink` attributes.

simple link

A simple link is a link that has exactly two resources, and is outbound (moves from a local resource to a remote resource). The `<a>` tag specifies a simple link (see Example 7–1). We'll look at this in more detail later.

EXAMPLE 7–1 THE SIMPLEST LINK

```
<myLink xlink:type="simple" xlink:href="effects.xml"/>
```

extended link

An extended link is a link that connects any number of resources. These resources can be any combination of local and remote resources.

This means that a simple link is actually a specific type of an extended link. The two are separated for convenience—a simplified syntax for a simple link makes life easier for XML developers (see Example 7–2).

EXAMPLE 7–2 AN EXTENDED LINK WITH MULTIPLE LOCATIONS

```
<myLink xlink:type="extended"
    title="effects to side effects">
  <sideEffects xlink:type="location"
    xlink:href="side.xml"
    xlink:label="side"/>
  <effects xlink:type="location"
    xlink:href="effects.xml"
    xlink:label="effects" />
  <bind xlink:type="arc"
    xlink:from="effects"
    xlink:to="effects" />
</myLink>
```

Don't worry about what's happening here—we'll cover this in detail later.

linkbases

A linkbase, also known as a link database, is a document that holds collections of inbound and third-party links. Linkbases are often used for link management, since finding remote resources isn't always easy.

◆ Usage

All XLink elements must include the `xlink:type` attribute. There are several different values you can use: `simple`, extended, resource, location, arc, and title. Using `xlink:type="simple"` defines your element as a simple link, and using `xlink:type="extended"` defines your element as an extended link. The proper names for these elements are *simple-type element* and *extended-type element*, respectively. The other types of elements are labeled in the same way—resource-type element, arc-type element, and so on.

Some of these XLink elements can contain other XLink elements. Table 7–1 shows which elements can be child elements.

Those are all the possible values for the type attribute. Now let's look at all the other attributes that are part of XLink.

◆ Attributes

Table 7–2 has a list of all the attributes you can use, along with a short description. We'll look at these attributes in more detail later—this is just a quick look to give you an idea of what's ahead.

TABLE 7–1 Elements and Allowed Child Elements (from W3C)

Parent Type	Significant Child Type
simple	None
extended	locator, arc, resource, title
locator	title
arc	title
resource	None
title	None

TABLE 7–2 Allowable Attributes and Descriptions

Attribute	Description
type	Mandatory attribute for all XLink elements—determines what kind of element it is.
href	A URI (used to be called a URL), just like HTML.
role	A URI that leads to a resource that describes the intended property.
arcrole	Like the role attribute, this must be a URI, but it's used to link to a linkbase (we'll cover this in detail later).
title	A human-readable string that describes the element (and yes, there's also a title-type element).
label	An XML-valid name that you attach to resource-type and location-type elements. A label allows other elements to refer to it.
show	Determines where the ending resource appears. Appropriate values are new, replace, other, none, and embed.
actuate	Determines the timing of when the link is traversed. Allowable values are onLoad, onRequest, other, and none.

◆ Elements and Their Attributes

XLink elements are restricted in the kind of attributes they can or must contain. Let's look at a summary in Table 7–3. This is just to give you an overview—we'll get into detail later. This table is from the W3C specification. Required attributes are denoted by R, and optional attributes are denoted by O.

TABLE 7–3 Elements and Their Attributes

	Element Types					
Attributes	simple	extended	locator	arc	resource	title
type	R	R	R	R	R	R
href	O		R			
role	O	O	O		O	
arcrole	O			O		
title	O	O	O	O	O	
show	O			O		
actuate	O			O		
label			O		O	
from				O		
to				O		

◆ Simple Links

Simple links are the kind of links you've seen before in HTML. Also known as a simple-type element, a simple link is a link between exactly two resources, a local starting resource and a remote ending resource. Example 7–3 shows a simple syntax.

EXAMPLE 7–3 SIMPLE LINK SYNTAX

```
<myLink xlink:type="simple"
    xlink:href="ending_resource_URI">
    starting resource text
</myLink>
```

HOW THE CODE WORKS

This is almost identical to the `<a>` tag in HTML. Notice that we only have two attributes: `type`, which is required for all XLink elements, and `href`, which is optional (I recommend always using it even if it is optional—otherwise, your link is untraversable).

Example 7–4 shows a simple link with all of the optional attributes.

EXAMPLE 7–4 TYPICAL SIMPLE LINK

```
<drugLink xlink:type="simple"
    xlink:href="http:/www.shelleybio.com/products"
    xlink:show="replace"
    xlink:actuate="onRequest"
    xlink:title="List of pharm. products"
    xlink:role="http://www.shelleybio.com/productdesc/"
    xlink:arcrole="http://www.shelleybio.com/xml/linkbase">
    Shelley Biotech's pharmaceutical products
</drugLink>
```

HOW THE CODE WORKS

This link, despite its plethora of attributes, is still a simple link from the text "Shelley Biotech's pharmaceutical products" to the URL *http://www.shelleybio.com/products*. Let's look at all of these attributes:

type

Every XLink element must have a `type` attribute—it's the only way of identifying the purpose of the element. In this case, `type="simple"`, so this is a simple type element.

href

Just like HTML, the value of an `href` attribute must be a URI (a.k.a. URL).

show

The `show` attribute determines where the ending resource is placed in the window/frame/panel. Only certain values are allowed: `new`, `replace`, `embed`, `other`, and `none`. In this case, we're using the value of `replace`, which means "replace the starting resource with the ending resource." This is the default way HTML links work: Starting Web pages are replaced by ending Web pages. (It's like saying `target="_self"` in an `<a>` tag.)

Using a value of `new` creates a new window/frame/panel and places the ending resource in it, much like `target="_blank"` in an `<a>` tag.

Setting a value of `embed` requests the ending resource to place itself inside the document containing the starting resource and replace only the starting resource while leaving the rest of the document alone. This is analogous to embedding an image or a Flash file in a Web page.

Setting a value of `other` tells the XLink processor to continue looking in the XML document for instructions on what to do with the ending resource. There's no standard for what these further instructions look like, so it's dependent on what program is parsing your XLink code.

Choosing a value of `none` tells the XLink parser, "Do whatever you want." The `none` value really means "unconstrained." It's left to the application to decide what to do with the link.

actuate

The `actuate` attribute determines when the link is actually traversed. There are four allowable values: `onRequest`, `onLoad`, `other`, and `none`. We've chosen `onRequest`, which means that the user must do something before the link is traversed (like clicking on it). If we had chosen `onLoad`, the link would have been traversed as soon as the starting resource was loaded. Bringing images into an HTML page uses a property similar to `onLoad`: The images are loaded as soon as possible—the user doesn't have to do anything to load images onto the page. The values `other` and `none` mean the same thing as in the `show` attribute: `other` tells the XLink application to continue looking for instructions, and `none` lets the application decide when to traverse the link.

role

This attribute contains a URI that leads to a document that describes the role of the link. This can be useful if you need more room than a `title` attribute (or title-type element) can conveniently contain. There's no standard format for this document.

arcrole

An `arcrole` is more complicated (and you'd probably never use it in a simple link), so we'll look at `arcroles` in more detail when we cover extended type links in the next section.

◆ What Simple Links Can't Do

Simple links can't
- Support more than two resources.
- Support inbound or third-party resources (all simple links must be outbound).
- Associate a title with an arc.
- Associate a title or a role with a local resource.
- Associate a title or a role with the link as a whole.

To do any of these things, you need an extended-type link.

◆ Simple Links that Seem Like Errors, but Aren't

You can create what appear to be nonsensical simple links that don't produce an error, links with no starting resource and links with no `href` attribute.

Links without a Starting Resource

A link with no starting resource could look like this:

```
<myLink xlink:type="simple" xlink:href="http://foo.com" />
```

This is a valid simple type link, even though there's no starting resource. In this case, XLink applications are typically expected to insert some default content to alert the user that a link exists.

Links with no **href** Attribute

It's possible for a link to have no `href` attribute:

```
<myLink xlink:type="simple">zap!</myLink>
```

Surprisingly, this isn't an error—it simply creates an untraversable link, much like `<a>hi there</a>` in HTML.

Simple Links in a DTD

Since XLink is just XML, let's look at how we'd define a simple link and its attributes in a DTD, as in Example 7–5.

EXAMPLE 7–5 A SIMPLE LINK'S DTD

```
<!ELEMENT drugLink ANY>
<!ATTLIST drugLink
    xlink:type (simple) #FIXED "simple"
    xlink:href CDATA #IMPLIED
    xlink:role NMTOKEN #IMPLIED
    xlink:arcrole NMTOKEN #IMPLIED
    xlink:show (new|replace|embed|other|none) #IMPLIED
    xlink:actuate (onLoad|onRequest|other|none) #IMPLIED
    xlink:title CDATA #IMPLIED>
```

HOW THE CODE WORKS

You've seen DTDs before (unless you really skipped ahead), so you should be able to decipher this on your own. Note that this DTD creates an element called `drugLink` that must be a simple link, because of the mandatory attribute `type` and its mandatory value of `simple`.

So that's the world of simple type elements, or simple links. They're much like the links you've seen in HTML, with a few extra attributes thrown on. The next section deals with extended links, which are different beasts altogether. The biggest difference is that extended links can actually act as a collection of links: that is, an extended link can contain multiple resources and multiple connections among those resources.

◆ Extended-Type Elements (Extended Links)

An extended link is a link that associates an arbitrary number of resources. The resources in a link are called *participating resources*. The participating resources in a link can be any combination of local and remote resources, even if they're all local or all remote.

In other words, an extended link can be any collection of inbound, outbound, and third-party arcs.

This kind of seemingly esoteric link can be useful because extended links are often stored in a separate location than the resources they associate.

How do these extended links contain any number of resources and connections? They do it by holding child elements that describe the resources and traverses of the link. Let's take a quick overview of these child elements.

Locator-Type Elements

These elements define any remote resources that are involved in the link.

Resource-type elements

These elements define any local resources involved in the link.

Arc-type elements

These elements provide traversal rules—that is, they establish which resource is the starting resource and which is the ending resource. Remember that a traversal connects two resources, and an extended link can be a collection of traversals.

Title-type elements

This element contains a human-readable string, a chunk of text that is often used to describe the extended link.

SIDE NOTE

You can also nest simple type elements and extended-type elements inside extended-type elements. However, if you do this, the links have nothing to do with each other, even though they appear to be part of the same link. Nested links have no relationship with each other.

Any child elements of locator-, resource-, or arc-type elements have no relationship to the link that contains the locator-, resource-, or arc-type element (that is, their grandparent elements). Here's an abridged example:

```
<myLink xlink:type="extended">
   <local xlink:type="locator"
xlink:href="http://foo.com"
xlink:label="foo">
         <ignored>la la la</ignored>
   </local>
... [ other subelements ] ...
</myLink>
```

HOW THE CODE WORKS

The `<ignored>` tag is completely ignored by the XLink application—it has no relationship to the surrounding link at all.

A more realistic example has three resources, as in Example 7–6.

EXAMPLE 7–6 AN EXTENDED LINK

```
<drugLink xlink:type="extended">
    <!-- two local resources -->
    <chemName xlink:type="resource"
        xlink:label="chemicalName">
        hydrachloroniametahexacyocaine
    </chemName>
    <marName xlink:type="resource" xlink:label="marketName">
        BreatheEasy
    </marName>

    <!-- two remote resources -->
    <effects xlink:type="locator"
        xlink:href="http://www.shelleybio.com/effects"
        xlink:label="effects" />
    <sideEffect xlink:type="locator"
        xlink:href="http://www.shelleybio.com/sides"
        xlink:label="sideEffects" />

    <!-- three traversals -->
    <link1 xlink:type="arc"
        xlink:from="chemicalName"
        xlink:to="effects"
        xlink:show="replace"
        xlink:actuate="onRequest" />
    <link2 xlink:type="arc"
        xlink:from="marketName"
        xlink:to="effects"
        xlink:show="replace"
        xlink:actuate="onRequest" />
    <link3 xlink:type="arc"
        xlink:from="chemicalName"
        xlink:to="sideEffects"
        xlink:show="replace"
        xlink:actuate="onRequest" />
</drugLink>
```

HOW THE CODE WORKS

There are a total of four resources here. The two local resources are the resource-type elements named `chemName` and `marName`.

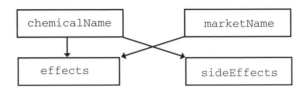

FIGURE 7–2 The resources and traversals of the extended link

The labels of these elements are `chemicalName` and `market-Name`, respectively. These two local resources are defined right in the elements themselves: `hydrachloroniametahexacyocaine` and `BreatheEasy`.

The two remote resources, resources that reside in another document, are located in the `effects` and `sideEffect` elements, and are located at *www.shelleybio.com/effects* and *www.shelleybio.com/sides*, respectively. The labels of these two remote resources are `effects` and `sideEffects`.

Once the resources are defined, it's time to connect them. In this link, we have three traversals. Both `chemicalName` and `marketName` are linked to `effects`, and `chemicalName` is linked to `sideEffects`. These relationships are shown in Figure 7–2.

◆ Extended Links and DTDs

What does the DTD for an extended link look like? Let's look at Example 7–7.

EXAMPLE 7–7 THE DRUGLINK DTD

```
<!ELEMENT drugLink (chemName | marName | effects |
    sideEffect | link1 | link2 | link3)*>
<!ATTLIST drugLink xlink:type (extended) #FIXED "extended">

<!ELEMENT chemName ANY>
<!ATTLIST chemName
    xlink:type (resource) #FIXED "resource"
    xlink:role  CDATA #IMPLIED
    xlink:label NMTOKEN #IMPLIED>

<!ELEMENT marName ANY>
<!ATTLIST marName
    xlink:type (resource) #FIXED "resource"
```

```
    xlink:role  CDATA #IMPLIED
    xlink:label NMTOKEN #IMPLIED>

<!ELEMENT sideEffect ANY>
<!ATTLIST sideEffect
    xlink:type (locator) #FIXED "locator"
    xlink:href CDATA #REQUIRED
    xlink:role CDATA #IMPLIED
    xlink:label NMTOKEN #IMPLIED>

<!ELEMENT effects ANY>
<!ATTLIST effects
    xlink:type (locator) #FIXED "locator"
    xlink:href CDATA #REQUIRED
    xlink:role CDATA #IMPLIED
    xlink:label NMTOKEN #IMPLIED>

<!ELEMENT link1 ANY>
<!ATTLIST link1
    xlink:type (arc) #FIXED "arc"
    xlink:from NMTOKEN #IMPLED
    xlink:to NMTOKEN #IMPLIED
    xlink:show (new|replace|embed|other|none) #IMPLIED
    xlink:actuate (onLoad|onRequest|other|none) #IMPLIED>

<!ELEMENT link2 ANY>
<!ATTLIST link2
    xlink:type (arc) #FIXED "arc"
    xlink:from NMTOKEN #IMPLIED
    xlink:to NMTOKEN #IMPLIED
    xlink:show (new|replace|embed|other|none) #IMPLIED
    xlink:actuate (onLoad|onRequest|other|none) #IMPLIED >

<!ELEMENT link3 ANY>
<!ATTLIST link3
    xlink:type (arc) #FIXED "arc"
    xlink:from NMTOKEN #IMPLIED
    xlink:to NMTOKEN #IMPLIED
    xlink:show (new|replace|embed|other|none) #IMPLIED
    xlink:actuate (onLoad|onRequest|other|none) #IMPLIED >
```

HOW THE CODE WORKS

As before, use your knowledge of DTDs to examine this code—it'll reinforce how these XLink elements are put together.

Now we're going to look at all of the possible subelements in an extended link in more detail. That is, resource-, locator-, arc-, and title-type elements.

◆ Resource-Type Elements

Resource-type elements specify local resources—in other words, resources that occur in the body of an XML document. Resource-type elements generally look like this:

```
<myRes xlink:type="resource"
    xlink:role="http://foo.com/resource-description"
    xlink:title="This is the text linking to the effects
        section"
    xlink:label="effectLink">
    Click here to see the effects!
</myRes>
```

The only mandatory attribute is `type`, but your resource can't be a part of any links unless you give it a label. Arc-type resources need a label name in order to establish a connection between resources. The optional attributes of a resource-type element are `role`, `title`, and `label`.

Here's a DTD describing a resource-type element.

```
<!ELEMENT myRes ANY>
<!ATTLIST myRes
    xlink:type (resource) #FIXED "resource"
    xlink:title CDATA #IMPLIED
    xlink:role CDATA #IMPLIED
    xlink:label NMTOKEN #IMPLIED>
```

As mentioned above, it is possible to have a local resource that has no content. If a link is meant to be traversed on user request (that is, `actuate="onRequest"`), and the starting local resource has no content, then the XLink application will typically generate some default content that will allow the user to initiate the traversal.

The naming here can be confusing: There are such things as local resources and remote resources, but the element that defines a local resource is a resource-type element, and the element that defines a remote resource is a locator-type element. The multiple uses of the word "resource" takes a little getting used to.

◆ Locator-Type Elements

A locator-type element defines a remote resource by pointing to that resource with a URI. The only meaningful child element that a locator-type element can contain is a title-type element. Any other child element won't have any relationship with the link. Also, a locator-type element must have an extended-type element for a parent, or the locator-type element isn't associated with a link.

Even though locator-type elements must contain an `href` attribute, they don't create links any more than resource-type elements do. All locator- and resource-type elements do is say, "Here's a resource." They say nothing about the connections between resources (creating those connections is the job of the arc-type elements).

The required attributes of a locator-type element are `type` and `href`—it's the only element that requires more than the `type` attribute. The optional attributes are `role`, `title`, and `label`. Even though `label` isn't a required attribute, you'll need it to create a traversal either to or from the remote resource (arc-type elements use the `label` attribute as references).

Here's an example of a locator-type element:

```
<farAway xlink:type="locator"
    xlink:href="http://www.shelleybio.com/effects"
    xlink:label="effects" />
```

And here's a piece of a DTD that defines a locator-type element.

```
<!ELEMENT farAway ANY>
<!ATTLIST farAway
    xlink:type (locator) #FIXED "locator"
    xlink:href CDATA #REQUIRED
    xlink:role CDATA #IMPLIED
    xlink:label NMTOKEN #IMPLIED>
```

Now that we've looked at the two kinds of elements that define the resources that can be in a link, it's time to look at the element that actually creates the connection, or traversal, between resources.

◆ Arc-Type Elements

Arc-type elements are the beasts that create the actual connections between resources. These connections are known as traversals. An "arc" is what contains information about the traversal: what resources it connects and what direction the traversal is in. All traversals have a beginning and an ending point.

Arc-type elements may have content, but that content is not related to the link.

Like all XLink elements, arc-type elements must have a `type` attribute. No other attributes are required. All other attributes (`to`, `from`, `show`, `actuate`, `arcrole`, `title`) are optional, but most likely you'll always use the `to` and `from` attributes, which set the starting and ending points of the traversal. The value of these two attributes comes from the `label` attribute of resource- and locator-type elements.

Let's look a simple example that connects two remote resources.

```
<eLink xlink:type="extended">
    <effects xlink:type="locator"
        xlink:href="http://www.shelleybio.com/effects"
        xlink:label="effects" />
    <sideEffects xlink:type="locator"
        xlink:href="http://www.shelleybio.com/side"
        xlink:label="sides" />
    <effectsArc xlink:type="arc"
        xlink:from="effects"
        xlink:to="sides"
        xlink:show="replace"
        xlink:actuate="onRequest"
        xlink:title="link from a drug's effects to its side
            effects" />
</eLink>
```

HOW THE CODE WORKS

The element `effectsArc` is the arc-type element that connects the two remote resources listed. Notice that the names of the elements are `effects` and `sideEffects`, while their `label` attribute values are `effects` and `sides`. Arc-type elements use the `label` values to set the starting and ending point of the traversal, so the values of the `to` and `from` attributes match the values of the `label` attributes.

Setting Several Traversals with a Single Arc

At first blush, it looks like arc-type elements can only connect pairs of elements, but they can actually connect any number of resources with a single element. How is this possible? Simple— you give multiple resources the same label. Let's look at an example: say you have two drivers and three cars. Each driver is capable of driving all three cars. Figure 7–3 shows what that relationship would look like.

From what we have learned, creating this link would take five elements to create the two driver resources and three car

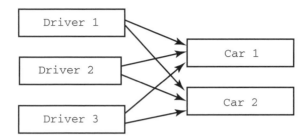

FIGURE 7–3 Relationship between drivers and cars

resources, and then six more arc-type elements to create the six traversals. However, with a little creative labeling, we can pare this down to a single arc-type element, as in Example 7–8.

EXAMPLE 7–8 MULTIPLE TRAVERSALS IN A SINGLE ARC-TYPE ELEMENT

```
<myGarage xlink:type="extended">
    <driver1 xlink:type="resource"
        xlink:label="driver">Bob</driver1>
    <driver2 xlink:type="resource"
        xlink:label="driver">Francine</driver1>
    <car1 xlink:type="resource"
        xlink:label="car">Mazda Miata</car1>
    <car2 xlink:type="resource"
        xlink:label="car">4Runner</car2>
    <car3 xlink:type="resource"
        xlink:label="car">Roadster</car3>
    <garageArcs xlink:type="arc"
        xlink:from="driver"
        xlink:to="car" />
</myGarage>
```

HOW THE CODE WORKS

Notice that we labeled the two `driver` elements as `driver`, and we labeled the three `car` elements as `car`. When the XLink application has to create a traversal from the `driver`-labeled element to the `car`-labeled element, it creates traversals in all possible combinations. That is, it creates the six traversals: driver1-car1, driver1-car2, driver1-car3, driver2-car1, driver2-car2, and driver2-car3. This can be a handy shortcut.

Remember that the `to` and `from` attributes are optional: what happens when one or both are omitted? An XLink application assumes that the missing label stands for *all* labels. Let's check this out.

```
<garageLinks xlink:type="arc" xlink:from="driver" />
```

Figure 7–4 shows the result of this code.

Whoa! What happened? By omitting the to attribute, we created the equivalent of the code below:

```
<garageLinks xlink:type="arc"
    xlink:from="driver" xlink:to="car" />
<garageLinks xlink:type="arc"
  xlink:from="driver" xlink:to="driver" />
```

Any traversal that can begin on any driver-labeled resource is created, including a traversal from a driver resource to itself. This creates a total of 15 traversals.

If you omit both the from and to attributes, then everything connects to everything else. This would create a total of 25 traversals.

```
<garageLinks xlink:type="arc" />
```

This method of creating traversals isn't used much, as you might guess.

You can also use an arc-type element to connect to a linkbase.

Using arcrole and Linkbases

A linkbase is a link database that holds collections of inbound and third-party links. Linkbases are often used for link management. In order to set up a call to a linkbase, add this attribute to an arc-type element:

```
arcrole="http://www.w3.org/1999/xlink/properties/linkbase"
```

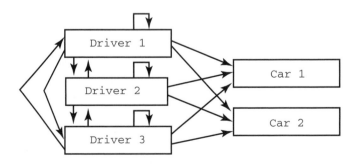

FIGURE 7–4 An omitted to attribute

Including this attribute in an arc-type element (and this exact value as well) is a signal to an XLink application to locate the appropriate linkbase and extract the appropriate link from the database. It's up to the XLink application to know where the appropriate linkbase is and where the appropriate link inside that linkbase is (or display a set of appropriate links). Determining the exact linkbase or the links inside the linkbase isn't something you're even allowed to code—the XLink application takes care of everything. All you as a programmer can do is use the code above, which is the same thing as announcing, "Use a linkbase now!" to the XLink application.

If you want to get fancy, this also allows you to potentially chain together linkbases.

That wraps up the necessary elements to create traversals between resources. There's one element left that can exist in an extended-type element: the title-type element.

◆ Title-Type Elements

The only purpose of a title-type element is to create a human-readable string. Why use a whole element instead of just using the `title` attribute? A title-type element can be longer, and can contain subelements.

```
<headline xlink:type="title">
    <english>Drug Effects</english>
    <espanol>Efectos de Drogas</espanol>
</headline>
```

HOW THE CODE WORKS

Any content can appear in a title-type element, and as you can see, it can be used for something like internationalization.

Simple vs. Extended Links

You may have realized that a simple link is just a kind of extended link. So why have a whole different kind of syntax? It's convenient. That's the only answer—the folks who put together XLink made our lives a little easier.

That's it for extended-type elements! And really, that's it for XLink. There is another section that covers in more detail all of the attributes that can be used, but it's elaboration of material you've already seen in this chapter. I do recommend at least skimming it, though: there's plenty of new stuff in this chapter, and the repetition will be good for you (trust me on this one).

◆ XLink Attributes

Time to look at all of the attributes and their properties.

type

The `type` attribute is the only attribute required by all XLink elements. The value of this attribute determines the purpose of the XLink element. Without setting `type`, you don't have an XLink element. The possible values are:

- `simple`: creates a link that contains a local starting point and a remote ending point
- `extended`: creates a link that may contain any number of resources and any manner of connections between them
- `resource`: creates a local resource
- `locator`: points to a remote resource
- `arc`: establishes a traversal between resources
- `title`: allows for a human-readable string that may contain child elements
- `none`: the element has no XLink-defined relationship to anything

href

The `href` attribute supplies the address of a remote resource. It may be in a simple type element (if it isn't the link is untraversable), and it must be in a locator-type element. Predictably, its value must be in the form of a URI. This attribute is also known as a *locator* attribute.

◆ Semantic Attributes (`title`, `role`, `arcrole`)

The role of semantic attributes is to describe resources.

title

The `title` attribute can appear in all XLink elements (except title-type elements). Its purpose is to provide a human-readable string for either programmers or some kind of display (or both).

role

The `role` attribute provides a URI that points to a resource (most likely, a document). This resource describes the element that the role attribute is a part of. The URI must be an absolute URI. Role attributes may be in extended-, simple-, locator-, and resource-type elements.

arcrole

Use the arcrole attribute to send your link to a linkbase—the XLink application should know where to go to find this linkbase. The URI must be an absolute URI. This attribute can only exist in locator-type elements.

◆ Behavior Attributes (show, actuate)

Both behavior attributes can exist only in simple- and arc-type elements. They're optional because these links may not be for users, but are intended for, say, other computer programs.

show

The show attribute determines where the ending point of the link appears. There are a few acceptable values:

- new: places the ending point in a new frame/window/panel. Analogous to target="_blank" in the <a> tag.
- replace: replaces the document containing the starting resource with the ending resource. Analogous to target= "_self" in the <a> tag.
- embed: loads the ending resource in place of the starting resource, without replacing the whole document. Analogous to the <img> tag.
- other: tells the XLink application to keep looking for instructions, which will determine what to do with the ending resource.
- none: really means "unconstrained"—tells the XLink application to decide what to do.

actuate

The actuate attribute describes when the link is traversed. It has a few allowable variables:

- onLoad: the link is traversed as soon as the starting resource is loaded
- onRequest: the link is traversed when the user initiates the traversal (often, the user does this by clicking on a link)
- other: tells the XLink application to keep looking for instructions, which will determine what to do with the ending resource

- none: really means "unconstrained"—tells the XLink application to decide what to do

◆ Traversal Attributes (`label`, `from`, `to`)

Traversal attributes describe the actual connection between resources.

label

This attribute gives a name to a resource that can be referenced elsewhere in the document. This name must be an XML-valid name (known as NMTOKEN in a DTD).

from

This attribute contains the name of the starting point of the traversal. It uses the name set in the `label` attribute. This attribute can only be found in arc-type elements.

to

This attribute contains the ending point of the traversal. Like the `from` attribute, `to` uses the name set in the `label` attribute. This attribute can only be found in arc-type elements.

◆ Recap

That's XLink! Remember that as of this writing, the XLink specification's status is "Last Call Working Draft," which means that it's a work in progress. It could change substantially from this point until it reaches "Recommendation" status, so make sure you check it before you implement anything. Chances are it won't change much, but check just to make sure.

8 XHTML: Create Working Web Pages in XML Now

IN THIS CHAPTER

- Purpose
- What XHTML Is
- User Agent Criteria
- Differences from HTML
- The XHTML DTDs
- Recap

So what is this XHTML thing anyway? Is it XML or HTML or what? The answer is, it's both. XHTML (Extensible HyperText Markup Language) is designed so that it's seen as HTML by all of the browsers available now, and as XML from user agents that can read XML. If you know HTML (I'm assuming that you do), then learning XHTML will probably take about 30 seconds. Go ahead and have a beer while you read this chapter—you'll need some brain cells, but not all of them.

◆ Purpose

The purpose of XHTML is to allow Web developers to make the transition from HTML to XML without sacrificing the ubiquity of HTML or the likely emergence of XML as a standard. It allows for both backward and forward compatibility.

XHTML adds XML extensibility and structure to HTML, while still allowing the code to double as HTML in current browsers.

Why Bother?

Why is the W3C messing with HTML? Clearly, HTML is amazingly popular, and its ease of use has helped make the Web the phenomenon it is. However, HTML was created to display technical documents. All other uses have been cobbled on top of this original purpose (starting with Marc Andresson adding an `<img>` tag to Mosaic, and continuing to `<iframe>` in Internet Explorer and `<layer>` in Netscape). Certainly, the use of HTML has far outstripped its purpose. Thus, HTML is in dire need of an overhaul into something more robust.

Most developers think XML is the answer, in part because of its flexibility. In an ideal world, HTML would magically disappear and be replaced by XML. Since this is not a perfect world (evidenced in part by the fact that I do not have a beachfront home in south Maui), the W3C has come up with a plan to ease HTML into XML. They've done this by creating a hybrid that is both HTML and XML at the same time: this is what XHTML is. It's a reformulation of HTML 4.0 as an XML-based language (that is, a series of XML tags).

XHTML is designed to be recognized as HTML by user agents that see HTML, such as Netscape and Internet Explorer. XHTML is also designed to be parsed as XML by any XML-aware user agents. This allows Web developers to create Web pages that incorporate both backwards and forwards compatibility.

Modularized XHTML

Since XHTML is a flavor of XML, it's easy to add new ideas to. It's also easy to break into modules. In fact, there's a new specification called Modularized XHTML that breaks XHTML into separate sections. It's then possible for documents to only call the chunks of XHTML that are needed at the time.

XHTML was also designed with general user agent operability in mind. One study predicts that by 2002, 75% of Internet documents will be viewed via alternative platforms like PDAs and cell phones. I think this number is too high, but the idea is still a solid one.

◆ What XHTML Is

XHTML is essentially HTML with some extra tags and syntax thrown in. Here's an example:

HTML

```
<p>Hi there.<p>My name is Irving.
<br><hr><br>
```

XHTML

```
<p>Hi there</p>
<p>My name is Irving</p>
<br /><hr /><br />
```

XHTML is just HTML with the rules of well-formed XML applied to it. We can get away with adding an extra forward slash to `<br>` and `<hr>` because HTML simply ignores what it doesn't understand. We'll look at the exact rules and differences between XHTML and HTML later on. For now, you should know that browsers can see `<br />` but not `<br/>`.

Developers can call the XML DOM or the HTML DOM, depending on what the user agent can see. Again, we'll look at scripting and DOMs later in this chapter (if the term is unfamiliar to you, DOM stands for Document Object Model, and it's a way that programming languages can peer into a document's structure).

XHTML documents should be viewable as text/html, text/xml, or application/xml MIME types.

◆ User Agent Criteria

If a user agent claims to parse and display XHTML documents, there are a few rules it must adhere to. An XHTML-compliant user agent must

1. Make sure the document is well-formed.
2. Validate the document against a DTD (we'll cover the XHTML DTDs later on).
3. Support the proper XHTML elements and attributes.
4. Recognize an ID-type attribute as a fragment identifier. That is, your attribute must be `id="foo"` in order to definitely identify that chunk of code. This means that the `name="bar"` attribute won't exclusively identify a section of code.
5. Render the content of unrecognized elements.
6. Ignore unrecognized attributes.
7. Replace unrecognized attribute values with default attribute values.
8. Render unrecognized entities literally. For example, `&bnb;` would appear on the screen as "&bnb;".

9. Render unrecognized characters or entities in such a way that it's clear to the user that normal rendering did not occur.

10. Remove trailing and leading white space.

11. Collapse sequences of white space into a single space.

12. Recognize the following entities:
    - space: `&#x0020;`
    - tab: `&#x0009;`
    - carriage return: `&#x000D;`
    - line feed: `&#x000A;`
    - form feed: `&#x000C;`
    - zero-width space: `&#x200B;`

These rules only apply to user agents that claim to fully conform to XHTML. Browsers like Netscape and IE can still parse and display XHTML, but they will only see it as HTML and apply HTML rules, not XHTML or XML rules, to the document.

◆ Differences from HTML

There are about a dozen differences between HTML and XHTML. Most of them you can already predict, but there are a few little surprises.

- Documents must be well-formed according to XML rules.
- Elements and attribute names must be in lower case. This is because XML is case-sensitive: `<li>` is a different tag than `<LI>` or `<Li>`.
- For nonempty elements, end tags are required. For example, `<p>Look! A duck!</p>`. Note that you cannot use `<p />` because `<p>` is not defined as an empty element. Instead, you must use `<p></p>`.
- Attribute values must be quoted. No more `border=0`. It must now be `border="0"`.
- No more attribute minimization. This means that valueless attributes like `NOSHADE` or `CHECKED` are no longer allowed in this form. They must appear as `noshade="noshade"` and `checked="checked"`. Don't use Boolean values with these attributes, as some browsers may react unpredictably.
- Empty elements must end with a space and a forward slash. So `<br />` is allowed, but `<br/>` is not. The space ensures that HTML browsers ignore the slash.
- The leading and trailing white space in attribute values is stripped.

TABLE 8-1 Tags Not to Nest

This Tag	Cannot Be Nested Inside These Tags
`a`	`a`
`pre`	`img`, `object`, `big`, `small`, `sub`, `sup`
`button`	`input`, `select`, `textarea`, `label`, `button`
`label`	`label`
`form`	`form`

- Script and style elements are defined as having a `#PCDATA` content. This means that the characters < and & are treated as markup, not content. As a result, those characters must be escaped using `&lt;` and `&amp;`. Since this is a monstrous pain, there is a workaround: wrap `CDATA` around your code:

```
<script>
<! [CDATA[
    … unescaped scripting code …
]]>
</script>
```

Another option is to use external script and style documents (this is what I prefer to do).

- Certain elements are not to be nested (you probably wouldn't try this anyway, but Table 8–1 shows the rules).
- Only ID attributes (which only include the `ID` attribute) act as identifiers—the name attribute does not. This means that `<a name="pants">` isn't technically an identifier.
- Don't use line breaks inside of attribute values—user agents handle them inconsistently.
- To specify a language, use both the `lang` and `xml:lang` attributes (`xml:lang` takes precedence).

Not too bad, right? It's mostly commonsense stuff, and you've probably been following some of these rules already.

There's one odd twist—you'd think that there was a single DTD for XHTML, wouldn't you? Well, there are three.

◆ The XHTML DTDs

The three XHTML DTDs are Strict, Transitional and Frameset. The Strict DTD only covers HTML tags that are part of HTML 4— no deprecated tags are included. XHTML's Transitional DTD contains everything the Strict DTD does, but it also includes these deprecated tags:

- `<iframe>`
- `<noframes>`
- `<menu>`
- `<dir>`
- `<center>`
- `<u>`
- `<s>`
- `<strike>`
- `<basefont>`
- `<font>`
- `<applet>`
- `<isIndex>`

The Frameset DTD contains everything the Transitional DTD contains including two frame-related elements: `<frameset>` and `<frame>`.

In other words:

Strict DTD + deprecated tags = Transitional DTD
Transitional DTD + `<frameset>` + `<frame>` = Frameset DTD

All XHTML documents have to begin with the standard XML declaration:

```
<?xml version="1.0" ?>
```

After that, include one of these three DOCTYPEs:

```
<!DOCTYPE HTML PUBLIC
    "-//W3C//DTD XHTML1.0 Strict//EN"
    SYSTEM
    "http://www.w3.org/TR/xhtml1/DTD/xhtml1-strict.dtd">
```

```
<!DOCTYPE HTML PUBLIC
    "-//W3C//DTD XHTML1.0 Transitional//EN"
    SYSTEM
    "http://www.w3.org/TR/xhtml1/DTD/xhtml1-
    transitional.dtd">
```

```
<!DOCTYPE HTML PUBLIC
    "-//W3C//DTD XHTML1.0 Frameset//EN"
    SYSTEM
    "http://www.w3.org/TR/xhtml1/DTD/xhtml1-frameset.dtd">
```

If you can, write your XHTML pages using the Strict DTD. If you have to use frames, use the Frameset DTD, but avoid deprecated tags if at all possible (deprecated means that the tags still work but won't be included in the next specification).

Let's look at some XHTML that includes a list, a table and a form in Example 8–1.

EXAMPLE 8–1 SOME XHTML

```
<?xml version ="1.0" ?>

<!DOCTYPE HTML PUBLIC "-//W3C//DTD XHTML1.0 Strict//EN" SYS-
TEM "http://www.w3.org/TR/xhtml1/DTD/xhtml1-strict.dtd">

<!-- <html> must always be the root element in XHTML -->
<html>
<head>
    <title>Shelley Biotech Contact Form</title>

    <!-- can't be an empty element -->
    <script language="javascript"
src="include/rollovers.js"></script>

    <!-- must be an empty element -->
    <link rel="stylesheet" href="include/shelley.css"
type="text/css" />

</head>
<body bgcolor="#333366" link="#0000CC" alink="#CC0099"
vlink="#993333">

<form name="contactForm" action="send_contact.php3"
method="post">

<table cellpadding="0" cellspacing="0" border="0">
    <tr>
        <td colspan="2" class="subhead">
            <p>Get Free Stuff!</p>
            <!-- notice the line items have an end tag
-->
            <ul>
                <li>A "My genome is better than yours"
T-shirt (XL only)</li>
                <li>A "Science, dammit!" travel
mug</li>
                <li>A Test Tube Beanie Baby</li>
            </ul>
            <p>Just fill out the contact form below!</p>
```

```
            </td>
      </tr>
      <tr>
            <td>Name</td>
            <td>
                  <!-- <input> is an empty tag -->
                  <input type="text" name="name" size="30" />
            </td>
      </tr>
      <tr>
            <td>Email</td>
            <td><input type="text" name="email" size="30"
/></td>
      </tr>
      <tr>
            <td>Company</td>
            <td><input type="text" name="company" size="30"
/></td>
      </tr>
      <tr>
            <td>Phone Number</td>
            <td><input type="text" name="phone" size="30"
/></td>
      </tr>
      <tr>
            <td>Any comments or questions?</td>
            <td><textarea name="comments" rows="5"
cols="30"></textarea></td>
      </tr>
</table>

</form>

</body>
</html>
```

◆ Recap

That wasn't too bad, was it? The all-inclusive Frameset DTD is listed in Appendix B, and all the special characters, symbols, and Latin characters are in Appendix C.

Be sure to check out the "XML well-formedness checker and validator" at *www.cogsci.ed.ac.uk/~richard/xml-check.html.*

9 Beginning XSLT: Xpath

IN THIS CHAPTER

- XSL Overview
- XPath Overview
- How XPath Sees the World
- Location Paths
- Predicates
- Functions
- Node-Set Functions
- String Functions
- Boolean Functions
- Number Functions
- Recap

You've probably heard about XSL, or Extensible Style Language. The purpose of this language is to provide a way to visually format XML data. The relationship between XSL and XML is analogous to the relationship between CSS (Cascading Stylesheets) and HTML, but with some important differences. First of all, XSL is a subset of XML. That is, XSL is a series of XML tags and attributes, much like XML Schema. An XSL processor is required to properly parse and format XML that has XSL applied to it. XML programmers have been looking forward to XSL for quite some time. In fact, it was taking so long to put XSL together, the W3C decided to split XSL into several separate parts.

◆ XSL Overview

The purpose of XSL is to allow a method of formatting XML documents. It was being built so slowly that the W3C divided XSL into several sections so that at least those sections could be accomplished quickly. One of these sections is called XSLT, or XSL Transformtions.

Another part of XSL is called XSL-FO, (Formatting Objects), which acts more like CSS than XSLT does.

XSLT

The purpose of XSLT is to create a way to transform one XML document into another—for example, transforming XML into XHTML. To accomplish this XML-to-XML translation, XSLT uses a two-part instruction. First, find an element or set of elements. Then, transform those elements into something else. Figure 9–1 illustrates this process.

In order to understand how XSL works, you need to know about XSLT, which is a large part of XSL. And in order to understand how XSLT works, you must first know how it selects elements.

XSLT uses a two-part process, the first part of which is selecting certain elements from the first XML document. How do you select elements in a document? You have to use a new language called XPath. Don't worry, this is a simple, compact language—it's designed to fit inside the value of an attribute. For example:

```
<xsl:template match="XPath_expression" />
```

This chapter will cover what goes inside *XPath_expression*.

Confused yet? XSLT is a part of XSL. XPath is a part of XSLT. Before we dive into XSLT, we must first look at XPath, and that's what this chapter is about.

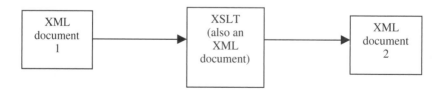

FIGURE 9–1 XML Transformation

◆ XPath Overview

XPath was created to provide a way to address parts of an XML document. Both XSLT and XPointer use XPath, both of which we'll examine later in this book. XPath is a W3C Recommendation, so it's stable, and not likely to change in the near future.

Using XPath allows you to pinpoint a certain element in an XML document or to establish a pattern that a number of elements fit into. The syntax XPath uses is not XML-based; it's entirely different, but not too hard to learn.

A chunk of working XPath is called an XPath expression. Whenever an XPath expression is evaluated, the result is an object. This object can be a number of things:

- A node-set: an unordered collection of nodes that doesn't have any duplicates
- A number
- A string
- A Boolean value

◆ How XPath Sees the World

Before we dive into the syntax of XPath, we need to know about its data model, which is how XPath views XML documents. In short, XPath sees nodes. XPath is node-happy. Here are the different kinds of nodes:

- root nodes
- element nodes
- attribute nodes
- text nodes
- namespace nodes
- processing instruction nodes
- comment nodes

These nodes are always placed in a tree structure, based on the structure of the XML document.

XPath also contains the concept of a context node, which is the node that has XPath's current attention at any given instant. Since an XPath expression always appears in an attribute value, that attribute always belongs to some element. Whatever that element is—whatever element contains the XPath expression—is the context node. All XPath expressions are based on this context. For example, if the XPath expression is

```
child::effects
```

this tells the XPath processor to look for all children `effects` elements of the context node. We'll cover this syntax in more detail later.

Root Nodes

When XPath looks at an XML document, the first thing it sees is the root node, even before it sees the root element (which in the XPath world is the top element node). For example, consider the following XML document.

```
<?xml version="1.0" ?>
<products>
    <product name="BreatheClear">
        <effect>bronchodialator</effect>
    </product>
    <product name="BeatClear">
        <effect>clears plaque on arterial walls</effect>
    </product>
</products>
```

The node tree for this code is illustrated in Figure 9–2.

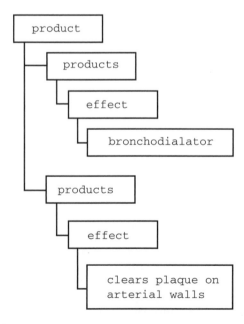

FIGURE 9–2 A node tree

Every node tree has a root node, and the root node never has a parent and always has exactly one element node (what we've been calling the root element). Don't get confused by the terms "root node" and "root element." In XPath, we don't use the term root element—just root node. Remember, XPath syntax isn't XML-based, so there are going to be some differences between XPath and XML. XPath has a root node and XML has a root element. XML's root element doesn't have a special name in XPath—it's just the only child element node of the root node.

In XPath, the root node is represented by a forward slash (/).

Element Nodes

For every regular element `<elementName>`, there is an element node. Element nodes can have child nodes and parent nodes. Children nodes of element nodes can be namespace nodes, other element nodes, and attribute nodes. Element nodes are the most common type of node.

Attribute Nodes

Attribute nodes are always children of element nodes. If the XML document doesn't include an attribute that has an #IM-PLIED state in the document's DTD, that attribute doesn't become a node. Default attributes are included, though. XPath doesn't care about the DTD—it only sees what's in the actual XML document.

Text Nodes

Text nodes are pretty simple. If the XML has this line:

```
<sideEffects>nausea, dizziness</sideEffects>
```

then the element node of `sideEffects` has a child text node of `nausea, dizziness`. Text nodes are always character data (CDATA).

Namespace Nodes

Namespace nodes are a little tricky. Element nodes are parents of namespace nodes, but namespace nodes are not children of parent nodes: it's a one-way relationship. (Those of you with teenagers may have experience with this.)

An element will have a namespace node under these conditions:

- For every attribute that begins with `xmlns:`
- For every attribute on an ancestor element whose name begins with `xmlns:`
- For an `xmlns` attribute in the element or any ancestor and the attribute is something other than `xmlns=""`

Processing Instruction Nodes

There's a single processing instruction node for every processing instruction the document.

Comment Nodes

Comment nodes are just comments.

```
<!--This draft updated 6/7/02 -->
```

◆ Location Paths

How exactly does XPath locate elements inside an XML document? It does this by building a location path that specifies a certain branch of the node tree. Location paths can further refine the location by adding something called a predicate, which we'll study in the next section.

There are two ways to specify a location path: using unabbreviated or abbreviated syntax. We'll look at the unabbreviated syntax first—it'll make more sense to you.

Unabbreviated Location Paths

Here are a whole slew of examples.

- `child::effects` selects all the `effects` elements that are children of the context node (that is, the current node).
- `child::*` selects all element children of the context node.
- `child::text()` selects all text-node children of the context node.
- `child::node()` selects all children of the context node, regardless of node type.
- `attribute::chemName` selects all `chemName` attributes of the context node.
- `attribute::*` selects all attributes of the context node.
- `descendent::effects` selects all `effects` elements that are descendents of the context node. (Descendents can be

anywhere inside the context node, as opposed to children, which must be only on the next level down.)

- `ancestor::product` selects all `product` ancestors of the context node.
- `ancestor-or-self::product` selects all `product` ancestors of the context node, and selects the context node as well if it's a `product` element.
- `descendent-or-self::effects` selects all `effects` descendents of the context node, including the context node itself if it's an `effects` element.
- `self::effects` selects the context node if it's an `effects` element—otherwise, nothing is selected.
- `child::product/descendent::effects` selects all `effects` descendents of the `product` element, if that `product` element is a child of the context node.
- `child::*/child::effects` selects all `effects` grandchildren of the context node.
- `/` selects the document root.
- `/descendent::product` selects all `product` elements in the document.
- `/descendent::product/child::effects` selects all `effects` elements that are children of `product` elements.

Parts of Location Paths

Before we look at the abbreviated syntax of location paths, let's make sure we know what we're looking at. You probably noticed that most of these paths involved

```
something :: something_else
```

The first part before the double colon is called an axis. The part after the double colon is called the node-test. The axis defines the relationship between the node selected and the context node. Here's a list of all the axes you can use:

- `child`
- `descendent`
- `parent`
- `ancestor`
- `following`
- `preceding`
- `attribute`
- `namespace`
- `self`
- `ancestor-or-self`

- `descendent-or-self`
- `following-sibling`
- `preceding-sibling`

The node-test can include any name of an element, along with these identifiers:

- `node()` returns true for any kind of node
- `text()` returns true for any text node
- `comment()` returns true for any comment node
- `processing-instruction()` returns true for any processing instruction

Abbreviated Location Paths

You can use abbreviated (Table 9–1) or unabbreviated syntax in your location paths. Do whatever's easiest for you.

TABLE 9–1 Location path abbreviations

Abbreviation	Stands For
(nothing)	`child::` (that is, `child::` can be omitted entirely)
@	`attribute::`
//	`/descendent-or-self::node()/`
.	`self::node()`
..	`parent::node()`

Let's look at the examples we saw above, but abbreviated:

- `effects` selects all the `effects` elements that are children of the context node (that is, the current node).
- `*` selects all element children of the context node.
- `text()` selects all text-node children of the context node.
- `node()` selects all children of the context node, regardless of node type.
- `@chemName` selects all `chemName` attributes of the context node.
- `@*` selects all attributes of the context node.
- `.//effects` selects all `effects` elements that are descendents of the context node (descendents can be anywhere inside the context node, as opposed to children, which must be only on the next level down).
- `.effects` selects the context node if it's an `effects` element. Otherwise, nothing is selected.
- `product//effects` selects all `effects` descendents of the `product` element, if that product element is a child of the context node.

- `*/effects` selects all `effects` grandchildren of the context node.
- `//product` selects all `product` elements in the document.
- `//product/effects` selects all `effects` elements that are children of `product` elements.

◆ Predicates

Predicates allow you to further refine your search for the right element. Using predicates, you can determine the exact position of the element or even use conditional logic. Predicates are separated from the rest of the location path by being placed in square brackets. A location path may have any number of predicates.

Unabbreviated Location Paths with Predicates

Here are a few examples of predicates in action.

- `child::effects[position()=1]` selects the first `effects` child of the context node.
- `child::effects[position()=last()]` selects the last `effects` child of the context node.
- `child::*[position()=1][self::effects]` selects the first child of the context node if it's an `effects` element. (Read this one and the first one closely—there's a subtle but important difference.) Note that you can use more than one predicate at once.
- `child::*[position()=last()][self::effects]` selects the last element of the context node if it is an `effects` element.
- `child::effects[position()=last()-1]` selects the next-to-last `effects` child of the context node.
- `child::effects[position()>1]` selects all the `effects` children of the context node except for the first one.
- `following-sibling::products[position()=1]` selects the next `products` sibling of the context node.
- `/descendent::effects[position()=34]` selects the 34th occurrence of the `effects` element in the document.
- `/descendent::category/child::product[position ()=2]/child::effects[position()=4]` selects the fourth `effects` element of the second product `element` in the `category` element.
- `child::effects[attribute::severity="mild"]` selects all the `effects` children of the context mode that have a `severity="mild"` attribute-value pair.

- `child::effects[attribute::severity="mild"][position()=4]` selects the fourth `effects` child element that has a `severity="mild"` attribute-value pair.
- `child::effects[position()=4][attribute::severity="mild"]` selects the fourth `effects` child element if that element has a `severity="mild"` attribute-value pair. (Compare and contrast with the example above—predicates are evaluated sequentially.)
- `child::product[child::marName]` selects all product elements that have a `marName` child element.
- `child::product[child::marName="BreatheClear"]` selects the `product` element that has a child element `marName` with a string-value of "`BreatheClear`". That is, the following element would be selected:

```
<contextNode>
<!--the product element is selected, not marName -->
    <product>
            <marName>BreatheClear</marName>
    </product>
</contextNode>
```

- `child::product[child::marName or child::chemName]` selects all `product` children of the context node that have either a `marName` child or a `chemName` child.

Well, that does it for our first look at predicates. Next, we'll look at what abbreviated predicates look like, and in later sections we'll look at all the conditionals and operators used in predicates, as well as all of the functions you can use.

Abbreivated Predicates

Here's the same list (mostly) as above, but with some shortening. The only real new abbreviation is that `postion()=` may be omitted.

- `effects[1]` selects the first `effects` child of the context node.
- `effects[last()]` selects the last `effects` child of the context node.
- `*[1][.effects]` selects the first child of the context node if it's an `effects` element. (Read this one and the first one closely—there's a subtle but important difference.)
- `*[last()][.effects]` selects the last element of the context node if its an `effects` element.
- `effects[last()-1]` selects the next-to-last `effects` child of the context node.

- `effects[position()>1]` selects all the `effects` children of the context node except for the first one. Note that we have to keep `position()` when we're using something other than =.
- `following-sibling::products[1]` selects the next `products` sibling of the context node.
- `//effects[34]` selects the 34th occurrence of the `effects` element in the document.
- `//category/product[2]/effects[4]` selects the fourth `effects` element of the second product `element` in the `category` element.
- `effects[@severity="mild"]` selects all the `effects` children of the context mode that have a `severity= "mild"` attribute-value pair.
- `effects[@severity="mild"][position()=4]` selects the fourth `effects` child element that has a `severity= "mild"` attribute-value pair.
- `effects[4][@severity="mild"]` selects the fourth effects child element if that element has a `severity= "mild"` attribute-value pair. (Compare and contrast with the example above—predicates are evaluated sequentially.)
- `product[marName]` selects all product elements that have a `marName` child element.
- `product[marName="BreatheEasy"]` selects the `product` element that has a child element `marName` with a string-value of "BreatheClear". That is, the following element would be selected:

```
<contextNode>
<!--the product element is selected, not marName -->
    <product>
            <marName>BreatheClear</marName>
    </product>
</contextNode>
```

- `product[marName or chemName]` selects all `product` children of the context node that have either a `marName` child or a `chemName` child.

Are you getting the hang of predicates? If you're still a little confused, try making a few up yourself. It's a good way to see exactly where the holes in your understanding (or my teaching) are.

Now let's look at ways to introduce some more conditional logic into your predicates.

Conditionals and Operators

Here are all of the conditional operators that you can use in a predicate. You've seen some of them already.

- `<=`, `<`, `>=`, `>`
- `=`, `!=`
- `and`
- `or`

This is also the order of precedence (most important first). The arithmetic operators are as follows:

- `+`
- `-`
- `div` (for division)
- `mod` (same as the `%` operator from Java and JavaScript)

And no, I didn't forget multiplication—there's no way to multiply in XPath. (Strange, huh?)

Now let's look at all of the functions you can use inside a predicate. (You've already seen `position()` and `last()`.)

◆ Functions

Use of these functions in predicates can give you some serious control over which elements your XPath expression can locate. The rest of this chapter is something like a reference manual—many of these functions are specific and somewhat self-explanatory, so we won't be looking at too many examples.

◆ Node-Set Functions

Node-set functions look at the actual nodes and what's around them.

last()

The `last()` function returns the number of sibling elements of the current node (plus the current node).

position()

This function returns a number equal to the context node's position among its siblings.

count(location_path)

This function returns the number of nodes that exist by the location path in the argument.

id("id_name")

This function selects the element that has the ID attribute of id_name. For example, id("drug5") selects the element that has the unique identifier of drug5. You'll see more of this in the XPointer chapter.

local-name(location_path)

This function returns the local name of an element. The local name is the name of the element, including any prefixes. The argument is optional, and if it's omitted, then the name of the context node is returned.

namespace-uri(location_path)

This function returns the name of the URI if the node is part of a namespace. If the node isn't part of a namespace, then an empty string is returned. The argument is optional, and if it's omitted, then the namespace of the context node is used.

name(location_path)

This function returns the name of the nodes in the node set, including the URI of the namespace if there is one. The combination of local and namespace name is called the expanded name of the node. For all nodes except element and attribute nodes, this function returns the same string as local-name(). The argument is optional, and if it's omitted, then the context node is used.

◆ String Functions

Use these functions to manipulate or create strings.

string(object)

The string function converts an object into a string in the following ways:

- If the argument is a node-set, then the function returns the first string-value it finds (a string-value being the first text node found).

- A number is converted into a string according to these rules:
  - NaN is converted into the string "NaN"
  - Positive infinity is converted into "Infinity"
  - Negative infinity is converted into "-Infinity"
  - Otherwise, a number is converted into a string of numbers
- Boolean values are converted into "true" or "false"

If the argument is omitted, then the context node is used as the default.

concat(string1, string2, ..., stringn)

This function concatenates all of the strings in the argument and returns that string.

starts-with(baseString, substring)

This function returns true or false, depending on whether baseString begins with substring or not.

contains(baseString, substring)

Returns true or false, depending on whether baseString contains substring.

substring-before(baseString, substring)

Returns the portion of the string baseString that exists before the occurrence of substring.

substring-after(baseString, substring)

Returns the portion of the string baseString that exists after the occurrence of the substring.

substring(string, startPositon, substringLength)

This function returns the substring based on string, starting at position startPosition. (Unlike Java and JavaScript, XPath starts counting at 1 instead of 0.) The substringLength argument is optional. If omitted, the substring continues to the end of the string.

string-length(string)

This function returns the number of characters in the argument. If the argument is omitted, then the string-value of the context node is used.

normalize-space(string)

This function strips white space in the string according to a few rules:

- Beginning white spaces are removed.
- Any sequences of white spaces inside the string are collapsed into a single space.
- Trailing spaces at the end of the string are removed.

translate(baseString, startTrans, endTrans)

This function returns a string after replacing the characters of *baseString* listed in *startTrans* with the characters in *endTrans*. For example, `translate("pants", "pan", "PAN")` results in `PANts`. If any characters listed in the *startTrans* string don't have a counterpart in *endTrans*, then those characters are not part of the returned string. For example, `translate("pants", "pan", "PA")` results in `PAts`.

◆ Boolean Functions

Use these functions to create or manipulate Boolean values.

boolean(object)

This function returns true or false, based on these rules:

- If the object is a number, the function returns `true` only if the number isn't negative, zero, or NaN.
- If the object is a node-set, the function returns `true` if the set isn't empty.
- If the object is a string, the function returns `true` only if the string has at least one character.

not(boolean)

This function returns `true` if the argument is `false`, and `false` if the argument is `true`.

true( )
This function always returns `true`.

false( )
This function always returns `false`.

lang(string)

This function returns `true` if the language in the string is the same language as set by the `xml:lang` attribute.

◆ Number Functions

Use these functions to manipulate or create numbers.

number(object)

This function returns a number based on the object, according to the following rules:

- Boolean values of `true` are converted to 1, `false` values to 0.
- A node-set is first converted to a string, and then that string is converted to a number
- Strings are converted to their mathematical value

sum(node-set)

This function returns the sum of all of the string-values in the node set.

ceiling(number)

This function returns the largest number that is not less than the argument and is an integer. (In other words, it rounds up.)

floor(number)

This function returns the largest number that is not more than the argument and is an integer. (In other words, it rounds down.)

round(number)

This function returns the nearest integer to the argument.

◆ Recap

That's XPath! You now know how to locate just about any element in any XML document using this language. This was a pretty dense chapter. Go ahead and take a walk, get a drink of water, and give it some time to sink in. Don't forget to stretch. Now, using these concepts, you're ready to dive into XSLT! Ready?

10 XSLT: An Overview

Now that you've waded through the new language of XPath, you're ready to jump into XSLT proper. Remember that XSLT is a part of XSL (Extensible Stylesheet Language). XSLT stands for Extensible Stylesheet Language—Transformations. There are other parts of XSL, including XSL-FO and XPointer.

◆ Overview of XSL

XSL stands for Extensible Style Language. It's a stylesheet language for XML. XSL has three different parts: XSLT (this chapter), XPath (the last chapter), and XSL-FO (XSL Formatting Objects). XSL's purpose in life is to provide a way to format or transform the raw data of one XML document into another form, whether that involves altering data or making text bold.

◆ Purpose of XSLT

XSLT's only purpose in life is to transform one XML document into another XML document. These two XML documents may look similar to each other, or they can be completely different—it's all up to the XSLT document. Right now, XSLT is mainly used to transform an XML document into XHTML so it can be displayed on the Web. Example 10–1 shows two XML files: the source XML, and what it looks like after XSLT has gone over it.

EXAMPLE 10–1 BEFORE AND AFTER XML

```
<!-- initial XML -->
<shelleyBiotech>
    <product_list>
        <product chemName="hydroBlah" marName="Breathe-
Clear">
            <effects>bronchodialator</effects>
            <sideEffects>nausea, dizziness</sideEffects>
        </product>
        <product chemName="hydroBlah1" marName="BeatEasy">
            <effects>artery wall plaque remover</effects>
            <sideEffects>nausea, joint soreness</side-
Effects>
        </product>
    </product_list>
</shelleyBiotech>

<!-- resulting XHTML -->
<html>
<head>
    <title>Shelley BioProducts</title>
</head>

<body bgcolor="#FFFFFF">
    <h1>Shelley BioProducts</h1>
    <p>
    <table>
        <tr>
            <td><b>Name</b>
            <td><b>Effects</b></td>
            <td><b>Side Effects</b></td>
        </tr>
        <tr>
            <td>BreatheClear (hydroBlah)</td>
```

```
            <td>Bronchodialator</td>
            <td>nausea, dizziness</td>
        </tr>
        <tr>
            <td>BeatEasy (hydroBlah1)</td>
            <td>artery wall plaque remover</td>
            <td>nausea, joint soreness</td>
        </tr>
    </table>
</body>
</html>
```

Transforming the original XML document into the XHTML document is what XSLT does

◆ How XSLT Works

So how does this XSLT thing really work? First, we start with two documents: the source XML document and the XSLT document. An XSLT processor is also required. Once this processor reads and starts executing the XSLT document, it first dissects the XML document and creates a source tree, which is a tree-like structure based on the structure of the original XML document. For example, part of the source tree for the XML document above would look something like Figure 10–1.

The sections of this tree are called nodes, just like in XPath. Notice that attributes are child nodes of the element they belong to, and text nodes are children of the element that contains them (for example, `bronchodialator` is a child of `effects`).

Once this source tree is created, the XSLT processor looks through the XSLT document, searching for instructions. These instructions occur in groups called "template rules." Each template rule matches a node or a pattern of nodes in the XML document. This node or set of nodes is what's set by an XPath expression. A set of nodes is called a *node-set*. For example, a template rule could be applicable only to the first `product` node, to all `product` nodes, or only to text nodes that have the substring "broncho" in them. An XSLT document can have any number of template rules. Here's the syntax for a template rule:

```
<xsl:template match="node-set">
    …instructions and/or literal elements…
</xsl:template>
```

The node-set used in the match attribute is something in the XPath that specifies a single node or a set of nodes. It says,

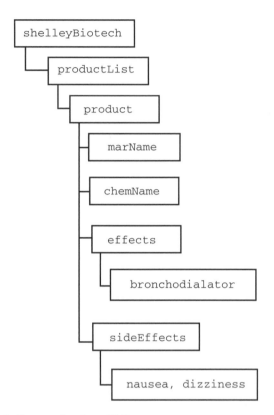

FIGURE 10–1 Tree node of our XML

"Apply the following instructions to any node that matches this XPath expression."

The XSLT processor takes all the instructions and literal elements and outputs them into something called the result tree, which usually results in another XML document.

As you can see, XSLT is expressed by being in a namespace that we're calling "xsl," even though the language is XSLT. An XSLT processor (which can be a part of a more generic XML processor) will see the namespace of these XSLT elements and will treat them differently that other XML elements.

Let's look briefly at what these instructions can look like.

Instructions

Once inside the template rule, the XSLT processor may encounter instructions, which are XSLT-specific elements that extract specific information from the source tree, or may create brand-new elements and attributes. Here's an example of an instruction that pulls the value from an attribute:

```
<xsl:value-of select="@marName" />
```

This line looks for the attribute called `marName` that occurs in the node-set. If our full template rule was:

```
<xsl:template match="product">
    <xsl:value-of select="@marName"/>
</xsl:template>
```

The XSL processor would search the source tree for a `product` element. Once found, it would then look for an attribute called `marName` in that node, and the value of that attribute would be output. Since there is more than a single occurrence of a `product` node, all nodes fitting into the node-set would be processed. Thus, the values of both `marName` attributes would be output:

```
BreatheClear
BeatEasy
```

Instructions aren't the only things that can appear in template rules. You can also include non-XSLT elements—these are known as *literal elements*.

Literal Elements

Here's an example of some literal elements around an instruction:

```
<xsl:template match="product">
    Marketing Name: <br />
    <b><xsl:value-of select="@marName"/></b>
    <p></p>
</xsl:template>
```

Everything in this example that doesn't begin with `xsl:` is a literal element. Literal elements are output exactly as is. In this case, the output would be:

```
Marketing Name: <br  />
<b>BreatheClear</b>
<p></p>
Marketing Name: <br />
<b>BeatEasy</b>
<p></p>
```

Template rules may contain only instructions, only literal elements, or a combination of the two.

Executing template rules isn't as straightforward as you might guess. An XSLT processor automatically runs only a single kind of template rule. All other template rules must be explicitly called by this first template rule. This first template rule is called the *root template* and it looks like this:

```
<xsl:template match="/">
    …instructions, literal elements…
    …calls to other templates…
</xsl:template>
```

The root template is the only template rule that is automatically run by the XSLT processor. Let's take a closer look at this all-important template.

◆ Root Templates

We're going to start our examination of root templates with a super-simple template rule and then get more complex, adding instructions and literal elements.

Example 10–2 shows a short XML document, an even shorter XSLT document that does nothing but output a single line, and the resulting output (which is just a single blank line).

EXAMPLE 10–2 NO LITERAL ELEMENTS OR XSLT INSTRUCTIONS

```
<!-- source XML document -->
<?xml version="1.0" ?>
<shelleyBiotech>
    <product_list>
        <product chemName="hydroBlah" marName="Breathe-
Clear">
            <effects>bronchodialator</effects>
            <sideEffects>nausea, dizziness</sideEffects>
        </product>
        <product chemName="hydroBlah1" marName="BeatEasy">
            <effects>artery wall plaque remover</
effects>
            <sideEffects>nausea, joint soreness</side-
Effects>
        </product>
    </product_list>
</shelleyBiotech>
```

```
<!-- Your first XSLT document -->
<?xml version="1.0" ?>
<xsl:stylesheet
    xmlns:xsl="http://www.w3.org/1999/XSL/Transform">
    <xsl:template match="/">

    </xsl:template>
</xsl:stylesheet>

<!--
    The XML result is just a single blank line.
    Nothing from the source XML document shows up,
    because we didn't specifically include
    instructions to.
-->
```

HOW THE CODE WORKS

The XSLT processor first creates a source tree out of our little XML document. It then looks for the root template in the XSLT document. It finds it, and outputs the one blank line it finds. That's it! The XSLT processor has finished without breaking a sweat.

You may have also noticed the line of code that establishes the XSLT namespace:

```
<xsl:stylesheet
xmlns:xsl="http://www.w3.org/1999/XSL/Transform">
```

This line is necessary, but it doesn't really matter what the prefix is. I'm using xsl, but it could be anything.

Let's take this to the next step—we'll throw in some literal elements, but no XSLT instructions yet. This means that the XSLT processor will output exactly what it sees in the root template, but it won't reference the source tree at all. The only reason it would access the source tree is if we wanted to extract some information from the source tree. Since we're only using literal elements, we don't care what's in the source tree. Example 10–3 illustrates this.

EXAMPLE 10–3 LITERAL ELEMENTS ONLY—NO XSLT INSTRUCTIONS

```
<!-- source XML document -->
<?xml version="1.0" ?>
<shelleyBiotech>
    <product_list>
        <product chemName="hydroBlah" marName="Breathe-
Clear">
            <effects>bronchodialator</effects>
```

```
                    <sideEffects>nausea, dizziness</sideEffects>
            </product>
            <product chemName="hydroBlah1" marName="BeatEasy">
                    <effects>artery wall plaque remover</
effects>
                    <sideEffects>nausea, joint soreness</side-
Effects>
            </product>
        </product_list>
</shelleyBiotech>


<!-- Your second XSLT document: -->
<?xml version="1.0" ?>
<xsl:stylesheet
xmlns:xsl="http://www.w3.org/1999/XSL/Transform">
        <xsl:template match="/">
            <html>
            <head>
                    <title>Shelley BioProducts</title>
            </head>
            <body>
                    It worked!
            </body>
            </html>
        </xsl:template>
</xsl:stylesheet>


<!-- The XML result (it's XHTML) -->
<html>
<head>
    <title>Shelley BioProducts</title>
</head>
<body>
    It worked!
</body>
</html>
```

Those are the basics of the root template. To make our XSLT useful, let's see how to call multiple template rules.

◆ Applying Multiple Templates

An XSLT processor will automatically run only the root template rule. If you have any other template rules, those need to be explicitly called. The way to explicitly call a template is to add an xsl:apply-template element.

The syntax of this element follows.

```
<xsl:apply-templates select="node-set" />
```

This instruction works like so:

1. The XSLT processor finds the nodes in the source tree that correspond to the node-set.
2. The processor then looks in the XSLT document to see which template rule is the most appropriate to use. Even if multiple template rules could apply to the node-set, only one template rule is chosen, based on rules that we won't get into right now.
3. The `xsl:apply-template` line is replaced by the output of the chosen template rule.

Example 10–4 shows what happens when you have several template rules, but forget to call them within the root template.

EXAMPLE 10–4 SEVERAL TEMPLATE RULES, LITERAL ELEMENTS ONLY

```
<!-- source XML document -->
<?xml version="1.0" ?>
<shelleyBiotech>
    <product_list>
        <product chemName="hydroBlah" marName="Breathe-
Clear">
            <effects>bronchodialator</effects>
            <sideEffects>nausea, dizziness</sideEffects>
        </product>
        <product chemName="hydroBlah1" marName="BeatEasy">
            <effects>artery wall plaque remover</
effects>
            <sideEffects>nausea, joint soreness</side-
Effects>
        </product>
    </product_list>
</shelleyBiotech>


<!--XSLT document - multiple templates -->
<?xml version="1.0" ?>
<xsl:stylesheet
xmlns:xsl="http://www.w3.org/1999/XSL/Transform">
    <xsl:template match="/">
        <html>
        <head>
            <title>Shelley BioProducts</title>
        </head>
```

```
            <body>
                    It worked!
            </body>
            </html>
        </xsl:template>

        <xsl:template match="product">
                Product info goes here.
        </xsl:template>
</xsl:stylesheet>
```

```
<!-- The XML result (it's XHTML) -->
<html>
<head>
    <title>Shelley BioProducts</title>
</head>
<body>
    It worked!
</body>
</html>
```

Well, that didn't help us very much. Notice that the second template was never run. To actually make sure the product template rule becomes a part of the result tree, we must add an `xsl:apply-template` to the root template rule as in Example 10–5.

EXAMPLE 10–5 APPLYING A TEMPLATE

```
<!-- XSLT document with xsl:apply-template -->
<?xml version="1.0" ?>
<xsl:stylesheet
xmlns:xsl="http://www.w3.org/1999/XSL/Transform">
    <xsl:template match="/">
            <html>
            <head>
                    <title>Shelley BioProducts</title>
            </head>
            <body>
                    It worked!<p></p>
                    <xsl:apply-templates select="product" />
            </body>
            </html>
        </xsl:template>

        <xsl:template match="product">
                Product info goes here.<br />
        </xsl:template>
</xsl:stylesheet>
```

```
<!-- result -->
<html>
<head>
    <title>Shelley BioProducts</title>
</head>
<body>
    It worked!<p></p>

    Product info goes here.<br />
    Product info goes here.<br />
</body>
</html>
```

HOW THE CODE WORKS

Yes! The second template rule was called. However, even though we have only one template rule that matches the "product" node, that rule seems to have been called twice. Why did this happen? When we called the product template rule with `<xsl:apply-templates select="product" />`, we asked the processor to find all the nodes that match the "product" node. Since there are two nodes that match that description, the template rule was applied twice.

All template rules can call other template rules, as long as there is no circular reference. In Example 10–6, there are a total of four template rules.

EXAMPLE 10–6 MULTIPLE TEMPLATES, MULTIPLE CALLING

```
<!-- source XML document -->
<?xml version="1.0" ?>
<shelleyBiotech>
    <product_list>
        <product chemName="hydroBlah" marName="Breathe-
Clear">
            <effects>bronchodialator</effects>
            <sideEffects>nausea, dizziness</sideEffects>
        </product>
        <product chemName="hydroBlah1" marName="BeatEasy">
            <effects>artery wall plaque remover</
effects>
            <sideEffects>nausea, joint soreness</side-
Effects>
        </product>
    </product_list>
</shelleyBiotech>


!-- XSLT document: multiple templates, multiple applications
-->
```

```
<?xml version="1.0" ?>
<xsl:stylesheet
xmlns:xsl="http://www.w3.org/1999/XSL/Transform">
    <xsl:template match="/">
          <html>
          <head>
                <title>Shelley BioProducts</title>
          </head>
          <body>
                It worked!<p></p>
                <xsl:apply-templates select="product" />
          </body>
          </html>
    </xsl:template>

    <xsl:template match="product">
          <b><xsl:value-of select="@marName" /></b> :
          <i><xsl:value-of select="@chemName" /></i>
          <p></p>
          <xsl:apply-tempaltes select="effects" /><br />
          <xsl:apply-templates select="sideEffects" />
          <p></p>
    </xsl:template>

    <xsl:template match="effects">
          Effects: <xsl:value-of select="effects" />
    </xsl:template>

    <xsl:template match="sideEffects">
          Side Effects: <xsl:value-of select="sideEffects" />
    </xsl:template>

</xsl:stylesheet>



<!-- The XML result (it's XHTML) -->
<html>
<head>
    <title>Shelley BioProducts</title>
</head>
<body>
    It worked!<p></p>

    <b>BreatheClear</b> : <i>hrdroBlah</i>
    <p></p>
    Effects: Bronchodialator<br />
    Side Effects: nausea, dizziness
    <p></p>
    <b>BeatEasy</b> : <i>htdroBlah1</i>
    <p></p>
```

```
        Effects: artery plaque remover<br />
        Side Effects: nausea, swollen joints
        <p></p>
  </body>
  </html>
```

HOW THE CODE WORKS

Are you following this? It can get tricky. The root template calls the template rule that is associated with the node-set of product (that is, `<xsl:apply-templates select="product" />`). Inside the product template rule, two more templates are called: one for `effect` and one for `sideEffects`.

You can see that when the root template calls the product template rule, it is applied twice because there are two product elements. Inside the product template rule, we call `effect` and `sideEffects`. Each of those two templates is called once.

At this point, you may be asking why `effects` and `sideEffects` are only called once—after all, there are two `effects` elements and two `sideEffects` elements. It seems like there should be four appearances of those elements in the output—twice for every `product` element. Why are there only two?

The answer is that when the `product` template rule looks for the `effects` and `sideEffects` elements, it only looks inside its current node-set. That is, it only looks inside the current node. The XSLT processor only looks for the `effects` and `sideEffects` elements inside the current `product` node.

◆ Instructions

Instructions are elements in the `xsl` namespace that look at the source XML document and usually extract certain values from it, whether from text nodes or attribute values. Instructions can also create elements and attributes out of nowhere. You saw some examples of instructions in earlier examples.

xsl:value-of

```
<xsl:value-of select=string-selection
  disable-output-escaping = "yes" | "no" />
```

You've seen this instruction before—it allows you to extract a string from somewhere in the source tree. The string selection value is simply an XPath expression that points to a text node or the value of an attribute.

```
<xsl:value-of select="product/effects" />
<xsl:value-of select="product/@chemName" />
```

xsl:strip-space

```
<xsl:strip-space elements="token list" />
```

This instruction takes a white space–separated list of element names as its argument. The value of that node, whether it's a text node or an attribute value, has its trailing and preceding white space removed, and any sequences of white space in the node are collapsed into a single space.

xsl:preserve-space

```
<xsl:preserve-space elements="token list" />
```

This instruction takes a white space–separated list of element names. The value of that node, whether it's a text node or an attribute value, has all of its white space preserved.

xsl:sort

```
<xsl:sort select = string-expression
    lang = { nmtoken }
    data-type = { "text" | "number" | name }
    order = { "ascending" | "descending" }
    case-order = { "upper-first" | "lower-first" } />
```

This instruction sorts nodes that arrive as a result of the xsl:apply-templates or xsl:for-each instructions. That is, the codes are processed in the order specified by xsl:sort instead of in the order they appear in the XML document. Here's an example.

```
<xsl:template match="products">
    <ol>
       <xsl:apply-templates select="product">
           <xsl:sort select="@chemName"/>
           <xsl:sort select="@marName"/>
       </xsl:apply-templates>
    </ol>
</xsl:template>
```

In this case, the templates are called according to the alphabetical order of the chemName attribute and then secondarily sorted by the marName attribute.

The syntax that you haven't seen, which is used in the first `xsl:sort` example, is the use of the curly braces. These braces allow you to use variables or XPath expressions to create values.

Since these braces are new, let's look at an example. Say this is your source code (this is taken from the W3C XML spec):

```
<photograph>
    <href>headquarters.jpg</href>
    <size width="300"/>
</photograph>
```

The XSLT document is as follows.

```
<xsl:variable name="image-dir">/images</xsl:variable>
<xsl:template match="photograph">
    <img src="{$image-dir}/{href}" width="{size@width}"/>
</xsl:template>
```

And here's the result:

```
<img src="/images/headquarters.jpg" width="300"/>
```

See how that works? Look at `xsl:variable` if you could use some more information. Remember that `$image-dir` is a variable.

xsl:include

```
<xsl:include href="uri-reference" />
```

You can include an external stylesheet in your document's stylesheet using `xsl:include`. This element can only be a direct child of `xsl:stylesheet`. All of the children of the external file's `xsl:stylesheet` element replace the `xsl:include` line. Stylesheets are not allowed to directly or indirectly include themselves. The template rules in the original document take precedence over any rules in the included document, so if there's any overlap between your file and the included one, the included file's rules are run and yours are ignored.

xsl:import

```
<xsl:import href="uri-reference" />
```

You can import an external stylesheet in your document's stylesheet using `xsl:import`. This instruction must be a direct child of `xsl:stylesheet`, and it must precede all other children.

The difference between `xsl:import` and `xsl:include` is that the rules in the imported element take precedence over the original document's rules, so your file's rules always take precedence over anything in the included file.

xsl:apply-imports

```
<xsl:apply-imports />
```

Use this instruction if you want the original document's template rule to override the imported document's rule. Just add this instruction inside the template rule you want to be used.

xsl:apply-templates

```
<xsl:apply-templates select="node-set"
    mode="name">
        [ xsl:sort | xsl:with-param ]
</xsl:apply-templates>
```

This element calls the most appropriate template rule for the indicated node set. If the `select` attribute is not included (that is, `<xsl:apply-templates/>`), then all of the children of the current node are processed.

`xsl:apply-templates` can not refer to itself: `<xsl:apply-templates select="." />` may cause a nonterminating loop, depending on the XSLT processor you're using.

The `mode` attribute is a little funny. When you create a template rule, you can give that rule a `mode` attribute, which acts as a kind of secondary identifier. The `mode` attribute doesn't do anything unless there's a `xsl:apply-template` that uses that same mode. In that case, only the appropriate template rules that share the same `mode` value are applied.

xsl:call-template

```
<xsl:call-template named="name">
    [ xsl:with-param ]
</xsl:call-template>
```

`xsl:call-template` is similar to `xsl:apply-template` in that they both invoke a template rule. The only differences are

1. `xsl:call-template` can only call a template via a matching `name` attribute.
2. `xsl:call-template` does not change the current node.

xsl:copy

```
<xsl:copy use-attribute-sets = "names">
   ...content...
</xs;:copy>
```

This instruction allows you to copy the current node into the result tree.

xsl:copy-of

```
<xsl:copy-of select=expression />
```

This instruction allows you to insert a piece of the source tree into the result tree without converting it into a string, like xsl:value-of does.

xsl:for-each

```
<xsl:for-each select="node-set">
   ...content and xsl:sort...
</xsl:for-each>
```

This instruction creates a loop that has as many steps as there are nodes in the node-set. For example, if this was the source XML:

```
<shelley>
    <product_list>
      <product>...</product>
      <product>...</product>
      <product>...</product>
      <product>...</product>
    </product_list>
</shelley>
```

and this is the XSLT:

```
<xsl:template match="shelley">
    <xsl:for-each select="product_list/product">
        chemical name:
        <xsl:value-of select="@chemName"/><br />
        marketing name: <xsl:value-of select="@marName"/>
        <p></p>
    </xsl:for-each>
</xsl:template>
```

this would result in a paragraph for each `product` child element of the `product_list` element.

xsl:if

```
<xsl:if test="boolean-expression">
    …content…
</xsl:if>
```

If the Boolean expression evaluates to `true` then the XSLT processor executes the content inside the `xsl:if` element.

```
<xsl:if test="position()>4">
  narc
</xsl:if>
```

xsl:choose

```
<xsl:choose>
    [ <xsl:when> | <xsl:otherwise> ]
</xsl:choose>
```

This instruction tells the XSLT processor to choose a single element from among a number of alternatives. In most programming languages, this is known as a case statement. These alternatives can be `xsl:when` elements and an optional `xsl:otherwise` element. Here's how the format could look:

```
<xsl:choose>
    <xsl:when test="foo">blah blah</xsl:when>
    <xsl:when test="bar">wonk wonk</xsl:when>
    <xsl:otherwise>pants george</xsl:otherwise>
</xsl:choose>
```

xsl:when

```
<xsl:when test="boolean-expression">
    …content…
</xsl:when>
```

This instruction is just like `xsl:if`. The only difference is that `xsl:when` occurs inside an `xsl:choose` element.

xsl:otherwise

```
<xsl:otherwise>
    …content…
</xsl:otherwise>
```

This instruction is analogous to an `xsl:else` statement in many other languages. It's simply the last `xsl:when` that doesn't need a Boolean test.

xsl:variable

```
<xsl:variable name="name"
    select="expression">
            ...variable value...
</xsl:variable>
```

This instruction creates a variable. In other words, it binds a name to a value. These variables can then be accessed by other XSLT instructions by placing the variable name in curly braces {} and preceding the variable with a dollar sign. See the definition for `xsl:element` on page 161 for an example.

xsl:param

```
<xsl:param name="name"
    select="expression">
    ...variable value...
</xsl:param>
```

This instruction creates a variable if and only if that variable hasn't been created already. If no variable has been created, this instruction acts just like `xsl:variable`.

xsl:with-param

```
<xsl:with-param name="name" select="expression">
    ...content...
</xsl:with-param>
```

This instruction lets you pass a variable to a template rule. It's allowed inside `xsl:apply-templates` and `xsl:call-template` elements. Use `xsl:with-param` when you want a template rule to be able to use a variable or a template. When you use this element, the instructions in the template rule can use the passed parameter as a variable.

xsl:decimal-format

```
<xsl:decimal-fomat name="name"
    decimal-separator = "char"
    grouping-separator = "char"
    infinity = "string"
    minus-sign = "char"
    minus-sign = "char"
```

```
NaN = "string"
percent = "char"
per-mile = "char"
zero-digit = "char"
pattern-separator = "char" />
```

This instruction declares a decimal-format, which you can use to visually format numbers. In more technical terms, it controls the interpretation of a format pattern used by the `format-number` function. Let's look at some of the attributes.

decimal-separator
Specifies the character used for the decimal sign—the default is the period (.).

grouping-separator
Specifies the character used as a grouping separator (for example, the comma in 10,000)—the default value is the comma.

percent
Specifies the character used as a percent sign—the default is %.

per-mile
Specifies the character used as the per mile sign—the default is the Unicode per-mile sign (#x2030).

zero-digit
Specifies the character used as the digit zero—the default is 0.

digit
Specifies the character used for a digit in the format pattern—the default is #.

pattern-separator
Specifies the character used to separate positive and negative subpatterns in a pattern—the default is the semi-colon (;).

xsl:template

```
<xsl:template match="node-set"
    name="name"
    priority="number"
    mode="name">
        ...content...
</xsl:template>
```

This instruction defines a template rule. The `match` attribute defines which parts of the source tree are to be affected by the rule. The `match` attribute is mandatory (unless the `name` attribute is used).

xsl:namespace-alias

```
<xsl:namespace-alias
    stylesheet-prefix = "prefix" | "#default"
    result-prefix = "prefix" | "#default" />
```

This instruction allows you to create an alias for a namespace. The `stylesheet-prefix` attribute is the alias that you're creating, and the `result-prefix` attribute is the real attribute. If you're dealing with the default namespace, use the `"#default"` value as the prefix.

◆ Creating Nodes

XSLT allows you to create your own elements based on information in the XML source tree. This is different from literal elements, which are hard-coded.

xsl:element

```
<xsl:element name = { name }
    namespace = { uri-reference }
    use-attribute-sets = "names">
        ...content...
</xsl:element>
```

This instruction allows you to create an element with a computed name.

xsl:attribute

```
<xsl:attribute name = { name }
    namespace = { uri-reference }>
        ...content...
</xsl:attribute>
```

This instruction allows you to create an attribute that can have a computed name, much like `xsl:element`.

xsl:attribute-set

```
<xsl:attribute-set name="name"
    use-attribute-sets = "names">
        ... xsl:attribute elements...
</xsl:attribute-set>
```

This element allows you to create a group of attributes.

```
<xsl:attribute-set name="drugNames">
    <xsl:attribute name="chemName">hydroBlah</xsl:attribute>
    <xsl:attriubte name="marName">hydroBlah</xsl:attribute>
</xsl:attribute-set>
```

xsl:text

```
<xsl:text disable-output-escaping = "yes" | "no">
    ...#PCDATA...
</xsl:text>
```

This instruction allows you to create a text node.

```
<xsl:text>nausea, dizziness</xsl:text>
```

xsl:processing-instruction

```
<xsl:processing-instruction name= { name }>
...content...
</xsl:processing-instruction>
```

Here's an example:

```
<xsl:processing-instruction>name="xml-
stylesheet">href="shelley.css" type="text/css"</xsl:process-
ing-instruction>
```

will result in

```
<?xml-stylesheet href="shelley.css" type="text/css"?>
```

xsl:number

```
<xsl:number
    level = "single" | "multiple" | "any"
    count = "pattern"
    from = "pattern"
    value = "number-expression"
    format = { string }
    lang = { nmtoken }
    letter-value = { "alphabetic" | "traditional" }
    grouping-separator = { char }
  grouping-size = { number } />
```

This instruction is used to output a formatted number into the result tree. Let's look at some of the potential attributes, as in this example from the W3C XSLT specification:

TABLE 10–1 Format Tokens

Format token	Description
1	Generates a sequence of 1, 2, 3, ..., 10, 11, ...
01	Generates a sequence of 01, 02, 03, ..., 10, 11, ...
A	Generates a sequence of A, B, C, ..., Z, AA, AB, AC
a	Generates a sequence of a, b, c, ..., z, aa, ab, ac
I	Generates a sequence of I, II, III, IV, V, VI, VII, VIII, ...
i	Generates a sequence of i, ii, iii, iv, v, vi, vii, viii, ...

```
<xsl:template match="item_list">
    <xsl:for-each select="item">
        <xsl:sort select="."/>
        <p>
        <xsl:number value="position()" format="1. "/>
        </p>
    </xsl:for-each>
</xsl:template>
```

This would result in a series of numbers, one for each `item` child in the `item_list` element.

Format Tokens

How to run the format tokens is shown in Table 10–1.

xsl:comment

```
<xsl:comment>
    ...content...
</xsl:comment>
```

This instruction creates an XML comment.

```
<xsl:comment>Here's the comment</xsl:comment>
```

results in

```
<!-- Here's the comment -->
```

◆ Functions

These functions can be used in XSLT instructions to further refine your search for the appropriate elements to transform, or to create, precise conditions for `xsl:if` and `xsl:when`.

These functions are extensions to the core XPath language, which we looked at in the last chapter.

document()

```
document(uri_or_node-set [, node-set] )
```

This function allows you to pull information from an XML document other than the source XML document. This extra XML information is parsed and placed into a data model just like the source XML document. This function returns a node-set.

If you use a node-set instead of a URI for the first argument, then the XSLT processor will look for the string-value of the first node in your node-set, and look for a URI there. It will then act as if the remaining node-set (without the first node) is actually the second argument (most folks just use a URI here).

Use the second argument (*node-set*) to specify which node-set in the external XML document that you want to use.

format-number()

```
format-number(number, formatPattern [, decimalPattern ])
```

This function takes a number and formats it according to the second (and optional third) arguments. A string with the formatted number is returned. Format patterns belong to a Java subclass and are not in the scope of this book. However, you can find information about format patterns (also called DecimalFormat) at *java.sun.com/ products/jdk/1.1/docs/api/java.text.DecimalFormat.html*.

Instructions for *decimalPattern* are found in the entry for xsl:decimal-format above.

current()

```
current()
```

This simple function returns a node-set with only the current node in the set. The abbreviated version of this function is the period (.).

For example,

```
<xsl:value-of select="current()"/>
```

is the same as

```
<xsl:value-of select="."/>
```

unparsed-entity-uri()

```
unparsed-entity-uri(entityName)
```

This function returns the URI where the unparsed entity with the name of *entityName* is. If there is no such entity, then an empty string is returned.

generate-id()

```
generate-id([node-set])
```

This function returns a string that uniquely identifies the first node in the argument node-set. It's up to the XSLT processor to decide what this identifier is, and there's no rule that XSLT processors have to return the same identifier every time they look at the same XML document. If the *node-set* argument is omitted, then the XSLT processor uses the current node.

system-property()

```
system-property(elementName)
```

This function returns several properties of the element in the argument:

- xsl:version returns a number giving the version of XSLT implemented by the XSLT processor.
- xsl:vendor returns a string identifying the vendor of the XSLT processor.
- xsl:vendor-url usually returns the URL of the vendor's home page.

element-available()

```
element-available(elementName)
```

This function searches the XSLT document for an element named *elementName*. If one is found, true is returned. Otherwise, false is returned.

function-available()

```
function-available(functionName)
```

Similar to element-available() above, this function returns true if there is a function in the function library called *functionName*. Otherwise, false is returned.

◆ Recap

You made it this far? Woo hoo! Well done. This was a pretty tough chapter—it can take a while to get your head around how transformations work. We'll take it a little easier in the next chapter—we'll just be looking at XPointer, which is an extension to XPath. It's something you can use in your XLink documents to increase their flexibility.

11 XPointer: XLinking to XML Fragments

IN THIS CHAPTER

- Purpose of XPointer
- What XPointer Is
- XLink Basics
- XPointer Concepts and Terminology
- XPointer Basics
- XPointer Functions
- Recap

Yep, it's time for another X(something). In this chapter, we look at XPointer, or XML Pointing Language. XPointer is a repurposing of XPath so that it works with XLink. Don't worry, it's not as esoteric as it sounds. In fact, this is one of the lighter chapters—not as simple as XHTML, but pretty easy on the brain if you've read the chapters on XLink and XPath.

◆ Purpose of XPointer

XPointer's purpose in life is to give XLink a little more flexibility. Remember XLink? It's that set of tags that lets you create links from one XML document to another. The only problem with XLink is that you can only link to a single document, not to a specific place within a document. Even HTML lets you link to a place within another document by using anchors, like <a

href="product.html#order">. XPointer exists to allow XLink to link to any position, text string, or node inside another XML document.

XPointer has something grander than just copying some HTML functionality, though. In HTML, when you want to link to a specific place inside a document, you need two pieces:

1. A marker in the target document like `<a name="order"> </a>`.

2. A link to that marker: `<a href="product.html #order">`.

For the highly technical folks who created XPointer, this is a problem: We're mixing markup and content, and that's a bad thing. Ideally, we shouldn't need any sort of marker in the target document. The target document should have content and nothing but content. There should be some way to link to a fragment inside a document that doesn't require anything special inside that target document. XPointer provides this.

◆ What XPointer Is

XPointer is an extension of XPath. In other words, XPointer = XPath + some new functions. When we create a chunk of code in XPointer, it's called an XPoint expression. Here's an abbreviated example:

```
<link xlink:type="simple"
    xlink:href="products.xml#beatClear"/>
```

HOW THE CODE WORKS

XPointer expressions always occur in the `xlink:href` attributes and they occur after a number sign (#), just like HTML. XPointer expressions can be more complex than this, though. The above is the abbreviated form of XPointer, and it looks just like HTML. The longer form, also called the full form, can look like this:

```
<link xlink:type="simple"
xlink:href="products.xml#xpointer(id('beatClear'))"/>
```

This code accomplishes the same thing as the code above. XPointer works well whether you're pointing at a single point in a document or a whole range of information.

To easily absorb XPointer, we'll need to do a quick review of ID-type attributes and a quick review of XLink basics.

◆ ID-Type Attributes

ID-type attributes can only contain values that exist nowhere else in the XML document. If we wanted to create a `<div>` element that had an ID-type attribute called `id`, this would appear in our DTD:

```
<!ELEMENT div ANY>
<!ATTLIST div id ID #REQUIRED>
```

This section of a DTD specifies an ID-type attribute called `id`. In our XML, the following is allowed because the two `div` elements have different values for their `id` attributes:

```
<div id="header">BeatClear</div>
<div id="subheader">Drastically reduce risks of a second
heart attack</div>
```

The following two lines of code cannot exist inside a valid XML document, because the `id` attribute values are the same:

```
<div id="header">BeatClear</div>
<div id="header">BreatheEasy</div>
```

XPointer is exceptionally good at finding the values of ID-type attributes—we'll examine how good soon. But first, we'll have a quick review of XLink basics.

◆ XLink Basics

Remember XLink? It's a way to define links with starting and ending resources and build traversals between them. Simple links are those with a local starting resource and a remote ending resource (just like a link in HTML). Complex links are actually collections of links, and they can start or end anywhere. In XLink, you can only designate entire documents as external resources—you can't say, "Go to a certain part of this external document."

That's it! You don't need any more review. Let's look at how XPointer views the XML world.

◆ XPointer Concepts and Terminology

XPointer can see nodes and elements, just like XPath, but it can see more, too. XPointer can also recognize points, ranges, and locations.

Points

Points are single spots in an XML document. Technically, points have no width—they exist between characters in an XML document. As an example, in the string "woof," there can be five points (designated by P): "PwPoPoPfP." Or, as in Figure 11–1, the arrows point to where the points would be.

Ranges

A range is a set of XML information that goes from one point to another. Ranges can include the more familiar "node" from XPath. In the example below, a range is in bold:

```
<shelleyBiotech>
    <product_list>
        <product chemName="hydroBlah" marName="Breathe-
Clear">
            <effects>bronchodialator</effects>
            <sideEffects>nausea, dizziness</sideEffects>
        </product>
        <product chemName="hydroBlah1" marName="BeatEasy">
            <effects>artery wall plaque remover</
effects>
            <sideEffects>nausea, joint soreness</side-
Effects>
        </product>
    </product_list>
</shelleyBiotech>
```

In this example, the starting point occurs just before the product node and the end point occurs just after the second `</product>`.

FIGURE 11–1 Where points are located

Location

A location is a generalization of the concept of a node, except that it includes points and ranges. A location could be a single point, a node, or a range. For example, a location could be the range below:

```
<shelleyBiotech>
    <product_list>
        <product chemName="hydroBlah" marName="Breathe-
Clear">
            <effects>bronchodialator</effects>
            <sideEffects>nausea, dizziness</sideEffects>
        </product>
        <product chemName="hydroBlah1" marName="BeatEasy">
            <effects>artery wall plaque remover</
effects>
            <sideEffects>nausea, joint soreness</side-
Effects>
        </product>
    </product_list>
</shelleyBiotech>
```

Location-Set

A location-set is an ordered list of locations. These locations don't need to be next to each other. For example, a location-set could be only the effects elements and the first sideEffects element, as well as the word "nausea" in the second sideEffects element.

```
<shelleyBiotech>
    <product_list>
        <product chemName="hydroBlah" marName="Breathe-
Clear">
            <effects>bronchodialator</effects>
            <sideEffects>nausea, dizziness</sideEffects>
        </product>
        <product chemName="hydroBlah1" marName="BeatEasy">
            <effects>artery wall plaque remover</
effects>
            <sideEffects>nausea, joint soreness</side-
Effects>
        </product>
    </product_list>
</shelleyBiotech>
```

Singleton

A singleton is a location-set that contains only a single location, such as a single or a range. In standard computer jargon, a singleton is a set with a single member.

Subresource

A resource is an XML document, and a subresource is any part of a resource that is identified by an XPointer expression. An XPointer expression can identify a point, range, node, location, or location-set. Thus, a subresource can be almost any combination of different parts of a resource.

Fragment

A fragment is a more general XML term that stands for any contiguous section of XML code.

◆ XPointer Basics

It took a few pages, but now you're ready to look at XPointer more closely. XPointer is at its best when it's looking for elements that have a certain ID-type attribute, like we saw in earlier examples.

Let's say we have the following code in our DTD:

```
<!ELEMENT product ANY>
<!ATTLIST product marName ID #REQUIRED>
```

This means that in our XML, any `product` element must have a `marName` attribute, and all those attributes must have different values. If the following is our target XML document:

```
<shelleyBiotech>
    <product_list>
        <product chemName="hydroBlah" marName="Breathe-
Clear">
            <effects>bronchodialator</effects>
            <sideEffects>nausea, dizziness</sideEffects>
        </product>
        <product chemName="hydroBlah1" marName="BeatEasy">
            <effects>artery wall plaque remover</
effects>
            <sideEffects>nausea, joint soreness</side-
Effects>
        </product>
    </product_list>
</shelleyBiotech>
```

Notice that there are two product elements. Let's say that we want to link to the product with a marketing name of "Beat-Easy". There are two ways to link to this element: abbreviated and full form. We'll look at the abbreviated form first:

```
xlink:href="products.xml#BeatEasy"
```

When you're looking for an element with a certain value for an ID-type attribute, all you need to do is follow the number sign with the value of the attribute. Now let's say that we want to find the second child element of the beatEasy element:

```
xlink:href="products.xml#BeatEasy/2"
```

If we want to ignore any sort of ID-type attribute and just focus on children, we can do that too. If we want to link to the second child of the second child of the first element, here's the code we'd use:

```
#/1/2/2
```

Here's a little test to see if you understand: Does the following XPointer expression make sense?

```
#start/3/4/beat/3/17
```

In other words, XPointer looks for the ID of "start," then looks down three children, down four children, looks for the ID "beat," down three children, and down 17 children. This expression, though it would work, is longer than it needs to be. The exact same result can be achieved with

```
#beat/3/17
```

Why? Because all ID values must be unique within the whole XML document, which means that there can only be a single "beat" ID, no matter where it is.

That covers what can be abbreviated in XPointer: only ID values and child positions. If you need to use other qualifiers to get to the desired element or string, you must use the full form of XPointer.

Full-Form XPointer

The syntax for a full-form XPointer expression looks like this:

```
#xpointer(expression)
```

Once you use the full form, you can't use any abbreviations—the whole expression must be in full form.

Let's start by looking at the full-form versions of the abbreviated expressions we looked at earlier. If the abbreviated form is

```
#BeatEasy
```

the full form is:

```
#xpointer(id('BreatEasy'))
```

XPointer is full of functions and lots of nested parentheses. Be careful—it's easy to lose track of how many parentheses you have.

If the abbreviated expression is

```
#beat/3/7
```

then the full-form expression is

```
#xpointer(id('BeatEasy')/*[position()=3]/*[position()=7])
```

Hopefully, this looks a little familiar to you from your understanding of XPath. You may also remember that XPath has a few abbreviations of its own. The line of code above can also be written as

```
#xpointer(id('BeatEasy')/*[3]/*[7])
```

So we've just seen three ways to write the same piece of code. It can be a little confusing, so if you're scratching your head right now, reread the above lines of code until they start to make sense. (They will, I promise.)

You may have realized that finding an ID-type attribute in an XML document means that there has to be a DTD: Otherwise, there's no way to determine whether an attribute is an ID-type or not. However, when you're writing your XPointer, you may not know whether your target document will have a DTD or not. Fortunately, there's a way to deal with this ambiguity:

```
#xpointer(id('BeatEasy'))xpointer(//*[marName='BeatEasy'])
```

If there is no DTD, then the first XPointer expression fails, and the second one is tried. If there is a DTD and the first

XPointer expression can be invoked, then the second XPointer expression is ignored.

If you need to locate an element with an attribute of a certain value, but that attribute is not an ID-type attribute, you can use this format:

```
#xpointer(//*[@chemName='hydroBlah1'])
```

You've seen this before in XPath.
What happens when we have the below XML:

```
<shelleyBiotech>
    <product>...</product>
    <product>...</product>
    <address>...</address>
</shelleyBiotech>
```

and our Xpointer expression is:

```
#xpointer(//shelleyBiotech/product)
```

We get the following location-set (bold stands for the part that's selected by XPointer):

```
<shelleyBiotech>
    <product>...</product>
    <product>...</product>
    <address>...</address>
</shelleyBiotech>
```

Escaping

Since parentheses are such an integral part of XPointer, they have to be escaped with a circumflex (^). For example, if you were looking for the text string "(start", you'd have to do this:

```
#xpointer(string-range('^(start'))
```

If you need to look for a circumflex in your string, escape it like this: ^^. Also, the less-than sign (<) needs to be escaped as <. If you're looking for the first three children of an element, here's what it would look like:

```
#xpointer(//product_list/product(position() &lt; 4))
```

Table 11–1 shows a summary.

TABLE 11–1 Escaping in XPointer

Character	Escaped as
(	^ (
^	^ ^
<	<

And no, I don't know why XPointer doesn't use a backslash, like every other language.

◆ XPointer Functions

In addition to all the functions that XPath provides (like `posi-tion()`), XPointer extends XPath by introducing a number of its own functions. Table 11–2 lists a summary, and then we'll look at each one in detail.

TABLE 11–2 XPointer functions

Function	Description
`start-point`	Finds the first point (zero-width) in a range.
`end-point`	Finds the last point (zero-width) in a range.
`string-range`	Finds the text string in the function's argument.
`range`	Returns the range in the function's argument.
`range-inside`	Much like `range`, returns the range in the function's argument, unless the range is a single element. In that case, the function returns whatever's inside the element.
`range-to`	Creates a range from a starting point to an ending point.
`origin`	Returns the node where the user program initiated the link to the target document.
`here`	Returns the location-set of the node that contains the XPointer expression.

`start-point`

Let's look at how to locate a specific point as marked by the big P in the following example:

```
<shelleyBiotech>P
    <product>...</product>
    <product>...</product>
</shelleyBiotech>
```

There are two ways to link to this point. The simplest way is this:

```
#xpointer(start-point(//shelleyBiotech))
```

Notice that the point is inserted directly after the element itself. You can also couple the `start-point` function with the range function (which we'll cover in detail later):

```
#xpointer(start-point(range(//shelleyBiotech/product[1])))
```

In this case, the point is inserted before the range indicated. This is a little odd, since the point was inserted after the element `shelleyBiotech` in the code above. I'm assuming that this is an oddity that will be worked out (or at least explained sufficiently) when XPointer finally gets to Recommendation status.

end-point

This function finds the ending point of a range or a node. Let's place a point in the following place:

```
<shelleyBiotech>
    <product>...</product>
    <product>...</product>P
    <address>...</address>
</shelleyBiotech>
```

Using `end-point`, here's what we'd do:

```
#xpointer(end-point(range(//shelleyBiotech/product[2])))
```

HOW THE CODE WORKS

First, we find the range that encompasses the second `product` child of `shelleyBiotech`. We then place the point at the end of that range. Fortunately, this is pretty intuitive.

You might see a way to link to this point using the `start-point` function. It would look like this:

```
#xpointer(start-point(range(//shelleyBiotech/address)))
```

That wraps it up for the point functions. Now let's look at some ways to target text strings using `string-range`.

string-range

The syntax for the string-range function is

```
string-range(range, string [,start [,length]])
```

There are a few different ways to use this function. We'll be looking at all of them, and this is the target XML we'll be linking to.

```
<shelleyBiotech>
    <product>hydroBlah1</product>
    <product>cholorhydronitrate</product>
    <product>nitro-1-hydroxide</product>
</shelleyBiotech>
```

If we wanted to find all occurrences of the phrase "hydro" in this XML, here's our XPointer code:

```
#xpointer(string-range(//*, 'hydro'))
```

The selected location-set is in bold below:

```
<shelleyBiotech>
    <product>hydroBlah1</product>
    <product>cholorhydronitrate</product>
    <product>nitro-1-hydroxide</product>
</shelleyBiotech>
```

Notice that all three occurrences of "hydro" are part of the location-set.

We can also combine functions. Say we want to look at points that occur just before all the "hydro"s in the document. Here's what our XPointer would look like:

```
#xpointer(starting-point(string-range(//*, 'hydro')))
```

Here's what the location-set would look like (again, using a big P to indicate where the points would go):

```
<shelleyBiotech>
    <product>PhydroBlah1</product>
    <product>cholorPhydronitrate</product>
    <product>nitro-1-Phydroxide</product>
</shelleyBiotech>
```

HOW THE CODE WORKS

XPointer first located all the "hydro" strings in the document and then placed points at the beginning of all of those strings.

If we decided that we only want the "dro" part of "hydro" here's what our Xpointer would look like:

```
#xpointer(string-range(//*,'hydro',3))
```

The resulting selected XML would look like this:

```
<shelleyBiotech>
    <product>hydroBlah1</product>
    <product>cholorhydronitrate</product>
    <product>nitro-1-hydroxide</product>
</shelleyBiotech>
```

HOW THE CODE WORKS

XPointer started by finding all occurrences of "hydro" in the document. Then it counted down the "hydro" string, and chose from the third character on to the end of the string. Note that XPointer, unlike many other languages, starts counting the string at 1 instead of 0.

On the off chance that you'd want to select only the "dr" part of "hydro" in the document, your XPointer expression would look something like this:

```
#xpointer(string-range(//*, 'hydro', 3, 2))
```

The resulting XML would look like this:

```
<shelleyBiotech>
    <product>hydroBlah1</product>
    <product>cholorhydronitrate</product>
    <product>nitro-1-hydroxide</product>
</shelleyBiotech>
```

HOW THE CODE WORKS

XPointer found all the "hydro"s in the XML document, started counting at the third character, and only counted two characters, yielding a little "dr" occurring three times.

Now that you've seen the basics of string-range, let's get a little fancy. Can you guess what the following XPointer would produce?

```
#xpointer(string-range(string-range(//*, 'hydro'), ''))
```

Pretty odd, eh? Here's the result:

```
<shelleyBiotech>
    <product>PₕPᵧPₐPᵣPₒPBlah1</product>
    <product>cholorPₕPᵧPₐPᵣPₒPnitrate</product>
    <product>nitro-1-PₕPᵧPₐPᵣPₒPxide</product>
</shelleyBiotech>
```

HOW THE CODE WORKS

We start by finding the three "hydro"s in the document. Those three "hydro"s then become the location-set for the outer `string-range` function. The function finds every zero-width character in those strings—essentially, it locates all of the points within the three "hydro" strings. Those points exist between the characters, both before and after.

A mellower way to select a point using `string-range` is to force the length of the string to be zero. Here's an example:

```
#xpointer(string-range(//sheleyBiotech/product[2], 'hydro',
1, 0))
```

This will place a point before the "hydro" in the second `product` element, like so:

```
<shelleyBiotech>
    <product>hydroBlah1</product>
    <product>cholorPhydronitrate</product>
    <product>nitro-1-hydroxide</product>
</shelleyBiotech>
```

There's one more thing we're going into look at in this section: combining locations. Check out this XPointer expression:

```
#xpointer( start-point(string-range(//shelleyBiotech/
product[1],'hydro')) | //ShelleyBiotech/address | string-
range(//*, 'nitro'))
```

Whoa! What's all this? It might be easier to digest in this form:

```
#xpointer( location1 | location2 | location3 )
```

This is a combination of several XPointer expressions that specify several locations. Here's what would be selected in the target XML.

```
<shelleyBiotech>
    <product>PhydroBlah1</product>
    <product>cholorhydronitrate</product>
    <product>nitro-1-hydroxide</product>
    <address>1234 Main Street</address>
</shelleyBiotech>
```

range-to

This function specifies a whole range inside an XML document. Here's the syntax:

```
#xpointer(node-set1/range-to(node-set2))
```

Let's say we want to select the first two products in the shelleyBiotech element:

```
<shelleyBiotech>
    <product>hydroBlah1</product>
    <product>cholorhydronitrate</product>
    <product>nitro-1-hydroxide</product>
    <address>1234 Main Street</address>
</shelleyBiotech>
```

Here's what the XPointer expression would look like:

```
#xpointer(//shelleyBiotech/product[1]/range-to(//shelley-
Biotech/product[2]))
```

This function is pretty simple. We don't need to go through a lot of offbeat examples to show you how it works.

range-inside

This function returns everything that's just inside the node-set in the function's argument. For example, if the XPointer expression is the following:

```
#xpointer(range-inside(//SheleyBiotech/product[2]))
```

The result would be this set:

```
<shelleyBiotech>
    <product>hydroBlah1</product>
    <product>cholorhydronitrate</product>
    <product>nitro-1-hydroxide</product>
    <address>1234 Main Street</address>
</shelleyBiotech>
```

Notice that everything inside the second product element is selected, not including the actual `<product>` tags.

range

This function is so simple it's a little hard to grasp: It simply returns what's in the argument. That's it. For example, if your expression was:

```
#xpointer(range(//ShelleyBiotech/product[2]))
```

this would choose the second `product` element inside `shelleyBiotech`.

here

This function returns the node that actually contains the XPointer expression. For example, if the full element that contains the expression is this:

```
<link xlink:type="simple"
xlink:href="#xpointer(here()/ancestor::product_list/
product[2])"/>
```

this selects the indicated element.

```
<product_list>
    <product>...</product>
    <product>...</product>
    <product>
        <product_links>
            <link
                xlink:type="simple" xlink:href="#
                xpointer(here()/ancestor::product_list
                /product[2])"/>
        </product_links>
    </product>
<product_list>
```

This function is more useful in selecting node-sets inside the document that contains the link that XPointer expression is attached to.

origin

This function returns the node that actually initiated the link to the target document. In the case of a simple link, `origin()` acts much like `here()`.

```
<link xlink:type="simple"
xlink:href="#xpointer(origin()/ancestor::product_list/
product[2])"/>
```

This selects the indicated element.

```
<product_list>
    <product>…</product>
    <product>…</product>
    <product>
        <product_links>
            <link
                xlink:type="simple" xlink:href="#
                xpointer(origin()/ancestor::product_li
                st/product[2])"/>
        </product_links>
    </product>
<product_list>
```

◆ Recap

And that's XPointer! Hopefully, this chapter wasn't too painful for you. XPointer simply takes the functionality of XPath (being able to point to places within an XML document) and gives that functionality for use in XLink. Remember that this is based on a Last Call Working Draft, and XPointer may go through some changes before it becomes a full-fledged recommendation. Be sure to check out *www.w3.org* for the latest information.

Legal Note

There's a technology-patent brouhaha bubbling around XPointer. It turns out that in 1997, Sun Microsystems and usability guru Jakob Nielsen were granted a patent for the "Method and system for implementing hypertext scroll attributes." What does this groundbreaking patent specify? It describes the process of using a string to define an external anchor for an HTML document. The string is defined in the link to the HTML document, and upon loading the HTML document, the Web browser scrolls to the first occurrence of the text string within the document. Seriously, they received a patent for this. (I believe the process of skipping flat stones across water is still open—patent it now before someone else does.)

When XPointer became a Candidate Recommendation in June 2000, the bits hit the fan. Sun published its terms and conditions under which XPointer could be implemented. The XML community immediately had a completely appropriate hissy fit that continues today, with such XML luminaries as Elliotte Rusty Harold and Tim Bray calling for the death of the XPointer specification if Sun doesn't seriously relax their legal chokehold on XPointer. This may seem extreme, but it's completely logical—the goal is to build open standards. If there's something in the way that prevents a specification from being open, then its primary goal is not being met, and the specification should give way to something else that does meet the goal.

12 Common Examples of XML

So now you know everything you need to become an XML visionary. There are other visionaries out there, and they've come up with some really interesting and powerful ways to use XML. We'll be looking at three

XML-based languages. First in line is SMIL, which is a language that lets you choreograph the timing and placement of multimedia elements in a presentation. Then, we'll take a gander at SVG, whose purpose in life is to describe vector-based images and animations—SVG players produce images and animations that look like Flash movies. Finally, we'll look at WDDX, a much shorter but equally powerful language that lets you transmit complicated data structures like multidimensional arrays via XML.

◆ SMIL

SMIL stands for Synchronized Multimedia Integration Language, and its purpose in life is

1. To control the temporal behavior of media (including some simple animations).
2. To control the layout of media objects.

Media objects are video clips, audio clips, animations, static images (both raster and vector), text, and streaming text. Controlling these chunks of multimedia temporally means affecting their timing—when they start, when they stop, how often they repeat, and so on. Controlling their layout means controlling their position. You can control an object's position, remove it completely, or move it along a path.

SMIL, like any other XML-based language, is simply a collection of elements and attributes, all defined by a DTD. The elements and attributes don't do anything by themselves, but require a SMIL processor (often called a SMIL Player). Players for SMIL 1.0 included Apple's QuickTime and RealNetwork's RealPlayer. However, the W3C has recently made SMIL 2.0 a Proposed Recommendation, which means that it will likely become a static standard within a few months (hopefully by the time you read this book). SMIL 2.0 is substantially different than SMIL 1.0—it's much more robust, and designed to be included in other XML-based languages. Thus, the version of SMIL than we'll examine today is version 2.0. It's possible that there will be some small changes between this version and the final version of SMIL, so before you write any big SMIL documents, make sure you check the W3C Web site (*www.w3.org*) to examine the final specification.

◆ Modularization

There are so many elements and attributes in SMIL that the authors decided to place similar elements and attributes in separate groups called modules. For example, there's a BasicAnimation module that contains all the elements you need to perform simple animations. There's an AudioLayout module that contains everything you need to properly adjust the sound level.

Some modules contain more advanced abilities than others, and in some of those cases, the advanced modules contain more basic modules within them. For example, the SplineAnimation module gives you lots of control over the pacing of an animation, and the module contains everything in the BasicAnimation module. Other modules share some elements and attributes—these modules overlap. What does this overlapping mean? It only means that the modules have some elements and attributes in common—nothing more.

◆ Why Bother with Modularization?

Modularization forces organization on SMIL, which makes it easier to learn and understand, but that's not all. The existence of modules makes it easier for other XML-based languages, like XHTML and SVG, to import bits and pieces of SMIL that would be useful, without having to import every single element and attribute. Modules are those bits and pieces. So, other XML languages can import one, some, or all of the SMIL attributes for their own use.

This practice of creating an XML-based language by combining chunks of other languages is known as profiling, and it allows authors to tailor languages to their specific needs.

SIDE NOTE
XHTML also involves modularization in a separate specification called "Modularized XHTML."

There are 44 modules in SMIL. This is a lot (one of them only consists of a single attribute, though). The authors of SMIL decided to add another layer of organization on top of the modularization, and have placed some of the modules into larger groups. For example, the Animation group contains both the

BasicAnimation and SplineAnimation modules. Let's take a look at these groups (there are 10 of them) and a brief description. We'll look at them in detail along with some code samples later. A list of all these groups and their description follows in Table 12–1.

TABLE 12–1 SMIL module groups

Name of Module Group	Description
Animation Modules	Allow authors to animate the position, width, length and color of any media object. No complicated animation, such as a person walking, is possible, but you can affect: 1. Horizontal and vertical stretching of object 2. Animate motion from point A to point B along a path
ContentControl Modules	Allow authors to test certain aspects of a user's system in order to display the appropriate layout or media object. Aspects that can be tested include speed of Internet connection and processor type. Authors may also create their own tests (based on pre-existing ones) and control the preloading of media objects.
Layout Modules	These modules control the position of visual elements and audio volume. Visual positioning includes multiple windows and nested regions. (Think nested layers from DHTML.*)
Linking Modules	These modules contain elements and attributes used for hyperlinking media objects. Links can be triggered by user events or temporal events (like a movie clip ending). Many formats are supported (XLink, XPointer, and XML Base), but the links usually look like XHTML.
Timing and Synchronization Module	This module provides a number of ways to control and manipulate the timing of media objects. It uses elements known as "time containers" to contain other time-related elements.
MediaObjects Modules	These modules contain the actual elements that contain media objects: video clips, audio clips, animations, images (both raster and vector), text and streaming text.
Metainformation Module	This is a single module that contains the `<meta>` element and uses RDF to describe SMIL documents (RDF stands for "Resource Description Format"—it's a language designed to describe documents).

Name of Module Group	Description

Structure Module	This module describes the overall structure of SMIL documents. In short, here it is:
	
	`<smil … >`
	`  <head>…</head>`
	`  <body>…</body>`
	`</smil>`

TimeManipulations Modules	This module gives to the author advanced control over time behavior, such as setting motion acceleration, deceleration, and autoReverse. The acceleration and deceleration are known as "Ease-In" and "Ease-Out" if you're used to working with Flash.
TransitionEffects Modules	This set of modules allows authors to implement and control filter behaviors known as "wipes," which are transitions from one scene to another.

*If you'd like a refresher, by all means feel free to pick up my DHTML book, *Essential CSS & DHTML for Web Professionals*, 2nd edition.

◆ Animation Modules

The animation modules are comprised of two modules I mentioned already: BasicAnimation and SplineAnimation. Both modules contain attributes and elements for incorporating animation into a timeline and composing the effects of multiple animations.

The basic syntax of animating an object involves placing one or more of the animation elements as children of the object to be animated. For example,

```
<rect width="25px" length="100px">
    <animate attributeName="width" from="25px"
        to="100px" begin="0s" dur="10s"/>
    <animate attributeName="length" from="100px"
        to="40px" begin="4s" dur="6s"/>
</rect>
```

HOW THE CODE WORKS

We've created a simple rectangle using a simplified tag from SVG (which we'll look at in the next section) that defines a rectangle. We then added two SMIL elements from the BasicAnimation module `<animate>`. In the first `animate` element, we're instructing the SMIL player to affect the width of the rectangle by taking its width from 25 pixels to 100 pixels. This scaling animation is to begin as soon as the rectangle is loaded (that's the begin="0s"—s stands for "seconds"). The animation is to last for 10 seconds—dur is short for "duration." Notice that we didn't specify frame rate, just how long the animation should take. In general, SMIL doesn't concern itself with frame rate—that's up to the application to decide. Also, you shouldn't count on the application that is playing your SMIL animations to be exact—applications can be unpredictable.

Next, we decide to animate the length of the rectangle and take it from 100 pixels to 40 pixels. Notice that we don't want the animation to start until the rectangle has been on the screen for four seconds. Then, the animation is to take only six seconds instead of 10. This way, the animation starts later than the width animation, but it happens faster, so at the end of 10 seconds, both the width and length of the rectangle have been altered and are in their final position.

You should note that these animations don't change the rectangle's length and width as far as the DOM is concerned. That is, if you wanted to access the rectangle using the DOM, then it would see a rectangle that's 25 pixels wide and 100 pixels long—it only knows about the object's original values.

You can also repeat animations over and over using the `repeatCount` attribute. And if you repeat an animation, are you repeating it from its original state, or are you adding to the animation? For example, let's say you're animating motion of an object:

```
<animateMotion path="somePathValues" accumulate="sum" re-
peatcount="4"/>
```

HOW THE CODE WORKS

In this code, some object (we're not sure what) is moved along some path that could be a straight line, an arc, or whatever. We can tell that this animation is repeated four times. What we don't know is whether this animation builds on itself and continues to move across the screen in four movements, or whether at the end of each animation, the object returns to its original position. You may have guessed that by using `accumulate="sum"`, we're not returning the object to its original position but rather moving it across the screen, with each animation building on the ending position of the previous animation.

There's much more to the BasicAnimation module, but this is an introduction, and further description is beyond the scope of this book.

SplineAnimation Module

This module contains everything in the BasicAnimation module, as well as some extra attribute values that allow developers to control the pacing of the animation, such as acceleration and deceleration. This can help your animations look more realistic and not as jerky.

◆ ContentControl Modules

There are four ContentControl modules: BasicContentControl, CustomTestAttributes, PrefetchControl, and SkipContentControl. All of the modules allow developers to examine the characteristics of the user's system and display appropriate content based on those characteristics.

BasicContentControl Module

This module is the foundation of content control, as it defines which conditions can be tested. Here's what developers can examine:

- `systemBitRate` indicates the speed of the user's Internet connection in bits.
- `systemCaptions` sets whether to display close-captioned text on the screen.
- `systemAudioDesc` sets whether to play audio closed-captioned material.
- `systemComponent` indicates URI that specifies the components of a playback system, number of audio channels, MPEG decoder, and so on.
- `systemCPU` returns which processor is being used—for example, ppc, vax, m68k, alpha, etc.
- `systemLanguage` shows a list separated by commas of names that the player tries to match to user preferences.
- `systemOverdubOrSubtitile` determines whether the player, if it must decide, plays an overdub track or displays text subtitles.
- `systemRequired` shows a list of extensions that are required to run the document (often a list of namespace prefixes.

- `systemScreenDepth` returns a positive integer (usually 1, 4, 8, 24 or 32) that specifies the depth of the screen color palette in bits.
- `systemScreenSize` (this is a helpful one) returns `true` or `false`, depending on if the user has the same screen size as the value of the attribute. For example, `systemScreen-Size="800x600"` would either be `true` or `false`.

CustomTestAttributes Module

This module introduces the elements `customAttributes` and `customTest`, which allow the developer to define his or her own custom test attributes. It also allows for an `override` setting, so that certain attributes cannot be changed at runtime by the application processing the SMIL elements.

PrefetchControl Module

This module controls the preloading of any media objects into the document, which can ensure a smoother user experience. If you're a Web page developer, this is exactly like using JavaScript to preload images so image rollovers will work smoothly. The good news is that you can choose exactly when you want to preload an object, so you can wait until the right moment, when the user is occupied with some other task, to load an object. You can even preload part of an object at a time, pause, and then resume loading it.

SkipContentControl Module

This tiny little module contains a single attribute: `skipContent`. If `skipContent` is `true`, then the content of an element is evaluated. If its value is `false`, then that element is ignored.

◆ Layout Modules

There are four layout modules: BasicLayout, AudioLayout, Multi-WindowLayout, and HierarchicalLayout. They're all pretty simple, especially if you've ever positioned elements using CSS in a Web page.

BasicLayout Module

This module contains all of the essential elements and attributes necessary to place elements anywhere on the screen. All of the layout information in a SMIL document must take place within the <head> element. There are a few ways to specify layout information, such as placing it all within an element or using syntax very similar to CSS. Below is the same information displayed in both ways. First, let's look at displaying everything in an element.

```
<layout>
    <region id="links" top="15px" left="90px"
        width="300px" height="600px"/>
</layout>
```

Now, using CSS:

```
<layout type="text/css">
    [region="links"] {
        top: 15px;
        left: 90px;
        width: 300px;
        height: 600px;
    }
</layout>
```

In the second example, notice the type attribute in the layout element. There's more you can do in this module, but this is just an introduction.

AudioLayout Module

This is another wee little module. It only has a single attribute: soundLevel. The value of this attribute is a percentage of the recorded sound level. For example, if the value is "100", then the sound will play at the same level at which it was recorded. If the value is "200", then it will play twice as loud.

MultiWindowLayout Module

This module allows you to control the position of various top-level windows (that's windows, not objects). You can control the layout of these windows using a new element called <topLayout>. Here's how you would use it:

```
<layout>
    <topLayout id="allProducts" title="ShelleyBioProducts"
        width="300px" height="500px"/>
        <region .../>
    </topLayout>
```

```
<topLayout …>
      <region …/>
  </topLayout>
</layout>
```

HierarchicalLayout Module

This module allows you to nest regions inside of each other. Regions are simple chunks of content. If you've worked in the DHTML world, these are the same thing as nested layers. To control the layout of these nested regions, a new element is introduced: <regPoint>, which controls the relative placement of a new region within a larger one.

◆ Linking Modules

The linking modules define elements and attributes used for hyperlinking media objects. These links can be triggered by user events like clicking on a link, or by temporal events, like a movie finishing playing. There are three modules involved: Linking-Attributes, BasicLinking, and ObjectLinking. The good news is that you can use XLink and XPointer syntax in these modules, which means you don't have to learn anything new. (About time you caught a break, eh?) All linking is also structured to look as much like XHTML as possible, so you'll be dealing with familiar <a> tags.

LinkingAttributes Module

This module is just a collection of attributes that deal with the sources and destinations of links. Here are a few examples:

- sourcePlaystate controls the temporal behavior of the presentation containing the link, once the link is traversed. Possible values are play, pause, and stop.
- show determines where the destination of the link appears, either in a new window or replacing the content that contains the link. (This is how Web pages work: The new one replaces the one with the link.)
- actuate determines when link is traversed. (You saw this in the Xlink chapter.) Possible values are onLoad and onRequest.

A link in SMIL may look exactly like XHTML:

```
<a href="professor.qt" target="showWindow">Dr. Moxon ex-
plains the metabolic processes.</a>
```

BasicLinking Module

This module contains all of the actual elements that contain the attributes in the LinkingAttributes module. For example, `<a>` and `<area>` are in this module. As it turns out, the `<map>` element is unnecessary because the area elements can be nested inside media elements, like so:

```
<video … >
    <area href="foo" begin="0s" end="5s"/>
    <area href="bar" begin="5s" end="10s"/>
</video>
```

ObjectLinking Module

This module extends what you can do in the BasicLinking module by allowing developers to link to fragments within media objects. It's not worth it to get into detail as to what this actually means—just file it away in your head and when you have to actually do it, it'll make some sense to you.

◆ Timing and Synchronization Module

This module is enormous, and one of the most vital for SMIL, since it contains all of the necessary elements and attributes for dealing with time. An important concept for this module is that of a "time container." These are containers are simple elements that references to media objects. Here are some simplified examples:

```
<seq>
    <video … />
    <video … />
    <audio … />
</seq>
```

"Seq" stands for "sequence," which means that the two videos and the audio clip will play one at a time, right after each other. The `seq` element is a time container. The two other time containers are `par` (short for "parallel," which runs the media objects all at the same time), and `excl`, which plays the media one at a time, but not in any particular order.

There are two kinds of duration: simple and active. A simple duration is the natural, intrinsic length of a media object. For example, a sound that plays for four seconds has a simple duration of four seconds. An active duration is the duration with the effects of any repeating of the media. A sound that plays for four seconds but is repeated three times has an active duration of 12 seconds.

The most common basic timing attributes are `begin`, `dur`, and `end`, which are usually specified in seconds. Table 12–2 contains a partial list and short description of the other basic timing attributes.

This module is so large that bits and pieces of its elements and attributes are available in separate submodules. We won't

TABLE 12-2 Partial List of Basic Timing Attributes

Attribute	Description
min	Specifies the minimum value of the active duration
max	Specifies the maximum value of the active duration
endSynch	Controls the point where all the affected media must end. Possible values are `first` (all child element media end when the first media ends), `last` (they end when the last element ends), `all`, `media`, and `id`.
repeatCount	Specifies the number of times the simple duration is to be repeated. This can be a decimal value.
repeatDur	Specifies how long the media is to be repeated.
fill	Specifies what to do with an element once its active duration is done. Usually, this means either removing it from display, holding it in place, or moving it back to its origin.
restart	Specifies when to rerun the active duration of the media, as if it never occurred. Possible values are `always`, `whenNotActive`, `never`, and `default`.
syncBehavior	Controls the synchronization relationship defined by the time contained (that is, in sequence, in parallel, etc.); allows developer to override time container.
syncTolerance	Defines how tolerant the synchronization behavior is if at runtime, the application is forced to alter the timing of the objects.
syncMaster	Can force all the other elements in the time container to synchronize their playback to a single media object.
timeContainer	Specifies that any element in the XML language is a time container. Allowable values are `par`, `seq`, `excl`, and `none`.
timeAction	Provides control over the effect of timing on an attribute.

go over them here, but it'd be useful for you to see a listing of them, so you can see how many different aspects there are to this large module.

- AccessKeyTiming
- BasicInlineTiming
- BasicTimeContainers
- EventTiming
- ExclTimeContainers
- FillDefault
- MediaMarkerTiming
- MinMaxTiming
- MultiArcTiming
- RepeatTiming
- RepeatValueTiming
- RestartDefault
- RestartTiming
- SyncBehavior
- SyncBehaviorDefault
- SyncbaseTiming
- SyncMaster
- TimeContainerAttributes
- WallclockTiming

◆ MediaObjects Modules

This module is more grounded—it's all of the elements and attributes that actually describe media objects, like videos, sound clips, and animations. The seven modules (we won't examine all of them) are BasicMedia, MediaParam, MediaClipping, MediaClipMarkers, BrushMedia, MediaAccessibility, and MediaDescription.

BasicMedia Module

The media elements are `ref` (for general media), `animation`, `audio`, `img` (for both raster and vector images), `text`, `textstream` (like it sounds, for streaming text), and `video`. The only attributes provided by this module are `src` and `type`.

The other modules provide ways to include such information as clipping (what parts of the media are visible), copyright, author, title, language, and links to descriptions of the media object.

◆ Metainformation Module

This module provides a way to include information about your SMIL document, much like the `<meta>` tags in HTML. In fact, this module also uses meta elements in much the same way. It also allows for use of RDF, which is a language especially designed to provide metainformation—it even stands for "Resource Definition Framework." RDF is an attempt to standardize metadata throughout the Web, so that it's much easier to search for something, instead of just hoping that the Google search engine is doing a good job (which is what most of you are probably doing). We won't go into RDF, but you should know that it's a good thing, and it's gaining in popularity.

SIDE NOTE

I'm not disparaging Google. I use it all the time. Google is my (and many other programmers') friend.

◆ Structure Module

This is another easy module—it simply states that the overall structure of a SMIL document must look like this:

```
<smil … >
    <head>…</head>
    <body>…</body>
</smil>
```

That's it. No big concepts here.

◆ TimeManipulations Modules

This module allows for advanced manipulation of time behavior, such as acceleration, deceleration, autoReverse, and overall speed of the media object. If you're a Flash person, the accelerating and deceleration effects are better known to you as "Easing Out" and "Easing In."

◆ TransitionEffects Modules

A common public description heard about SMIL is that it allows authors to bring television-like content to the Web. Well, we've all heard that claim before, but SMIL does contain transitions—

that is, graphical animations to go from scene to scene. These are also called "wipes," because the animation often wipes away one scene, replacing it with another.

SMIL has dozens of predetermined wipes available to use—everything from star wipes to fades to eye wipes. All the effects are available in the SMIL specification at *www.w3.org*. You can either use these effects as they are, or you can affect their timing or speed (a transition using this level of control is known as "in-line transition").Well, that does it for SMIL—you now have a solid foundation to build on, if you ever need to create a SMIL document.

◆ SVG

SVG stands for Scalar Vector Graphics, and its goal in life is to describe all manner of two-dimensional vector graphics, such as

- lines
- shapes
- fills
- strokes
- Bezier curves
- gradients
- text
- images (you can import raster images)
- effects

You may be thinking that this is a lot of detail for a text-based language, and you're right. The specification for SVG is over 500 pages long—it's a monster. As it turns out, that's not really a problem, because actual humans aren't really intended to have to deal with SVG text directly. It's more or less assumed that different vector-based programs like Flash and Illustrator will both be able to export and import SVG documents. As a developer, it's unlikely you'll spend much time actually coding anything in SVG. In fact, Illustrator 9 can already export documents in SVG, and Adobe has released the second version of an SVG-viewing browser plug-in. I expect that future versions of Flash, LiveMotion, and Freehand will support SVG, among other file formats.

So why bother learning any SVG if you can rely on applications to both read and write it for you? Technically, there is no need. However, I think it's a good idea to have an idea of the limitations, capabilities, and structure of what you're producing. For example, I wish more people out there using Dreamweaver and

GoLive to create Web pages knew at least a little HTML. I'm convinced we'd have better-quality Web sites out there if they did.

Quirks of SVG

As I mentioned earlier, SVG is an XML-based language that describes two-dimensional objects. SVG describes shapes, paths, text and effects. SVG is not a verbose language. In fact, much of its data is very condensed and difficult to read. Here's an example of a simple curvy line:

```
<path id="squiggle" d="M 100 100 L 104 120 Q 25 0 L 140 150
Q 25 0 L 160 180 z"/>
```

Huh? Not exactly the easy-to-read XML we've seen up until this point. What does d mean? And what's this list of numbers and letters? As it turns out, this is a line with some curves and some straight segments that is closed off at the end.

What you're seeing doesn't really meet the human-readability goal of XML. In fact, SVG even introduces a new syntax that isn't XML-based. That list of numbers and letters is a brand new syntax that's SVG-specific.

So why did the authors of SVG do this? Why add a new syntax and attributes that are impossible to decipher? As it turns out, they actually had a good reason: file size. Without these short attributes and path syntax, the length of these SVG files would be much, much larger. Since the goal is to create files that can be easily transferred between various applications, and it's unlikely that actual humans will be coding much SVG, the brevity of the code is more important than its readability. There's still some distress about this in the XML community, and it's well-founded. While many people disagree with the choices of the editors of SVG, the editors get major kudos for describing their decision-making process in public.

SVG Examples

In this section, we'll quickly cover some samples of simple SVG, enough to give you an idea of what the language looks like, but we won't go deep into detail.

Here's how to call the current SVG DTD:

```
<? xml version="1.0">
<!DOCTYPE svg PUBLIC "-//W3C//DTD SVG 20000303 Stylable//EN"
"http://www.w3.org/TR/2000/03/WD-SVG-20000303/DTD/svg-
20000303-stylable.dtd">
```

```
<svg xml:space="preserve" width="5in" height="2.5in">
    … text and shapes …
</svg>
```

SVG is currently a Candidate Recommendation, not a full W3C Recommendation, which means that it could change a little bit from now until it becomes an official standard. Once SVG reaches Recommendation status, this DTD call will probably look a little different. To check the status of SVG, check out *www.w3 .org/Graphics/SVG/*.

Let's start examining some of the simpler things you can build with SVG.

Rectangle

To create a blue rectangle, enter in Example 12-1.

EXAMPLE 12-1 AN SVG RECTANGLE

```
<?xml version="1.0"?>
<!DOCTYPE svg PUBLIC "-//W3C//DTD SVG 20000303 Stylable//EN"
"http://www.w3.org/TR/2000/03/WD-SVG-20000303/DTD/svg-
20000303-stylable.dtd">
<svg xml:space="preserve" width="5.5in" height="2in">
    <rect style="fill:blue;" width="250" height="100"/>
</svg>
```

HOW THE CODE WORKS

This is a pretty simple SVG document. We start with your basic XML declaration and set the DTD to use. We then set the SVG element and set two attributes that preserve any white space we use in the document, and create a something called a viewport that's 5.5 inches across and 2 inches tall. This viewport is our window into the SVG document.

We then create a blue rectangle that is 250 pixels wide and 100 pixels high.

Using any browser (except IE for Macintosh), and Adobe's SVG plug-in (get it at *www.adobe.com/svg*), you should get a result something like Figure 12-1.

Circle

You can also create a circle in SVG, as in Example 12-2 (I left out the XML declaration and the DOCTYPE, but you'll need them to make this example work).

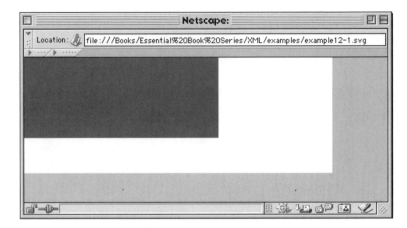

FIGURE 12-1 A blue SVG rectangle

EXAMPLE 12-2 AN SVG CIRCLE

```
<svg xml:space="preserve" width="500" height="400">
    <circle style="fill:yellow;stroke:black;" cx="200"
cy="200" r="75"/>
</svg>
```

HOW THE CODE WORKS

We changed the size of the viewport to be 500 pixels wide and 400 pixels tall. We also added a different stroke color to the circle, instead of a simple fill. We set the center of the circle with the cx and cy attribues, and set the radius with r. This results in Figure 12-2.

Paths

Of course, SVG can also handle irregular shapes. Example 12–3 shows how to draw an off-center triangle:

EXAMPLE 12-3 AN SVG TRIANGLE

```
<svg xml:space="preserve" width="500" height="400">
    <path d="M 50 25
             L 400 20
             L 300 120 z"
        style="fill:lightgrey;
               stroke-width:10;
               stroke:black;"/>
</svg>
```

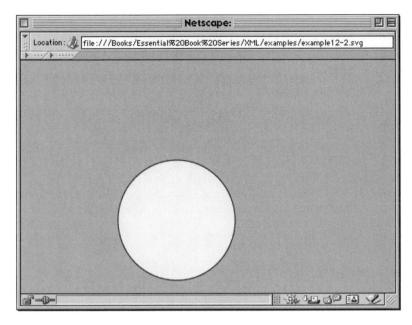

FIGURE 12–2 A yellow circle with a black border

HOW THE CODE WORKS

It's all about the path element and the values inside the d at-tribute. Here's how to translate: M stands for "move to," as in "move the drawing tool to this coordinate." So whatever is about to be drawn starts at coordinates (50,25). The L stands for "draw a line to," so lines are drawn from (50,25) to (400,20) and from (400,20) to (300,120). The path finishes up at z, which means "close the path," so a third line is drawn from (300,120) to the origin at (50,25). We also added a new value the style attribute: stroke-weight. Put together, everything looks like Figure 12–3.

There are many other ways to define a path, but a detailed examination is beyond the scope of this book.

Text Along a Path

Let's get a little more complicated, and wrap some text around a path. Example 12–4 involves defining a path, then drawing a thick and a thin line along that path and wrapping some text around the path. Ready?

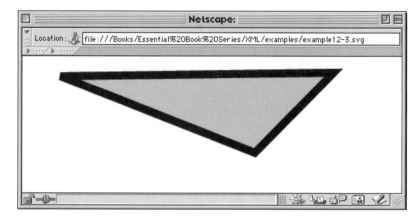

FIGURE 12–3 Off-center gray triangle

EXAMPLE 12–4 TEXT ALONG A PATH

```
<svg xml:space="preserve" width="500" height="400">

<defs>
  1.<path id="swoop" d="M -100 0 c 0 -100 200 -100 200
0"/>
</defs>

2.<g id="textSwoop" transform="translate(200,200)">
  3.<use xlink:href="#swoop"
       style="stroke:yellow; stroke-width:15;
fill:none;"/>
  4.<use xlink:href="#swoop"
       style="stroke:blue; stroke-width:1; fill:none;"/>

  5.<text style="font-family:arial;
             font-size:75;
             font-weight:700;
             fill:blue;">

     6.<textPath xlink:href="#swoop" startOffset="0">
          Howdy!
       </textPath>
  </text>
</g>
</svg>
```

HOW THE CODE WORKS

1. We begin by defining a path without actually displaying it. This is accomplished by placing the path definition inside a <def> tag (it stands for "definition"). Thus, we have a path that can be reused whenever we want to. Notice that this path actually starts 100 pixels off the left of the screen.

2. We then create a group of objects (g is short for "group") called textSwoop, and we move everything in this group over 200 pixels and down 200 pixels.

3. Here's where we draw our thick line around the path. We use a new element, appropriately called use, and link to the path with xlink:href, which should look familiar to you. We make this a fat, yellow line.

4. We draw a line along the path again using the use element, except that we make this line skinny and blue.

5. Then, we announce that we're about to display some text. It's big, bold Arial text.

6. Using textPath, we spell out that the text needs to follow a certain path, and that the text should begin at the beginning of the text.

Figure 12–4 shows what it looks like:

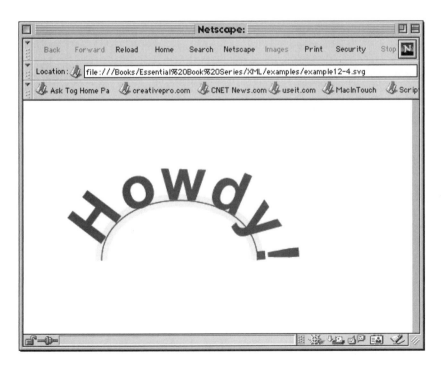

FIGURE 12–4 Wrapped text

That'll do it for SVG. These examples give you an idea of what the language is about, but like I said, the specification is over 500 pages long, so if you're really curious, you now have plenty to keep you busy.

The most interesting things about SVG that we did not cover are its animation capabilities (which look exactly like SMIL animation elements) and its ability to change properties on the fly. That is, you can create JavaScript functions that alter the appearance or behavior of parts of an SVG document (like using Action-Script for Flash movies).

◆ WDDX

WDDX is a very compact XML-based language whose elements and attributes allow developers to transform data structures such as date-time values, null values, arrays and query recordsets into XML. It's a simple language, but quite powerful. It allows you to pass highly structured data common to most programming languages, like arrays, to other applications via the text-only format of XML.

WDDX stands for "Web Distributed Data Exchange," and it's the invention of some bright folks at Allaire (now Macromedia). WDDX is open-source, and parsing of this language is built into Cold Fusion, a middleware language that many readers of this book probably have some experience with (it's also part of PHP). I've found WDDX to be easy to use and darn useful. The brevity of its DTD also impresses me. In fact, here it is:

```
<!--
******************************************************************
************
        WDDX DTD

        Editor:                 Simeon Simeonov (simeons@
allaire.com)

        Contributing authors: Hussain Chinoy (hussain@
granularity.com)
                                Nate Weiss (nweiss@icesinc.com)

        Last modified:          October 19, 1999

        Copyright (c) 1998, 1999 Allaire Corp.
http://www.allaire.com
-->
<!ELEMENT wddxPacket (header, data)>
```

```
<!ATTLIST wddxPacket
         version CDATA #FIXED "1.0">

<!ELEMENT header (comment?)>

<!ELEMENT comment (#PCDATA)>

<!ELEMENT data (null | boolean | number | dateTime | string
| array | struct | recordset | binary)>

<!ELEMENT null EMPTY>
<!ATTLIST null
         type CDATA #IMPLIED>

<!ELEMENT boolean EMPTY>
<!ATTLIST boolean
         value (true | false) #REQUIRED
         type CDATA #IMPLIED>

<!ELEMENT string (#PCDATA | char)*>
<!ATTLIST string
         type CDATA #IMPLIED>

<!ELEMENT char EMPTY>
<!ATTLIST char
         code CDATA #REQUIRED>

<!ELEMENT number (#PCDATA)>
<!ATTLIST number
         type CDATA #IMPLIED>

<!ELEMENT dateTime (#PCDATA)>
<!ATTLIST dateTime
         type CDATA #IMPLIED>

<!ELEMENT array (null | boolean | number | dateTime | string
| array | struct | recordset | binary)*>
<!ATTLIST array
         length CDATA #REQUIRED
         type CDATA #IMPLIED>

<!ELEMENT struct (var*)>
<!ATTLIST struct
         type CDATA #IMPLIED>

<!ELEMENT var (null | boolean | number | dateTime | string |
array | struct | recordset | binary)>
<!ATTLIST var
         name CDATA #REQUIRED>

<!ELEMENT recordset (field*)>
<!ATTLIST recordset
```

```
          rowCount CDATA #REQUIRED
          fieldNames CDATA #REQUIRED
          type CDATA #IMPLIED>

<!ELEMENT field (null | boolean | number | dateTime | string
| binary)*>
<!ATTLIST field
          name CDATA #REQUIRED>

<!ELEMENT binary (#PCDATA)>
<!ATTLIST binary
          encoding CDATA #FIXED "base64"
          length CDATA #IMPLIED
          type CDATA #IMPLIED>
```

◆ Recap

There are a ton of XML-based languages out there that are quickly becoming finalized and gaining acceptance. SMIL synchronizes multimedia elements in a presentation and has been in use for over a year. SVG already has its own working browser plug-in, even though the specification isn't 100% complete. And WDDX is much, much shorter, but its laser-focused purpose makes it ideal to transfer complex data structures.

You're almost done! Just one more chapter on the XML DOM, and you're free to go!

13 Manipulating XML: The DOM

Last chapter! You're almost done! We'll end this book with a solid look at XML's Document Object Model, or DOM. You can write XML without ever knowing anything about the DOM, but you'll be a better programmer if you know what it is and how to use it.

◆ What the DOM Is and Does

DOM stands for Document Object Model, and unlike some other titles in the computer world, that's a pretty accurate one. DOM is a specification put forth by the W3C that creates a way for any programming language to navigate through and manipulate an XML or HTML document. That may not sound like much, but it's darn important.

It's in everybody's interest for programming languages to be able to parse through XML documents, and to be able to add, delete or modify any part of those documents. However, if every programming language implemented their own special way to browse through XML documents, it'd be chaos. You'd only be able to do certain things in certain languages, there'd be no consistency of syntax, and it'd just be a mess.

The DOM does two things that make life easier for programmers:

- It creates a logical structure for the document (also called the node tree).
- It provides a way to read through and manipulate the document.

The goal of the DOM is to provide a language-independent interface into all well-formed XML (and HTML) documents. Since this interface is between the XML document, and an application, the interface is known as an application programming interface (API).

The first thing a DOM does to your document is to create a node tree out of it, as you saw in the XPath chapter. DOM goes further than just creating a node tree, though—it looks at all of the nodes in the tree and places all of them into certain categories. All the nodes in your document will fit into one of these categories.

These categories are more than just containers. Many categories have a number of special properties and methods associated with them. For example, say your XML document has a text node and a regular empty element (an element node). These two nodes are placed in different containers. The container that holds all the text nodes has a method that lets you split the text node into two separate nodes. The container that contains the empty element doesn't have this capability. Thus, empty elements can't be split into two.

You don't get to decide which category your nodes go into. DOM decides that for you, and that's a good thing; it'd be a pain to have to do that yourself.

In official DOM parlance, these categories are called "interfaces." There are two kinds of interfaces: fundamental and extended. Fundamental interfaces are used for both XML and HTML documents. Extended interfaces are only for XML documents.

Before we get too deep into interfaces (and we will), let's look at the different kinds of nodes.

◆ Types of Nodes

DOM sees your document as a hierarchy of nodes. There are several different kinds of nodes, and these node types are allowed only certain children of certain node types. Table 13–1 lists all of the node types and their allowed children.

So these are the node types. You may be thinking, "So what?" It certainly isn't vital that you know this, but it's a nice introduction into how DOM sees your XML documents. Note that these

TABLE 13-1 Node Types and Children

Node Type	Allowable Children
Document	Element (maximum of one), ProcessingInstruction, Comment, DocumentType
DocumentFragment	Element, ProcessingInstruction, Comment, Text, CDATASection, EntityReference
DocumentType	no children
EntityReference	Element, ProcessingInstruction, Comment, Text, CDATASection, EntityReference
Element	Element, Text, Comment, ProcessingInstruction, CDATASection, EntityReference
Attr	Text, EntityReference
ProcessingInstruction	no children
Comment	no children
Text	no children
CDATASection	no children
Entity	Element, ProcessingInstruction, Comment, Text, CDATASection, EntityReference
Notation	no children

are node types, but that's different than categories (or interfaces). Interfaces are different, and even though there are some similarities between the node type and the categories DOM places your XML nodes in, they are different things.

◆ DOM Interfaces

There are a total of 19 node interfaces, and they're split into two groups: Fundamental and Extended. We'll be looking at all of them in some detail, but let's glance over all of them briefly. Table 13-2 contains all the Fundamental Interfaces, and Table 13-3 contains all the Extended Interfaces.

Fundamental Interfaces are likely to be used for both XML and HTML documents. Extended Interfaces are likely to only be used on XML documents.

TABLE 13–2 Fundamental Interfaces

Interface	Description
DOMException	This interface defines the cases in which the DOM encounters an error (also known as throwing an exception).
ExceptionCode	This interface matches an integer that indicates the kind of error encountered.
DOMImplementation	This interface provides methods that are document-wide. In other words, they are independent of any specific node.
DocumentFragment	This interface is a lightweight Document object. It exists because it's often preferable to work with a desired portion of a whole document than having to keep the entire document in memory.
Document	This interface represents the entire XML or HTML document. Conceptually, you can see it as the root node (not root element, remember) of the document tree. The methods in this interface allow you to create and retrieve elements and attributes.
Node	This interface represents a single node within the document. Its methods are adept at dealing with adding sibling elements and dealing with child elements.
NodeList	This interface provides a way to look into an ordered list of nodes.
NamedNodeMap	This interface maintains a collection of unordered nodes—these nodes may be referred to by name, whereas those in a NodeList are often referred to by position in the list.
CharacterData	This interface is an extension of the Node interface. It allows you to manipulate to navigate through sections of character data.
Attr	This interface represents an attribute within an element. The DOM does not consider attributes as children of the element that contains them. Rather, it sees them as a property of the element.
Element	This interface represents an actual element within a document. In the DOM world, there's a subtle difference between a node and an element (for example, comments are nodes, not elements). The methods of this interface are great at manipulating attributes and their values.
Text	This interface represents the textual content of an element or an attribute.
Comment	This interface represents the content of a comment. That is, everything between the "<!--" and "-->".

TABLE 13-3 Extended Interfaces

Interface	Description
CDATASection	CDATASections are those that are started with "CDATA" and end with "]]>." Remember those?
DocumentType	This interface represents a list of possible document types within your document. This interface is not seen as 100% complete, because no one has completely figured out how namespaces fit into the picture.
Notation	This read-only interface represents a notation used in the document.
Entity	This interface represents a parsed or unparsed entity in the document.
EntityReference	This interface represents the representation of an entity (as opposed to the entity itself).
ProcessingInstruction	This interface represents a processing instruction (the lines of code that begin with "<?").

◆ Properties and Methods

Now let's look at all of the interfaces that afford programmers various attributes and methods that can be used to navigate through and manipulate an XML (or HTML) document. Not all interfaces have attributes or methods, so not every one is included below.

DOMImplementation

The methods of this interface concern themselves with affecting the document as a whole, as opposed to any specific element or node.
There are no attributes in the DOMImplementation interface.

Method	Description
CreateDocument	Creates a brand new document object of the specified type.
CreateDocumentType	Creates an empty DocumentType node. (Remember that DocumentType is a type of node?) Currently, there's no way to actually create new document type, but it's expected that future versions of DOM will be able to.
HasFeature	Tests whether the current DOM implementation supports a specified version of a specified feature.

Document

The properties and methods of this interface deal with all aspects of the XML or HTML document, including the creation of attributes and elements.

Property	Description
Doctype	Reads the DTD of the document. If there is no DTD, then it returns null.
DocumentElement	Returns the root element of the document. In the case of an HTML document, this would always be <html>.
Implementation	Returns the DOCImplementation that handles the document.

Method	Description
CreateAttribute	Creates an attribute with the given name.
CreateAttributeNS	Creates an attribute with the specified local name and URI.
CreateCDATASection	Creates a section of character data in the document.
CreateComment	Creates a comment node.
createDocumentFragment	Creates an empty document fragment.
CreateElement	Creates an element of the specified type and with the specified name.
CreateElementNS	Creates an element with the given local name and URI.
createEntityReference	Creates an EntityReference object (EntityReference is a node type from earlier in the chapter).
CreateProcessing Instruction	Creates a processing instruction with the given name and data strings.
CreateTextNode	Creates a text node with the specified string.
GetElementById	Returns the element whose identifier is specified. If you've done some DHTML for Netscape 6, you've seen this method before.*

*If you want to learn more, be sure to check out my book, *Essential CSS & DHTML for Web Professionals*, 2nd edition. There's also code available at *www.wire-man.com/dhtml2*.

Method	Description
getElementsByTagName	Returns a list of all the nodes that have the specified tag name.
getElementsByTagNameNS	Returns a list of all the nodes that have the specified local name and URI.
importNode	Creates a copy of a node in another document and brings it into the current one.

Node and NodeType

The properties and methods of the Node and NodeType interfaces overlap somewhat, so we'll go at them in one big group—it's a little easier to understand this way.

Property	Description
attributes	Contains a list of all the attributes in the node. If there are no attributes, null is returned.
childNodes	Contains a list of all the children of the referenced node.
firstChild	Returns the node of the first child of the specified node.
lastChild	Returns the node of the last child of the specified node.
localName	Returns the local name of the namespace the node is a part of.
namespacedURI	Returns the namespace URI of the indicated node.
siblingNode	Returns the node immediately following the indicated node.
nodeName	Returns the name of the node, based on its type.
nodeType	Returns the kind of node it is.
nodeValue	Returns the value of the node (if it has one). If there is no value, then null is returned.
ownerDocument	Returns the Document object associated with the node.
parentNode	Returns the parent node of the indicated node.
prefix	Returns the namespace prefix of the indicated node.
previousSibling	Returns the node immediately preceding the indicated node.

Method	Description
appendChild	Adds a node as the last child of the current node.
cloneNode	Creates a copy of the specified node.
hasAttributes	Returns true if the nods has attributes, false if it does not.
hasChildNodes	Returns true if the nods has children, false if it does not.
insertBefore	Inserts a node immediately preceding the specified node.
isSupported	Tests whether the current DOM implementation supports a certain feature or not.
normalize	Restructures the XML document so that there are no empty text nodes, and adjacent text nodes are combined into a single node.
removeChild	Removes the specified child element.
replaceChild	Replaces the indicated child with a new one.

NodeList

The NodeList interface contains a single property and a single method.

Property	Description
Length	The number of nodes in a list.

Method	Description
Item	Returns the node that is in a specified position in the list.

NamedNodeMap

The NamedNodeMap also contains a list of nodes, but this list is unordered—the common way to access a node is to name it.

Property	Description
Length	The number of nodes in a mapping.

Method	Description
GetNamedItem	Retrieves a node with the specified name.
GetNamedItemNS	Retrieves a node in the specified namespace (both prefix and URI).
Item	Returns the node in the specified position (but since this list is unordered, there's no real way to tell beforehand which node is at that position).
RemoveNamedItem	Removes a node with the specified name.
RemoveNamedItemNS	Removes a node with the specified namespace prefix and URI.
SetNamedItem	Adds a node with the specified name. If the node to be added already exists, the old node is replaced by the new one.
SetNamedItemNS	Adds a node with the specified prefix and URI of a namespace. If the node to be added already exists, the old node is replaced by the new one.

CharacterData

This interface deals with any CDATA section in the document, and extends the Node node type.

Property	Description
data	The actual character data.
length	The number of characters in the character data string.

Method	Description
appendData	Appends the indicated string to the end of the character data portion of the node.
deleteData	Removes a range of characters from the character data.
insertData	Adds a string to the specified location within the character data section of the node.
replaceData	Replaces a range of characters with a specified string.
substringData	Extracts a range of characters from within the character data.

Attr

I'm not sure why this interface isn't called "Attribute." In any case, this interface deals with attributes. There are no methods, just properties, and `value` is the only property that can be altered.

Property	Description
Name	Returns the name of the attribute
OwnerElement	Returns the name of the element that contains the attribute.
Specified	Returns `true` if the attribute was given a specific value in the document. Otherwise, `false` is returned.
Value	The value of the specified attribute.

Element

This interface represents a window into any element within your document.

Property	Description
TagName	The name of the element's tag.

Method	Description
GetAttribute	Retrieves an attribute value by name.
getAttributeNS	Retrieves an attribute value by a specified namespace (both local name and URI).
getAttributeNode	Retrieves a complete attribute node.
getAttributeNodeNS	Retrieves an entire attribute node specified by the local name and URI of the attribute's namespace.
getElementsByTagName	Returns a list of all the nodes that have the specified tag name.
getElementsByTagNameNS	Returns a list of all the nodes that have the specified local name and URI.
hasAttribute	Returns `true` if the element has an attribute. If not, `false` is returned.

Method	Description
hasAttributeNS	Returns `true` if the element (specified by the local name and URI of a namespace) has an attribute. If not, `false` is returned.
removeAttribute	Removes the indicated attribute from the element.
removeAttributeNS	Removes an attribute specified by the local name and URI of a namespace.
removeAttributeNode	Removes the entire attribute node.
setAttribute	Adds an attribute to the element. If that attribute already exists, the new one replaces it.
setAttributeNS	Adds an attribute (specified by the local name and URI of a namespace) to the element. If that attribute already exists, the new one replaces it.
setAttributeNode	Adds a new attribute node to the element. If that attribute node already exists, the new one replaces it.
setAttributeNodeNS	Adds a new attribute (specified by the local name and URI of a namespace) node to the element. If that attribute node already exists, the new one replaces it.

Text

This interface represents the textual content of an element or an attribute.

Method	Description
splitText	Breaks the specified text node into two nodes.

DocumentType

This interface mostly provides access to a list of entities in the document. It is likely that references to namespaces will be a part of this interface in future versions of the DOM. For now, there are only a few properties, and no methods.

Property	Description
Entities	Returns an unordered list of all the entities in the document.
InternalSubset	Returns a string representing the internal subset. The actual content of this string is heavily implementation-dependent.
Name	Returns the name of the DTD (that is, the name immediately following "DOCTYPE").
Notations	Returns an unordered list of notations declared in the DTD.
PublicId	Returns the identifier of the external subset.
SystemId	Returns the system identifier of the external subset.

Notation

This interface looks a lot like a subset of the Entities interface. Presently, it can only offer a couple of read-only properties.

Property	Description
PublicId	Returns the identifier of the external subset.
SystemId	Returns the system identifier of the external subset.

Entity

This interface represents the actual entities, both parsed and unparsed, in the document. Currently, it can only offer three read-only properties.

Property	Description
notationName	Returns the name of the notation for unparsed entities.
publicId	Returns the public identifier of the specified entity.
systemId	Returns the system identifier of the specified entity.

ProcessingInstruction

The interface is pretty specific—it only deals with processing instructions, and currently only offers two read-only properties.

Property	Description
data	The actual instructions of the processing instruction, starting from the first white space, and ending just before "?>".
target	The target of the processing instruction.

◆ Recap

Hey! You did it! You just learned XML! You can now officially ask for a raise or charge your clients more. (Try it—it's fun!)

In this last chapter, we explored the DOM of XML, which is an API that allows programming languages to navigate through and manipulate both XML and HTML documents. We looked at all of the interfaces involved, as well as all of the properties and methods.

There's some good stuff in the appendices, so feel free to peruse them at your leisure. Also, all of the examples in this book are available at *www.wire-man.com/xml*. If you have any questions, feel free to email me at dan-xml@wire-man.com, and I'll help you in any way I can. (Feedback is also welcome!)

A XML 1.0 Specification

IN THIS CHAPTER

Here it is—the spec that started it all. You can also see this specification (and much more) on the World Wide Web Consortium's Web site at www.w3.org.

◆ Extensible Markup Language (XML) 1.0 (Second Edition)

W3C Recommendation 6 October 2000

This version:

> http://www.w3.org/TR/2000/REC-xml-20001006 (XHTML, XML, PDF, XHTML review version with color-coded revision indicators)

Latest version:

> http://www.w3.org/TR/REC-xml

Previous versions:

> http://www.w3.org/TR/2000/WD-xml-2e-20000814
> http://www.w3.org/TR/1998/REC-xml-19980210

Editors:

> Tim Bray, Textuality and Netscape <tbray@textuality.com>
> Jean Paoli, Microsoft <jeanpa@microsoft.com>
> C. M. Sperberg-McQueen, University of Illinois at Chicago and Text Encoding Initiative <cmsmcq@uic.edu>
> Eve Maler, Sun Microsystems, Inc. <eve.maler@east.sun.com> - Second Edition

Abstract

The Extensible Markup Language (XML) is a subset of SGML that is completely described in this document. Its goal is to enable generic SGML to be served, received, and processed on the Web in the way that is now possible with HTML. XML has been designed for ease of implementation and for interoperability with both SGML and HTML.

Status of this Document

This document has been reviewed by W3C Members and other interested parties and has been endorsed by the Director as a W3C Recommendation. It is a stable document and may be used as reference material or cited as a normative reference from another document. W3C's role in making the Recommendation is to draw attention to the specification and to promote its widespread deployment. This enhances the functionality and interoperability of the Web.

This document specifies a syntax created by subsetting an existing, widely used international text processing standard (Standard Generalized Markup Language, ISO 8879:1986(E) as amended and corrected) for use on the World Wide Web. It is a product of the W3C XML Activity, details of which can be found at http://www.w3.org/XML. The English version of this specification is the only normative version. However, for translations of this document, see http://www.w3.org/XML/#trans. A list of current W3C Recommendations and other technical documents can be found at http://www.w3.org/TR.

This second edition is not a new version of XML (first published 10 February 1998); it merely incorporates the changes dictated by the first-edition errata (available at http://www.w3 .org/XML/xml-19980210-errata) as a convenience to readers. The errata list for this second edition is available at http://www.w3 .org/XML/xml-V10-2e-errata.

Please report errors in this document to xml-editor@w3.org; archives are available.

NOTE:
C. M. Sperberg-McQueen's affiliation has changed since the publication of the first edition. He is now at the World Wide Web Consortium, and can be contacted at cmsmcq@w3.org.

◆ Table of Contents

Appendices

◆ 1 Introduction

Extensible Markup Language, abbreviated XML, describes a class of data objects called XML documents and partially describes the behavior of computer programs which process them. XML is an application profile or restricted form of SGML, the Standard Generalized Markup Language [ISO 8879]. By construction, XML documents are conforming SGML documents.

XML documents are made up of storage units called entities, which contain either parsed or unparsed data. Parsed data is made up of characters, some of which form character data, and some of which form markup. Markup encodes a description of the document's storage layout and logical structure. XML provides a mechanism to impose constraints on the storage layout and logical structure.

[Definition: A software module called an XML processor is used to read XML documents and provide access to their content and structure.] [Definition: It is assumed that an XML processor is doing its work on behalf of another module, called the application.] This specification describes the required behavior of an XML processor in terms of how it must read XML data and the information it must provide to the application.

1.1 Origin and Goals

XML was developed by an XML Working Group (originally known as the SGML Editorial Review Board) formed under the auspices of the World Wide Web Consortium (W3C) in 1996. It was chaired by Jon Bosak of Sun Microsystems with the active participation of an XML Special Interest Group (previously known as the SGML Working Group) also organized by the W3C. The membership of the XML Working Group is given in an appendix. Dan Connolly served as the WG's contact with the W3C.

The design goals for XML are:

1. XML shall be straightforwardly usable over the Internet.
2. XML shall support a wide variety of applications.
3. XML shall be compatible with SGML.
4. It shall be easy to write programs which process XML documents.
5. The number of optional features in XML is to be kept to the absolute minimum, ideally zero.
6. XML documents should be human-legible and reasonably clear.
7. The XML design should be prepared quickly.
8. The design of XML shall be formal and concise.
9. XML documents shall be easy to create.
10. Terseness in XML markup is of minimal importance.

This specification, together with associated standards (Unicode and ISO/IEC 10646 for characters, Internet RFC 1766 for language identification tags, ISO 639 for language name codes, and ISO 3166 for country name codes), provides all the information necessary to understand XML Version 1.0 and construct computer programs to process it.

This version of the XML specification may be distributed freely, as long as all text and legal notices remain intact.

1.2 Terminology

The terminology used to describe XML documents is defined in the body of this specification. The terms defined in the following list are used in building those definitions and in describing the actions of an XML processor:

may

[Definition: Conforming documents and XML processors are permitted to but need not behave as described.]

must

[Definition: Conforming documents and XML processors are required to behave as described; otherwise they are in error.]

error

[Definition: A violation of the rules of this specification; results are undefined. Conforming software may detect and report an error and may recover from it.]

fatal error

[Definition: An error which a conforming XML processor must detect and report to the application. After encountering a fatal error, the processor may continue processing the data to search for further errors and may report such errors to the application. In order to support correction of errors, the processor may make unprocessed data from the document (with intermingled character data and markup) available to the application. Once a fatal error is detected, however, the processor must not continue normal processing (i.e., it must not continue to pass character data and information about the document's logical structure to the application in the normal way).]

at user option

[Definition: Conforming software may or must (depending on the modal verb in the sentence) behave as described; if it does, it must provide users a means to enable or disable the behavior described.]

validity constraint

[Definition: A rule which applies to all valid XML documents. Violations of validity constraints are errors; they must, at user option, be reported by validating XML processors.]

well-formedness constraint

[Definition: A rule which applies to all well-formed XML documents. Violations of well-formedness constraints are fatal errors.]

match

[Definition: (Of strings or names:) Two strings or names being compared must be identical. Characters with multiple possible representations in ISO/IEC 10646 (e.g. characters with both precomposed and base+diacritic forms) match only if they have the same representation in both strings. No case folding is performed. (Of strings and rules in the grammar:) A string matches a grammatical production if it belongs to the language generated by that production. (Of content and content models:) An element matches its declaration when it conforms in the fashion described in the constraint [VC: Element Valid].]

for compatibility

[Definition: Marks a sentence describing a feature of XML included solely to ensure that XML remains compatible with SGML.]

for interoperability

[Definition: Marks a sentence describing a non-binding recommendation included to increase the chances that XML documents can be processed by the existing installed base of SGML processors which predate the WebSGML Adaptations Annex to ISO 8879.]

◆ 2 Documents

[Definition: A data object is an XML document if it is well-formed, as defined in this specification. A well-formed XML document may in addition be valid if it meets certain further constraints.]

Each XML document has both a logical and a physical structure. Physically, the document is composed of units called entities. An entity may refer to other entities to cause their inclusion in the document. A document begins in a "root" or document entity. Logically, the document is composed of declarations, elements, comments, character references, and processing instructions, all of which are indicated in the document by explicit markup. The logical and physical structures must nest properly, as described in 4.3.2 Well-Formed Parsed Entities.

2.1 Well-Formed XML Documents

[Definition: A textual object is a well-formed XML document if:]

1. Taken as a whole, it matches the production labeled document.
2. It meets all the well-formedness constraints given in this specification.
3. Each of the parsed entities which is referenced directly or indirectly within the document is well-formed.

Document

```
[1]    document   ::=   prolog element Misc*
```

Matching the document production implies that:

1. It contains one or more elements.
2. [Definition: There is exactly one element, called the root, or document element, no part of which appears in the content of any other element.] For all other elements, if the start-tag is in the content of another element, the end-tag is in the content of the same element. More simply stated, the elements, delimited by start- and end-tags, nest properly within each other.

[Definition: As a consequence of this, for each non-root element C in the document, there is one other element P in the document such that C is in the content of P, but is not in the content of any other element that is in the content of P. P is referred to as the parent of C, and C as a child of P.]

2.2 Characters

[Definition: A parsed entity contains text, a sequence of characters, which may represent markup or character data.] [Definition: A character is an atomic unit of text as specified by ISO/IEC 10646 [ISO/IEC 10646] (see also [ISO/IEC 10646-2000]). Legal characters are tab, carriage return, line feed, and the legal characters of Unicode and ISO/IEC 10646. The versions of these standards cited in A.1 Normative References were current at the time this document was prepared. New characters may be added to these standards by amendments or new editions. Consequently, XML processors must accept any character in the range specified for Char. The use of "compatibility characters", as defined in section 6.8 of [Unicode] (see also D21 in section 3.6 of [Unicode3]), is discouraged.]

Character Range

```
[2]    Char   ::=   #x9 | #xA | #xD | [#x20-#xD7FF] |
[#xE000-#xFFFD] | [#x10000-#x10FFFF]   /* any Unicode char-
acter, excluding the surrogate blocks, FFFE, and FFFF. */
```

The mechanism for encoding character code points into bit patterns may vary from entity to entity. All XML processors must accept the UTF-8 and UTF-16 encodings of 10646; the mechanisms for signaling which of the two is in use, or for bringing other encodings into play, are discussed later, in 4.3.3 Character Encoding in Entities.

2.3 Common Syntactic Constructs

This section defines some symbols used widely in the grammar.

S (white space) consists of one or more space (#x20) characters, carriage returns, line feeds, or tabs.

WHITE SPACE

```
[3]   S   ::=   (#x20 | #x9 | #xD | #xA)+
```

Characters are classified for convenience as letters, digits, or other characters. A letter consists of an alphabetic or syllabic base character or an ideographic character. Full definitions of the specific characters in each class are given in B Character Classes.

[Definition: A Name is a token beginning with a letter or one of a few punctuation characters, and continuing with letters, digits, hyphens, underscores, colons, or full stops, together known as name characters.] Names beginning with the string "xml", or any string which would match (('X'|'x') ('M'|'m') ('L'|'l')), are reserved for standardization in this or future versions of this specification.

NOTE:

The Namespaces in XML Recommendation [XML Names] assigns a meaning to names containing colon characters. Therefore, authors should not use the colon in XML names except for namespace purposes, but XML processors must accept the colon as a name character.

An Nmtoken (name token) is any mixture of name characters.

Names and Tokens

```
[4]   NameChar  ::=   Letter | Digit | '.' | '-' | '_' |
':' | CombiningChar | Extender
[5]   Name   ::=   (Letter | '_' | ':') (NameChar)*
[6]   Names  ::=   Name (S Name)*
[7]   Nmtoken  ::=   (NameChar)+
[8]   Nmtokens  ::=   Nmtoken (S Nmtoken)*
```

Literal data is any quoted string not containing the quotation mark used as a delimiter for that string. Literals are used for specifying the content of internal entities (EntityValue), the values of attributes (AttValue), and external identifiers (SystemLiteral). Note that a SystemLiteral can be parsed without scanning for markup.

Literals

```
[9]    EntityValue   ::=   '"' ([^%&"] | PEReference | Refer-
ence)* '"'
|   "'" ([^%&'] | PEReference | Reference)* "'"
[10]   AttValue   ::=   '"' ([^<&"] | Reference)* '"'
|   "'" ([^<&'] | Reference)* "'"
[11]   SystemLiteral   ::=   ('"' [^"]* '"') | ("'" [^']*
"'")
[12]   PubidLiteral   ::=   '"' PubidChar* '"' | "'" (Pubid-
Char - "'")* "'"
[13]   PubidChar   ::=   #x20 | #xD | #xA | [a-zA-Z0-9] | [-
'()+,./:=?;!*#@$_%]
```

NOTE:
Although the EntityValue production allows the definition of an entity consisting of a single explicit < in the literal (e.g., <!ENTITY mylt "<">), it is strongly advised to avoid this practice since any reference to that entity will cause a well-formedness error.

2.4 Character Data and Markup

Text consists of intermingled character data and markup. [Definition: Markup takes the form of start-tags, end-tags, empty-element tags, entity references, character references, comments, CDATA section delimiters, document type declarations, processing instructions, XML declarations, text declarations, and any white space that is at the top level of the document entity (that is, outside the document element and not inside any other markup).]

[Definition: All text that is not markup constitutes the character data of the document.]

The ampersand character (&) and the left angle bracket (<) may appear in their literal form only when used as markup delimiters, or within a comment, a processing instruction, or a CDATA section. If they are needed elsewhere, they must be escaped using either numeric character references or the strings "&" and "<" respectively. The right angle bracket (>) may be represented using the string ">", and must, for compatibility, be escaped using ">" or a character reference when it appears in the string "]]>" in content, when that string is not marking the end of a CDATA section.

In the content of elements, character data is any string of characters which does not contain the start-delimiter of any markup. In a CDATA section, character data is any string of characters not including the CDATA-section-close delimiter, "]]>".

To allow attribute values to contain both single and double quotes, the apostrophe or single-quote character (') may be represented as "'", and the double-quote character (") as """.

Character Data

```
[14]    CharData    ::=    [^<&]* - ([^<&]* ']]>' [^<&]*)
```

2.5 Comments

[Definition: Comments may appear anywhere in a document outside other markup; in addition, they may appear within the document type declaration at places allowed by the grammar. They are not part of the document's character data; an XML processor may, but need not, make it possible for an application to retrieve the text of comments. For compatibility, the string "—" (double-hyphen) must not occur within comments.] Parameter entity references are not recognized within comments.

Comments

```
[15]    Comment    ::=    '<!-' ((Char - '-') | ('-' (Char -
'-')))* '->'
```

An example of a comment:

```
<!-- declarations for <head> & <body> -->
```

Note that the grammar does not allow a comment ending in --->. The following example is not well-formed.

```
<!-- B+, B, or B--->
```

2.6 Processing Instructions

[Definition: Processing instructions (PIs) allow documents to contain instructions for applications.]

Processing Instructions

```
[16]    PI    ::=    '<?' PITarget (S (Char* - (Char* '?>'
Char*)))? '?>'
```

```
[17]   PITarget   ::=   Name - (('X' | 'x') ('M' | 'm') ('L'
| 'l'))
```

PIs are not part of the document's character data, but must be passed through to the application. The PI begins with a target (PITarget) used to identify the application to which the instruction is directed. The target names "XML", "xml", and so on are reserved for standardization in this or future versions of this specification. The XML Notation mechanism may be used for formal declaration of PI targets. Parameter entity references are not recognized within processing instructions.

2.7 CDATA Sections

[Definition: CDATA sections may occur anywhere character data may occur; they are used to escape blocks of text containing characters which would otherwise be recognized as markup. CDATA sections begin with the string "<![CDATA[" and end with the string "]]>":]

CDATA Sections

```
[18]   CDSect      ::=          CDStart CData CDEnd
[19]   CDStart     ::=            '<![CDATA['
[20]   CData    ::=   (Char* - (Char* ']]>' Char*))
[21]   CDEnd    ::=   ']]>'
```

Within a CDATA section, only the CDEnd string is recognized as markup, so that left angle brackets and ampersands may occur in their literal form; they need not (and cannot) be escaped using "<" and "&". CDATA sections cannot nest.

An example of a CDATA section, in which "<greeting>" and "</greeting>" are recognized as character data, not markup:

```
<![CDATA[<greeting>Hello, world!</greeting>]]>
```

2.8 Prolog and Document Type Declaration

[Definition: XML documents should begin with an XML declaration which specifies the version of XML being used.] For example, the following is a complete XML document, well-formed but not valid:

```
<?xml version="1.0"?> <greeting>Hello, world!</greeting>
```

and so is this:

```
<greeting>Hello, world!</greeting>
```

The version number "1.0" should be used to indicate confor-mance to this version of this specification; it is an error for a doc-ument to use the value "1.0" if it does not conform to this version of this specification. It is the intent of the XML working group to give later versions of this specification numbers other than "1.0", but this intent does not indicate a commitment to produce any future versions of XML, nor if any are produced, to use any par-ticular numbering scheme. Since future versions are not ruled out, this construct is provided as a means to allow the possibility of automatic version recognition, should it become necessary. Processors may signal an error if they receive documents labeled with versions they do not support.

The function of the markup in an XML document is to de-scribe its storage and logical structure and to associate attribute-value pairs with its logical structures. XML provides a mechanism, the document type declaration, to define constraints on the logical structure and to support the use of predefined stor-age units. [Definition: An XML document is valid if it has an as-sociated document type declaration and if the document complies with the constraints expressed in it.]

The document type declaration must appear before the first element in the document.

Prolog

```
[22]   prolog         ::=   XMLDecl? Misc* (doc-
typedecl Misc*)?
[23]   XMLDecl        ::=   '<?xml' VersionInfo Encod-
ingDecl? SDDecl? S? '?>'
[24]   VersionInfo    ::=   S 'version' Eq ("'" Ver-
sionNum "'" | '"' VersionNum '"')/* */
[25]   Eq             ::=   S? '=' S?
[26]   VersionNum     ::=   ([a-zA-Z0-9_.:] | '-')+
[27]   Misc           ::=   Comment | PI | S
```

[Definition: The XML document type declaration contains or points to markup declarations that provide a grammar for a class of documents. This grammar is known as a document type definition, or DTD. The document type declaration can point to an external subset (a special kind of external entity) containing markup declarations, or can contain the markup declarations di-rectly in an internal subset, or can do both. The DTD for a docu-ment consists of both subsets taken together.]

[Definition: A markup declaration is an element type decla-ration, an attribute-list declaration, an entity declaration, or a notation declaration.] These declarations may be contained in whole or in part within parameter entities, as described in the well-formedness and validity constraints below. For further information, see 4 Physical Structures.

Document Type Definition

```
[28]   doctypedecl   ::=   '<!DOCTYPE' S Name (S Exter-
nalID)? S? ('[' (markupdecl | DeclSep)* ']' S?)? '>'
    [VC: Root Element Type]
[WFC: External Subset]
/* */
[28a]  DeclSep       ::=   PEReference | S[WFC: PE Between
Declarations]
/* */
[29]   markupdecl    ::=   elementdecl | AttlistDecl | En-
tityDecl | NotationDecl| PI | Comment    [VC: Proper Decla-
ration/PE Nesting]
[WFC: PEs in Internal Subset]
```

Note that it is possible to construct a well-formed document containing a doctypedecl that neither points to an external subset nor contains an internal subset.

The markup declarations may be made up in whole or in part of the replacement text of parameter entities. The productions later in this specification for individual nonterminals (elementdecl, AttlistDecl, and so on) describe the declarations after all the parameter entities have been included.

Parameter entity references are recognized anywhere in the DTD (internal and external subsets and external parameter entities), except in literals, processing instructions, comments, and the contents of ignored conditional sections (see 3.4 Conditional Sections). They are also recognized in entity value literals. The use of parameter entities in the internal subset is restricted as described below.

Validity constraint: Root Element Type

The Name in the document type declaration must match the element type of the root element.

Validity constraint: Proper Declaration/PE Nesting

Parameter-entity replacement text must be properly nested with markup declarations. That is to say, if either the first character or the last character of a markup declaration (markupdecl above) is contained in the replacement text for a parameter-entity reference, both must be contained in the same replacement text.

Well-formedness constraint: PEs in Internal Subset

In the internal DTD subset, parameter-entity references can occur only where markup declarations can occur, not within markup declarations. (This does not apply to references that occur in external parameter entities or to the external subset.)

Well-formedness constraint: External Subset

The external subset, if any, must match the production for extSubset.

Well-formedness constraint: PE Between Declarations

The replacement text of a parameter entity reference in a DeclSep must match the production extSubsetDecl.

Like the internal subset, the external subset and any external parameter entities referenced in a DeclSep must consist of a series of complete markup declarations of the types allowed by the non-terminal symbol markupdecl, interspersed with white space or parameter-entity references. However, portions of the contents of the external subset or of these external parameter entities may conditionally be ignored by using the conditional section construct; this is not allowed in the internal subset.

External Subset

```
[30]    extSubset    ::=    TextDecl? extSubsetDecl
[31]    extSubsetDecl    ::=    ( markupdecl | conditionalSect
| DeclSep)*/*    */
```

The external subset and external parameter entities also differ from the internal subset in that in them, parameter-entity references are permitted within markup declarations, not only between markup declarations.

An example of an XML document with a document type declaration:

```
<?xml version="1.0"?> <!DOCTYPE greeting SYSTEM "hello.dtd">
<greeting>Hello, world!</greeting>
```

The system identifier "hello.dtd" gives the address (a URI reference) of a DTD for the document.

The declarations can also be given locally, as in this example:

```
<?xml version="1.0" encoding="UTF-8" ?>
<!DOCTYPE greeting [
```

```
<!ELEMENT greeting (#PCDATA)>
]>
<greeting>Hello, world!</greeting>
```

If both the external and internal subsets are used, the internal subset is considered to occur before the external subset. This has the effect that entity and attribute-list declarations in the internal subset take precedence over those in the external subset.

2.9 Standalone Document Declaration

Markup declarations can affect the content of the document, as passed from an XML processor to an application; examples are attribute defaults and entity declarations. The standalone document declaration, which may appear as a component of the XML declaration, signals whether or not there are such declarations which appear external to the document entity or in parameter entities. [Definition: An external markup declaration is defined as a markup declaration occurring in the external subset or in a parameter entity (external or internal, the latter being included because non-validating processors are not required to read them).]

Standalone Document Declaration

```
[32]   SDDecl   ::=   S 'standalone' Eq (("'" ('yes' | 'no')
"'") | ('"' ('yes' | 'no') '"')) [VC: Standalone Document
Declaration]
```

In a standalone document declaration, the value "yes" indicates that there are no external markup declarations which affect the information passed from the XML processor to the application. The value "no" indicates that there are or may be such external markup declarations. Note that the standalone document declaration only denotes the presence of external declarations; the presence, in a document, of references to external entities, when those entities are internally declared, does not change its standalone status.

If there are no external markup declarations, the standalone document declaration has no meaning. If there are external markup declarations but there is no standalone document declaration, the value "no" is assumed.

Any XML document for which standalone="no" holds can be converted algorithmically to a standalone document, which may be desirable for some network delivery applications.

Validity constraint: Standalone Document Declaration

The standalone document declaration must have the value "no" if any external markup declarations contain declarations of:

- attributes with default values, if elements to which these attributes apply appear in the document without specifications of values for these attributes, or
- entities (other than amp, lt, gt, apos, quot), if references to those entities appear in the document, or
- attributes with values subject to normalization, where the attribute appears in the document with a value which will change as a result of normalization, or
- element types with element content, if white space occurs directly within any instance of those types.

An example XML declaration with a standalone document declaration:

```
<?xml version="1.0" standalone='yes'?>
```

2.10 White Space Handling

In editing XML documents, it is often convenient to use "white space" (spaces, tabs, and blank lines) to set apart the markup for greater readability. Such white space is typically not intended for inclusion in the delivered version of the document. On the other hand, "significant" white space that should be preserved in the delivered version is common, for example in poetry and source code.

An XML processor must always pass all characters in a document that are not markup through to the application. A validating XML processor must also inform the application which of these characters constitute white space appearing in element content.

A special attribute named xml:space may be attached to an element to signal an intention that in that element, white space should be preserved by applications. In valid documents, this attribute, like any other, must be declared if it is used. When declared, it must be given as an enumerated type whose values are one or both of "default" and "preserve". For example:

```
<!ATTLIST poem  xml:space (default|preserve) 'preserve'>
```

```
<!-- -->
<!ATTLIST pre xml:space (preserve) #FIXED 'preserve'>
```

The value "default" signals that applications' default white-space processing modes are acceptable for this element; the value "preserve" indicates the intent that applications preserve all the white space. This declared intent is considered to apply to all elements within the content of the element where it is specified, unless overriden with another instance of the xml:space attribute.

The root element of any document is considered to have signaled no intentions as regards application space handling, unless it provides a value for this attribute or the attribute is declared with a default value.

2.11 End-of-Line Handling

XML parsed entities are often stored in computer files which, for editing convenience, are organized into lines. These lines are typically separated by some combination of the characters carriage-return (#xD) and line-feed (#xA).

To simplify the tasks of applications, the characters passed to an application by the XML processor must be as if the XML processor normalized all line breaks in external parsed entities (including the document entity) on input, before parsing, by translating both the two-character sequence #xD #xA and any #xD that is not followed by #xA to a single #xA character.

2.12 Language Identification

In document processing, it is often useful to identify the natural or formal language in which the content is written. A special attribute named xml:lang may be inserted in documents to specify the language used in the contents and attribute values of any element in an XML document. In valid documents, this attribute, like any other, must be declared if it is used. The values of the attribute are language identifiers as defined by [IETF RFC 1766], Tags for the Identification of Languages, or its successor on the IETF Standards Track.

NOTE:
[IETF RFC 1766] tags are constructed from two-letter language codes as defined by [ISO 639], from two-letter country codes as defined by [ISO 3166], or from language identifiers registered with the Internet Assigned Numbers Authority [IANA-LANGCODES]. It is expected that the successor to [IETF RFC 1766] will introduce three-letter language codes for languages not presently covered by [ISO 639].

(Productions 33 through 38 have been removed.)

For example:

```
<p xml:lang="en">The quick brown fox jumps over the lazy
dog.</p>
<p xml:lang="en-GB">What colour is it?</p>
<p xml:lang="en-US">What color is it?</p>
<sp who="Faust" desc='leise' xml:lang="de">
  <l>Habe nun, ach! Philosophie,</l>
  <l>Juristerei, und Medizin</l>
  <l>und leider auch Theologie</l>
  <l>durchaus studiert mit heißem Bemüh'n.</l>
</sp>
```

The intent declared with xml:lang is considered to apply to all attributes and content of the element where it is specified, unless overridden with an instance of xml:lang on another element within that content.

A simple declaration for xml:lang might take the form

```
xml:lang NMTOKEN #IMPLIED
```

but specific default values may also be given, if appropriate. In a collection of French poems for English students, with glosses and notes in English, the xml:lang attribute might be declared this way:

```
<!ATTLIST poem    xml:lang NMTOKEN 'fr'>
<!ATTLIST gloss   xml:lang NMTOKEN 'en'>
<!ATTLIST note    xml:lang NMTOKEN 'en'>
```

◆ 3 Logical Structures

[Definition: Each XML document contains one or more elements, the boundaries of which are either delimited by start-tags and end-tags, or, for empty elements, by an empty-element tag. Each element has a type, identified by name, sometimes called its "generic identifier" (GI), and may have a set of attribute specifications.] Each attribute specification has a name and a value.

Element

```
[39]   element   ::=    EmptyElemTag
| STag content ETag    [WFC: Element Type Match]
[VC: Element Valid]
```

This specification does not constrain the semantics, use, or (beyond syntax) names of the element types and attributes, except that names beginning with a match to (('X'|'x')('M'|'m') ('L'|'l')) are reserved for standardization in this or future versions of this specification.

Well-formedness constraint: Element Type Match

The Name in an element's end-tag must match the element type in the start-tag.

Validity constraint: Element Valid

An element is valid if there is a declaration matching element-decl where the Name matches the element type, and one of the following holds:

1. The declaration matches EMPTY and the element has no content.
2. The declaration matches children and the sequence of child elements belongs to the language generated by the regular expression in the content model, with optional white space (characters matching the nonterminal S) between the start-tag and the first child element, between child elements, or between the last child element and the end-tag. Note that a CDATA section containing only white space does not match the nonterminal S, and hence cannot appear in these positions.
3. The declaration matches Mixed and the content consists of character data and child elements whose types match names in the content model.
4. The declaration matches ANY, and the types of any child elements have been declared.

3.1 Start-Tags, End-Tags, and Empty-Element Tags

[Definition: The beginning of every non-empty XML element is marked by a start-tag.]

Start-tag

```
[40]    STag   ::=   '<' Name (S Attribute)* S? '>'
   [WFC: Unique Att Spec]
[41]    Attribute   ::=   Name Eq AttValue   [VC: Attribute
Value Type]
[WFC: No External Entity References]
[WFC: No < in Attribute Values]
```

The Name in the start- and end-tags gives the element's type. [Definition: The Name-AttValue pairs are referred to as the attribute specifications of the element], [Definition: with the Name in each pair referred to as the attribute name] and [Definition: the content of the AttValue (the text between the ' or " delimiters) as the attribute value.]Note that the order of attribute specifications in a start-tag or empty-element tag is not significant.

Well-formedness constraint: Unique Att Spec

No attribute name may appear more than once in the same start-tag or empty-element tag.

Validity constraint: Attribute Value Type

The attribute must have been declared; the value must be of the type declared for it. (For attribute types, see 3.3 Attribute-List Declarations.)

Well-formedness constraint: No External Entity References

Attribute values cannot contain direct or indirect entity references to external entities.

Well-formedness constraint: No < in Attribute Values

The replacement text of any entity referred to directly or indirectly in an attribute value must not contain a <.
An example of a start-tag:

```
<termdef id="dt-dog" term="dog">
```

[Definition: The end of every element that begins with a start-tag must be marked by an end-tag containing a name that echoes the element's type as given in the start-tag:]

End-tag

```
[42]    ETag    ::=    '</' Name S? '>'
```

An example of an end-tag:

```
</termdef>
```

[Definition: The text between the start-tag and end-tag is called the element's content:]

Content of Elements

```
[43]   content   ::=   CharData? ((element | Reference | CD-
Sect | PI | Comment) CharData?)*/* */
```

[Definition: An element with no content is said to be empty.] The representation of an empty element is either a start-tag immediately followed by an end-tag, or an empty-element tag. [Definition: An empty-element tag takes a special form:]

Tags for Empty Elements

```
[44]   EmptyElemTag   ::=   '<' Name (S Attribute)* S?
'/>'[WFC: Unique Att Spec]
```

Empty-element tags may be used for any element which has no content, whether or not it is declared using the keyword EMPTY. For interoperability, the empty-element tag should be used, and should only be used, for elements which are declared EMPTY.

Examples of empty elements:

```
<IMG align="left"
 src="http://www.w3.org/Icons/WWW/w3c_home" />
<br></br>
<br/>
```

3.2 Element Type Declarations

The element structure of an XML document may, for validation purposes, be constrained using element type and attribute-list declarations. An element type declaration constrains the element's content.

Element type declarations often constrain which element types can appear as children of the element. At user option, an XML processor may issue a warning when a declaration mentions an element type for which no declaration is provided, but this is not an error.

[Definition: An element type declaration takes the form:]

Element Type Declaration

```
[45]   elementdecl   ::=   '<!ELEMENT' S Name S contentspec
S? '>'   [VC: Unique Element Type Declaration]
[46]   contentspec   ::=   'EMPTY' | 'ANY' | Mixed |
children
```

where the Name gives the element type being declared.

Validity constraint: Unique Element Type Declaration

No element type may be declared more than once.
Examples of element type declarations:

```
<!ELEMENT br EMPTY>
<!ELEMENT p (#PCDATA|emph)* >
<!ELEMENT %name.para; %content.para; >
<!ELEMENT container ANY>
```

3.2.1 Element Content

[Definition: An element type has element content when elements of that type must contain only child elements (no character data), optionally separated by white space (characters matching the nonterminal S).][Definition: In this case, the constraint includes a content model, a simple grammar governing the allowed types of the child elements and the order in which they are allowed to appear.] The grammar is built on content particles (cps), which consist of names, choice lists of content particles, or sequence lists of content particles:

Element-content Models

```
[47]    children  ::=   (choice | seq) ('?' | '*' | '+')?
[48]    cp  ::=  (Name | choice | seq) ('?' | '*' | '+')?
[49]    choice  ::=   '(' S? cp ( S? '|' S? cp )+ S? ')'/*
*/
/* */
[VC: Proper Group/PE Nesting]
[50]    seq  ::=   '(' S? cp ( S? ',' S? cp )* S? ')'/* */
[VC: Proper Group/PE Nesting]
```

where each Name is the type of an element which may appear as a child. Any content particle in a choice list may appear in the element content at the location where the choice list appears in the grammar; content particles occurring in a sequence list must each appear in the element content in the order given in the list. The optional character following a name or list governs whether the element or the content particles in the list may occur one or more (+), zero or more (*), or zero or one times (?). The absence of such an operator means that the element or content particle must appear exactly once. This syntax and meaning are identical to those used in the productions in this specification.

The content of an element matches a content model if and only if it is possible to trace out a path through the content model, obeying the sequence, choice, and repetition operators and matching each element in the content against an element type in the content model. For compatibility, it is an error if an element in the document can match more than one occurrence of an element type in the content model. For more information, see E Deterministic Content Models.

Validity constraint: Proper Group/PE Nesting

Parameter-entity replacement text must be properly nested with parenthesized groups. That is to say, if either of the opening or closing parentheses in a choice, seq, or Mixed construct is contained in the replacement text for a parameter entity, both must be contained in the same replacement text.

For interoperability, if a parameter-entity reference appears in a choice, seq, or Mixed construct, its replacement text should contain at least one non-blank character, and neither the first nor last non-blank character of the replacement text should be a connector (| or ,).

Examples of element-content models:

```
<!ELEMENT spec (front, body, back?)>
<!ELEMENT div1 (head, (p | list | note)*, div2*)>
<!ELEMENT dictionary-body (%div.mix; | %dict.mix;)*>
```

3.2.2 Mixed Content

[Definition: An element type has mixed content when elements of that type may contain character data, optionally interspersed with child elements.] In this case, the types of the child elements may be constrained, but not their order or their number of occurrences:

Mixed-content Declaration

```
[51]      Mixed    ::=    '(' S? '#PCDATA' (S? '|' S?
Name)* S? ')*'
| '(' S? '#PCDATA' S? ')'    [VC: Proper Group/PE Nesting]
[VC: No Duplicate Types]
```

where the Names give the types of elements that may appear as children. The keyword #PCDATA derives historically from the term "parsed character data."

Validity constraint: No Duplicate Types

The same name must not appear more than once in a single mixed-content declaration.

Examples of mixed content declarations:

```
<!ELEMENT p (#PCDATA|a|ul|b|i|em)*>
<!ELEMENT p (#PCDATA | %font; | %phrase; | %special; |
%form;)* >
<!ELEMENT b (#PCDATA)>
```

3.3 Attribute-List Declarations

Attributes are used to associate name-value pairs with elements. Attribute specifications may appear only within start-tags and empty-element tags; thus, the productions used to recognize them appear in 3.1 Start-Tags, End-Tags, and Empty-Element Tags. Attribute-list declarations may be used:

- To define the set of attributes pertaining to a given element type.
- To establish type constraints for these attributes.
- To provide default values for attributes.

[Definition: Attribute-list declarations specify the name, data type, and default value (if any) of each attribute associated with a given element type:]

Attribute-list Declaration

```
[52]    AttlistDecl    ::=    '<!ATTLIST' S Name AttDef* S? '>'
[53]    AttDef         ::=    S Name S AttType S DefaultDecl
```

The Name in the AttlistDecl rule is the type of an element. At user option, an XML processor may issue a warning if attributes are declared for an element type not itself declared, but this is not an error. The Name in the AttDef rule is the name of the attribute.

When more than one AttlistDecl is provided for a given element type, the contents of all those provided are merged. When more than one definition is provided for the same attribute of a given element type, the first declaration is binding and later declarations are ignored. For interoperability, writers of DTDs may choose to provide at most one attribute-list declaration for a given element type, at most one attribute definition for a given attribute name in an attribute-list declaration, and at least one attribute definition in each attribute-list declaration. For interoperability, an XML processor may at user option issue a warning when more than one attribute-list declaration is provided for a given element type, or more than one attribute definition is provided for a given attribute, but this is not an error.

3.3.1 Attribute Types

XML attribute types are of three kinds: a string type, a set of tokenized types, and enumerated types. The string type may take any literal string as a value; the tokenized types have varying lexical and semantic constraints. The validity constraints noted in the grammar are applied after the attribute value has been normalized as described in 3.3 Attribute-List Declarations.

Attribute Types

```
[54]   AttType   ::=   StringType | TokenizedType |
EnumeratedType
[55]   StringType   ::=   'CDATA'
[56]   TokenizedType   ::=   'ID'   [VC: ID]
[VC: One ID per Element Type]
[VC: ID Attribute Default]
| 'IDREF' [VC: IDREF]
| 'IDREFS'   [VC: IDREF]
| 'ENTITY'   [VC: Entity Name]
| 'ENTITIES'   [VC: Entity Name]
| 'NMTOKEN'   [VC: Name Token]
| 'NMTOKENS'   [VC: Name Token]
```

Validity constraint: ID

Values of type ID must match the Name production. A name must not appear more than once in an XML document as a value of this type; i.e., ID values must uniquely identify the elements which bear them.

Validity constraint: One ID per Element Type

No element type may have more than one ID attribute specified.

Validity constraint: ID Attribute Default

An ID attribute must have a declared default of #IMPLIED or #REQUIRED.

Validity constraint: IDREF

Values of type IDREF must match the Name production, and values of type IDREFS must match Names; each Name must match the value of an ID attribute on some element in the XML document; i.e. IDREF values must match the value of some ID attribute.

Validity constraint: Entity Name

Values of type ENTITY must match the Name production, values of type ENTITIES must match Names; each Name must match the name of an unparsed entity declared in the DTD.

Validity constraint: Name Token

Values of type NMTOKEN must match the Nmtoken production; values of type NMTOKENS must match Nmtokens.

[Definition: Enumerated attributes can take one of a list of values provided in the declaration]. There are two kinds of enumerated types:

Enumerated Attribute Types

```
[57]    EnumeratedType   ::=   NotationType | Enumeration
[58]    NotationType     ::=   'NOTATION' S '(' S? Name (S?
'|' S? Name)* S? ')'         [VC: Notation Attributes]
[VC: One Notation Per Element Type]
[VC: No Notation on Empty Element]
[59]    Enumeration            ::=   '(' S? Nmtoken (S? '|' S?
Nmtoken)* S? ')'   [VC: Enumeration]
```

A NOTATION attribute identifies a notation, declared in the DTD with associated system and/or public identifiers, to be used in interpreting the element to which the attribute is attached.

Validity constraint: Notation Attributes

Values of this type must match one of the notation names included in the declaration; all notation names in the declaration must be declared.

Validity constraint: One Notation Per Element Type

No element type may have more than one NOTATION attribute specified.

Validity constraint: No Notation on Empty Element

For compatibility, an attribute of type NOTATION must not be declared on an element declared EMPTY.

Validity constraint: Enumeration

Values of this type must match one of the Nmtoken tokens in the declaration.

For interoperability, the same Nmtoken should not occur more than once in the enumerated attribute types of a single element type.

3.3.2 Attribute Defaults

An attribute declaration provides information on whether the attribute's presence is required, and if not, how an XML processor should react if a declared attribute is absent in a document.

Attribute Defaults

```
[60]    DefaultDecl   ::=       '#REQUIRED' | '#IMPLIED'
| (('#FIXED' S)? AttValue)   [VC: Required Attribute]
[VC: Attribute Default Legal]
[WFC: No < in Attribute Values]
[VC: Fixed Attribute Default]
```

In an attribute declaration, #REQUIRED means that the attribute must always be provided, #IMPLIED that no default value is provided. [Definition: If the declaration is neither #REQUIRED nor #IMPLIED, then the AttValue value contains the declared default value; the #FIXED keyword states that the attribute must always have the default value. If a default value is declared, when an XML processor encounters an omitted attribute, it is to behave as though the attribute were present with the declared default value.]

Validity constraint: Required Attribute

If the default declaration is the keyword #REQUIRED, then the attribute must be specified for all elements of the type in the attribute-list declaration.

Validity constraint: Attribute Default Legal

The declared default value must meet the lexical constraints of the declared attribute type.

Validity constraint: Fixed Attribute Default

If an attribute has a default value declared with the #FIXED keyword, instances of that attribute must match the default value.

Examples of attribute-list declarations:

```
<!ATTLIST termdef
        id      ID      #REQUIRED
        name    CDATA   #IMPLIED>
```

```
<!ATTLIST list
         type    (bullets|ordered|glossary)  "ordered">
<!ATTLIST form
         method  CDATA   #FIXED "POST">
```

3.3.3 Attribute-Value Normalization

Before the value of an attribute is passed to the application or checked for validity, the XML processor must normalize the attribute value by applying the algorithm below, or by using some other method such that the value passed to the application is the same as that produced by the algorithm.

1. All line breaks must have been normalized on input to #xA as described in 2.11 End-of-Line Handling, so the rest of this algorithm operates on text normalized in this way.
2. Begin with a normalized value consisting of the empty string.
3. For each character, entity reference, or character reference in the unnormalized attribute value, beginning with the first and continuing to the last, do the following:
   - For a character reference, append the referenced character to the normalized value.
   - For an entity reference, recursively apply step 3 of this algorithm to the replacement text of the entity.
   - For a white space character (#x20, #xD, #xA, #x9), append a space character (#x20) to the normalized value.
   - For another character, append the character to the normalized value.

If the attribute type is not CDATA, then the XML processor must further process the normalized attribute value by discarding any leading and trailing space (#x20) characters, and by replacing sequences of space (#x20) characters by a single space (#x20) character.

Note that if the unnormalized attribute value contains a character reference to a white space character other than space (#x20), the normalized value contains the referenced character itself (#xD, #xA or #x9). This contrasts with the case where the unnormalized value contains a white space character (not a reference), which is replaced with a space character (#x20) in the normalized value and also contrasts with the case where the unnormalized value contains an entity reference whose replacement text contains a white space character; being recursively processed, the white space character is replaced with a space character (#x20) in the normalized value.

All attributes for which no declaration has been read should be treated by a non-validating processor as if declared CDATA.

Following are examples of attribute normalization. Given the following declarations:

```
<!ENTITY d "&#xD;">
<!ENTITY a "&#xA;">
<!ENTITY da "&#xD;&#xA;">
```

the attribute specifications in the left column below would be normalized to the character sequences of the middle column if the attribute a is declared NMTOKENS and to those of the right columns if a is declared CDATA.

Attribute Specification.	a is NMTOKENS	a is CDATA
a="xyz"	x y z	#x20 #x20 x y z
a="&d;&d;A&a;&a;B&da;"	A #x20 B	#x20 #x20 A #x20 #x20 B #x20 #x20
a="A

B
"#	#xD #xD A #xA #xA B #xD #xA	#xD #xD A #xA #xA B #xD #xD

Attribute specification   a is NMTOKENS   a is CDATA
a="

xyz"x y z   #x20 #x20 x y z
A #x20 B   #x20 #x20 A #x20 #x20 B #x20 #x20
a=
"A

B
"#xD #xD A #xA #xA B #xD
    #xA #xD #xD A #xA #xA B #xD #xD

Note that the last example is invalid (but well-formed) if a is declared to be of type **NMTOKENS**.

3.4 Conditional Sections

[Definition: Conditional sections are portions of the document type declaration external subset which are included in, or excluded from, the logical structure of the DTD based on the keyword which governs them.]

```
Conditional Section
[61]    conditionalSect    ::=    includeSect | ignoreSect
[62]    includeSect    ::=    '<![' S? 'INCLUDE' S? '[' extSub-
setDecl ']]>'    /* */
[VC: Proper Conditional Section/PE Nesting]
[63]    ignoreSect    ::=    '<![' S? 'IGNORE' S? '[' ignore-
SectContents* ']]>'    /* */
[VC: Proper Conditional Section/PE Nesting]
[64]    ignoreSectContents    ::=    Ignore ('<![' ignoreSect-
Contents ']]>' Ignore)*
[65]    Ignore    ::=    Char* - (Char* ('<![' | ']]>') Char*)
```

Validity constraint: Proper Conditional Section/PE Nesting

If any of the "<![", "[", or "]]>" of a conditional section is contained in the replacement text for a parameter-entity reference,all of them must be contained in the same replacement text.

Like the internal and external DTD subsets, a conditional section may contain one or more complete declarations, comments, processing instructions, or nested conditional sections, intermingled with white space.

If the keyword of the conditional section is INCLUDE, then the contents of the conditional section are part of the DTD. If the keyword of the conditional section is IGNORE, then the contents of the conditional section are not logically part of the DTD. If a conditional section with a keyword of INCLUDE occurs within a larger conditional section with a keyword of IGNORE, both the outer and the inner conditional sections are ignored. The contents of an ignored conditional section are parsed by ignoring all characters after the "[" following the keyword, except conditional section starts "<![" and ends "]]>", until the matching conditional section end is found. Parameter entity references are not recognized in this process.

If the keyword of the conditional section is a parameter-entity reference, the parameter entity must be replaced by its content before the processor decides whether to include or ignore the conditional section.

An example:

```
<!ENTITY % draft 'INCLUDE' >
<!ENTITY % final 'IGNORE' >

<![%draft;[
<!ELEMENT book (comments*, title, body, supplements?)>
]]>
<![%final;[
<!ELEMENT book (title, body, supplements?)>
]]>
```

◆ 4 Physical Structures

[Definition: An XML document may consist of one or many storage units. These are called entities; they all have content and are all (except for the document entity and the external DTD subset) identified by entity name.] Each XML document has one entity called the document entity, which serves as the starting point for the XML processor and may contain the whole document.

Entities may be either parsed or unparsed. [Definition: A parsed entity's contents are referred to as its replacement text; this text is considered an integral part of the document.]

[Definition: An unparsed entity is a resource whose contents may or may not be text, and if text, may be other than XML. Each unparsed entity has an associated notation, identified by name. Beyond a requirement that an XML processor make the identifiers for the entity and notation available to the application, XML places no constraints on the contents of unparsed entities.]

Parsed entities are invoked by name using entity references; unparsed entities by name, given in the value of ENTITY or ENTITIES attributes.

[Definition: General entities are entities for use within the document content. In this specification, general entities are sometimes referred to with the unqualified term entity when this leads to no ambiguity.] [Definition: Parameter entities are parsed entities for use within the DTD.] These two types of entities use different forms of reference and are recognized in different contexts. Furthermore, they occupy different namespaces; a parameter entity and a general entity with the same name are two distinct entities.

4.1 Character and Entity References

[Definition: A character reference refers to a specific character in the ISO/IEC 10646 character set, for example one not directly accessible from available input devices.]

Character Reference

```
[66]    CharRef   ::=    '&#' [0-9]+ ';'
| '&#x' [0-9a-fA-F]+ ';'    [WFC: Legal Character]
```

Well-formedness constraint: Legal Character

Characters referred to using character references must match the production for Char.

If the character reference begins with "&#x", the digits and letters up to the terminating ; provide a hexadecimal representation of the character's code point in ISO/IEC 10646. If it begins just with "&#", the digits up to the terminating ; provide a decimal representation of the character's code point.

[Definition: An entity reference refers to the content of a named entity.] [Definition: References to parsed general entities use ampersand (&) and semicolon (;) as delimiters.] [Definition: Parameter-entity references use percent-sign (%) and semicolon (;) as delimiters.]

Entity Reference

```
[67]    Reference    ::=    EntityRef | CharRef
[68]    EntityRef    ::=    '&' Name ';'    [WFC: Entity
Declared]
[VC: Entity Declared]
[WFC: Parsed Entity]
[WFC: No Recursion]
[69]    PEReference    ::=    '%' Name ';'    [VC: Entity
Declared]
[WFC: No Recursion]
[WFC: In DTD]
```

Well-formedness constraint: Entity Declared

In a document without any DTD, a document with only an internal DTD subset which contains no parameter entity references, or a document with "standalone='yes'", for an entity reference that does not occur within the external subset or a parameter entity, the Name given in the entity reference must match that in an entity declaration that does not occur within the external subset or a parameter entity, except that well-formed documents need not declare any of the following entities: amp, lt, gt, apos, quot. The declaration of a general entity must precede any reference to it which appears in a default value in an attribute-list declaration.

Note that if entities are declared in the external subset or in external parameter entities, a non-validating processor is not obligated to read and process their declarations; for such documents, the rule that an entity must be declared is a well-formedness constraint only if standalone='yes'.

Validity constraint: Entity Declared

In a document with an external subset or external parameter entities with "standalone='no'", the Name given in the entity reference must match that in an entity declaration. For interoperability, valid documents should declare the entities amp, lt, gt, apos, quot, in the form specified in 4.6 Predefined Entities. The declaration of a parameter entity must precede any reference to it. Similarly, the declaration of a general entity must precede any attribute-list declaration containing a default value with a direct or indirect reference to that general entity.

Well-formedness constraint: Parsed Entity

An entity reference must not contain the name of an unparsed entity. Unparsed entities may be referred to only in attribute values declared to be of type ENTITY or ENTITIES.

Well-formedness constraint: No Recursion

A parsed entity must not contain a recursive reference to itself, either directly or indirectly.

Well-formedness constraint: In DTD

Parameter-entity references may only appear in the DTD.
Examples of character and entity references:
Type <key>less-than</key> (<) to save options.
This document was prepared on &docdate; and
is classified &security-level;.
Example of a parameter-entity reference:

```
<!-- declare the parameter entity "ISOLat2"... -->
<!ENTITY % ISOLat2
        SYSTEM "http://www.xml.com/iso/isolat2-xml
.entities" >
<!-- ... now reference it. -->
%ISOLat2;
```

4.2 Entity Declarations

[Definition: Entities are declared thus:]

Entity Declaration

```
[70]   EntityDecl   ::=   GEDecl | PEDecl
[71]   GEDecl   ::=   '<!ENTITY' S Name S EntityDef S? '>'
[72]   PEDecl   ::=   '<!ENTITY' S '%' S Name S PEDef S? '>'
[73]   EntityDef   ::=   EntityValue | (ExternalID
NDataDecl?)
[74]   PEDef   ::=   EntityValue | ExternalID
```

The Name identifies the entity in an entity reference or, in the case of an unparsed entity, in the value of an ENTITY or ENTITIES attribute. If the same entity is declared more than once, the first declaration encountered is binding; at user option, an XML processor may issue a warning if entities are declared multiple times.

4.2.1 Internal Entities

[Definition: If the entity definition is an EntityValue, the defined entity is called an internal entity. There is no separate physical storage object, and the content of the entity is given in the declaration.] Note that some processing of entity and character references in the literal entity value may be required to produce the correct replacement text: see 4.5 Construction of Internal Entity Replacement Text.

An internal entity is a parsed entity.

Example of an internal entity declaration:

```
<!ENTITY Pub-Status "This is a pre-release of the
specification.">
```

4.2.2 External Entities

[Definition: If the entity is not internal, it is an external entity, declared as follows:]

External Entity Declaration

```
[75]    ExternalID   ::=    'SYSTEM' S SystemLiteral
| 'PUBLIC' S PubidLiteral S SystemLiteral
[76]    NDataDecl    ::=    S 'NDATA' S Name    [VC: Notation
Declared]
```

If the NDataDecl is present, this is a general unparsed entity; otherwise it is a parsed entity.

Validity constraint: Notation Declared

The Name must match the declared name of a notation.

[Definition: The SystemLiteral is called the entity's system identifier. It is a URI reference (as defined in [IETF RFC 2396], updated by [IETF RFC 2732]), meant to be dereferenced to obtain input for the XML processor to construct the entity's replacement text.] It is an error for a fragment identifier (beginning with a # character) to be part of a system identifier. Unless otherwise provided by information outside the scope of this specification (e.g. a special XML element type defined by a particular DTD, or a processing instruction defined by a particular application specification), relative URIs are relative to the location of the resource within which the entity declaration occurs. A URI might thus be relative to the document entity, to the entity containing the external DTD subset, or to some other external parameter entity.

URI references require encoding and escaping of certain characters. The disallowed characters include all non-ASCII characters, plus the excluded characters listed in Section 2.4 of [IETF RFC 2396], except for the number sign (#) and percent sign (%) characters and the square bracket characters re-allowed in [IETF RFC 2732]. Disallowed characters must be escaped as follows:

1. Each disallowed character is converted to UTF-8 [IETF RFC 2279] as one or more bytes.
2. Any octets corresponding to a disallowed character are escaped with the URI escaping mechanism (that is, converted to %HH, where HH is the hexadecimal notation of the byte value).
3. The original character is replaced by the resulting character sequence.

[Definition: In addition to a system identifier, an external identifier may include a public identifier.] An XML processor attempting to retrieve the entity's content may use the public identifier to try to generate an alternative URI reference. If the processor is unable to do so, it must use the URI reference specified in the system literal. Before a match is attempted, all strings of white space in the public identifier must be normalized to single space characters (#x20), and leading and trailing white space must be removed.

Examples of external entity declarations:

```
<!ENTITY open-hatch
        SYSTEM "http://www.textuality.com/boilerplate/Open-
Hatch.xml">
<!ENTITY open-hatch
        PUBLIC "-//Textuality//TEXT Standard open-hatch
boilerplate//EN"

"http://www.textuality.com/boilerplate/OpenHatch.xml">
<!ENTITY hatch-pic
        SYSTEM "../grafix/OpenHatch.gif"
        NDATA gif >
```

4.3 Parsed Entities

4.3.1 The Text Declaration

External parsed entities should each begin with a text declaration.

Text Declaration

```
[77]    TextDecl   ::=   '<?xml' VersionInfo? EncodingDecl S?
'?>'
```

The text declaration must be provided literally, not by reference to a parsed entity. No text declaration may appear at any position other than the beginning of an external parsed entity. The text declaration in an external parsed entity is not considered part of its replacement text.

4.3.2 Well-Formed Parsed Entities

The document entity is well-formed if it matches the production labeled document. An external general parsed entity is well-formed if it matches the production labeled extParsedEnt. All external parameter entities are well-formed by definition.

Well-Formed External Parsed Entity

```
[78]    extParsedEnt   ::=   TextDecl? content
```

An internal general parsed entity is well-formed if its replacement text matches the production labeled content. All internal parameter entities are well-formed by definition.

A consequence of well-formedness in entities is that the logical and physical structures in an XML document are properly nested; no start-tag, end-tag, empty-element tag, element, comment, processing instruction, character reference, or entity reference can begin in one entity and end in another.

4.3.3 Character Encoding in Entities

Each external parsed entity in an XML document may use a different encoding for its characters. All XML processors must be able to read entities in both the UTF-8 and UTF-16 encodings. The terms "UTF-8" and "UTF-16" in this specification do not apply to character encodings with any other labels, even if the encodings or labels are very similar to UTF-8 or UTF-16.

Entities encoded in UTF-16 must begin with the Byte Order Mark described by Annex F of [ISO/IEC 10646], Annex H of [ISO/IEC 10646-2000], section 2.4 of [Unicode], and section 2.7 of [Unicode3] (the ZERO WIDTH NO-BREAK SPACE character, #xFEFF). This is an encoding signature, not part of either the markup or the character data of the XML document. XML processors must be able to use this character to differentiate between UTF-8 and UTF-16 encoded documents.

Although an XML processor is required to read only entities in the UTF-8 and UTF-16 encodings, it is recognized that other encodings are used around the world, and it may be desired for XML processors to read entities that use them. In the absence of external character encoding information (such as MIME headers), parsed entities which are stored in an encoding other than UTF-8 or UTF-16 must begin with a text declaration (see 4.3.1 The Text Declaration) containing an encoding declaration:

Encoding Declaration

```
[80]   EncodingDecl   ::=   S 'encoding' Eq ('"' EncName '"'
|  "'" EncName "'" )
[81]   EncName   ::=   [A-Za-z] ([A-Za-z0-9._] | '-')*   /*
Encoding name contains only Latin characters */
```

In the document entity, the encoding declaration is part of the XML declaration. The EncName is the name of the encoding used.

In an encoding declaration, the values "UTF-8", "UTF-16", "ISO-10646-UCS-2", and "ISO-10646-UCS-4" should be used for the various encodings and transformations of Unicode / ISO/IEC 10646, the values "ISO-8859-1", "ISO-8859-2", ... "ISO-8859-n" (where n is the part number) should be used for the parts of ISO 8859, and the values "ISO-2022-JP", "Shift_JIS", and "EUC-JP" should be used for the various encoded forms of JIS X-0208-1997. It is recommended that character encodings registered (as charsets) with the Internet Assigned Numbers Authority [IANA-CHARSETS], other than those just listed, be referred to using their registered names; other encodings should use names starting with an "x-" prefix. XML processors should match character encoding names in a case-insensitive way and should either interpret an IANA-registered name as the encoding registered at IANA for that name or treat it as unknown (processors are, of course, not required to support all IANA-registered encodings).

In the absence of information provided by an external transport protocol (e.g. HTTP or MIME), it is an error for an entity including an encoding declaration to be presented to the XML processor in an encoding other than that named in the declaration, or for an entity which begins with neither a Byte Order Mark nor an encoding declaration to use an encoding other than UTF-8. Note that since ASCII is a subset of UTF-8, ordinary ASCII entities do not strictly need an encoding declaration.

It is a fatal error for a TextDecl to occur other than at the beginning of an external entity.

It is a fatal error when an XML processor encounters an entity with an encoding that it is unable to process. It is a fatal error if an XML entity is determined (via default, encoding declaration, or higher-level protocol) to be in a certain encoding but contains octet sequences that are not legal in that encoding. It is also a fatal error if an XML entity contains no encoding declaration and its content is not legal UTF-8 or UTF-16.

Examples of text declarations containing encoding declarations:

```
<?xml encoding='UTF-8'?>
<?xml encoding='EUC-JP'?>
```

4.4 XML Processor Treatment of Entities and References

The table below summarizes the contexts in which character references, entity references, and invocations of unparsed entities might appear and the required behavior of an XML processor in each case. The labels in the leftmost column describe the recognition context:

Reference in Content

as a reference anywhere after the start-tag and before the end-tag of an element; corresponds to the nonterminal content.

Reference in Attribute Value

as a reference within either the value of an attribute in a start-tag, or a default value in an attribute declaration; corresponds to the nonterminal AttValue.

Occurs as Attribute Value

as a Name, not a reference, appearing either as the value of an attribute which has been declared as type ENTITY, or as one of the space-separated tokens in the value of an attribute which has been declared as type ENTITIES.

Reference in Entity Value

as a reference within a parameter or internal entity's literal entity value in the entity's declaration; corresponds to the nonterminal EntityValue.

Reference in DTD

as a reference within either the internal or external subsets of the DTD, but outside of an EntityValue, AttValue, PI, Comment, SystemLiteral, PubidLiteral, or the contents of an ignored conditional section (see 3.4 Conditional Sections).

		Entity Type			
			External		
		Internal	Parsed		
	Parameter	**General**	**General**	**Unparsed**	**Character**
Reference in Content	Not recognized	Included	Included if validating	Forbidden	Included
Reference in Attribute Value	Not recognized	Included in literal	Forbidden	Forbidden	Included
Occurs as Attribute Value	Not recognized	Forbidden	Forbidden	Notify	Not recognized
Reference in Entity Value	Included as literal	Bypassed	Bypassed	Forbidden	Included
Reference in DTD	Included as PE	Forbidden	Forbidden	Forbidden	Forbidden

4.4.1 Not Recognized

Outside the DTD, the % character has no special significance; thus, what would be parameter entity references in the DTD are not recognized as markup in content. Similarly, the names of unparsed entities are not recognized except when they appear in the value of an appropriately declared attribute.

4.4.2 Included

[Definition: An entity is included when its replacement text is retrieved and processed, in place of the reference itself, as though it were part of the document at the location the reference was recognized.] The replacement text may contain both character data and (except for parameter entities) markup, which must be recognized in the usual way. (The string "AT&T;" expands to "AT&T;" and the remaining ampersand is not recognized as an entity-reference delimiter.) A character reference is included when the indicated character is processed in place of the reference itself.

4.4.3 Included If Validating

When an XML processor recognizes a reference to a parsed entity, in order to validate the document, the processor must include its replacement text. If the entity is external, and the processor is not attempting to validate the XML document, the processor may, but need not, include the entity's replacement text. If a non-validating processor does not include the replacement text, it must inform the application that it recognized, but did not read, the entity.

This rule is based on the recognition that the automatic inclusion provided by the SGML and XML entity mechanism, primarily designed to support modularity in authoring, is not necessarily appropriate for other applications, in particular document browsing. Browsers, for example, when encountering an external parsed entity reference, might choose to provide a visual indication of the entity's presence and retrieve it for display only on demand.

4.4.4 Forbidden

The following are forbidden, and constitute fatal errors:
- the appearance of a reference to an unparsed entity.
- the appearance of any character or general-entity reference in the DTD except within an EntityValue or AttValue.
- a reference to an external entity in an attribute value.

4.4.5 Included in Literal

When an entity reference appears in an attribute value, or a parameter entity reference appears in a literal entity value, its replacement text is processed in place of the reference itself as though it were part of the document at the location the reference was recognized, except that a single or double quote character in the replacement text is always treated as a normal data character and will not terminate the literal. For example, this is well-formed:

```
<!-  ->
<!ENTITY % YN '"Yes"' >
<!ENTITY WhatHeSaid "He said %YN;" >
```

while this is not:

```
<!ENTITY EndAttr "27'" >
<element attribute='a-&EndAttr;>
```

4.4.6 Notify

When the name of an unparsed entity appears as a token in the value of an attribute of declared type ENTITY or ENTITIES, a validating processor must inform the application of the system and public (if any) identifiers for both the entity and its associated notation.

4.4.7 Bypassed

When a general entity reference appears in the EntityValue in an entity declaration, it is bypassed and left as is.

4.4.8 Included as PE

Just as with external parsed entities, parameter entities need only be included if validating. When a parameter-entity reference is recognized in the DTD and included, its replacement text is enlarged by the attachment of one leading and one following space (#x20) character; the intent is to constrain the replacement text of parameter entities to contain an integral number of grammatical tokens in the DTD. This behavior does not apply to parameter entity references within entity values; these are described in 4.4.5 Included in Literal.

4.5 Construction of Internal Entity Replacement Text

In discussing the treatment of internal entities, it is useful to distinguish two forms of the entity's value. [Definition: The literal entity value is the quoted string actually present in the entity declaration, corresponding to the non-terminal EntityValue.] [Definition: The replacement text is the content of the entity, after replacement of character references and parameter-entity references.]

The literal entity value as given in an internal entity declaration (EntityValue) may contain character, parameter-entity, and general-entity references. Such references must be contained entirely within the literal entity value. The actual replacement text that is included as described above must contain the replacement text of any parameter entities referred to, and must contain the character referred to, in place of any character references in the literal entity value; however, general-entity references must be left as-is, unexpanded. For example, given the following declarations:

```
<!ENTITY % pub    "&#xc9;ditions Gallimard" >
<!ENTITY    rights "All rights reserved" >
<!ENTITY    book   "La Peste: Albert Camus,
&#xA9; 1947 %pub;. &rights;" >
```

then the replacement text for the entity "book" is:

```
La Peste: Albert Camus,
© 1947 Éditions Gallimard. &rights;
```

The general-entity reference "&rights;" would be expanded should the reference "&book;" appear in the document's content or an attribute value.

These simple rules may have complex interactions; for a detailed discussion of a difficult example, see D Expansion of Entity and Character References.

4.6 Predefined Entities

[Definition: Entity and character references can both be used to escape the left angle bracket, ampersand, and other delimiters. A set of general entities (amp, lt, gt, apos, quot) is specified for this purpose. Numeric character references may also be used; they are expanded immediately when recognized and must be treated as character data, so the numeric character references "<" and "&" may be used to escape < and & when they occur in character data.]

All XML processors must recognize these entities whether they are declared or not. For interoperability, valid XML documents should declare these entities, like any others, before using them. If the entities lt or amp are declared, they must be declared as internal entities whose replacement text is a character reference to the respective character (less-than sign or ampersand) being escaped; the double escaping is required for these entities so that references to them produce a well-formed result. If the entities gt, apos, or quot are declared, they must be declared as internal entities whose replacement text is the single character being escaped (or a character reference to that character; the double escaping here is unnecessary but harmless). For example:

```
<!ENTITY lt     "&#38;#60;">
<!ENTITY gt     "&#62;">
<!ENTITY amp    "&#38;#38;">
<!ENTITY apos   "&#39;">
<!ENTITY quot   "&#34;">
```

4.7 Notation Declarations

[Definition: Notations identify by name the format of unparsed entities, the format of elements which bear a notation attribute, or the application to which a processing instruction is addressed.]

[Definition: Notation declarations provide a name for the notation, for use in entity and attribute-list declarations and in attribute specifications, and an external identifier for the notation which may allow an XML processor or its client application to locate a helper application capable of processing data in the given notation.]

Notation Declarations

```
[82]   NotationDecl  ::=   '<!NOTATION' S Name S (Exter-
nalID | PublicID) S? '>'   [VC: Unique Notation Name]
[83]   PublicID  ::=   'PUBLIC' S PubidLiteral
```

Validity constraint: Unique Notation Name

Only one notation declaration can declare a given Name.

XML processors must provide applications with the name and external identifier(s) of any notation declared and referred to in an attribute value, attribute definition, or entity declaration. They may additionally resolve the external identifier into the system identifier, file name, or other information needed to allow the application to call a processor for data in the notation described. (It is not an error, however, for XML documents to declare and refer to notations for which notation-specific applications are not available on the system where the XML processor or application is running.)

4.8 Document Entity

[Definition: The document entity serves as the root of the entity tree and a starting-point for an XML processor.] This specification does not specify how the document entity is to be located by an XML processor; unlike other entities, the document entity has no name and might well appear on a processor input stream without any identification at all.

◆ 5 Conformance

5.1 Validating and Non-Validating Processors

Conforming XML processors fall into two classes: validating and non-validating.

Validating and non-validating processors alike must report violations of this specification's well-formedness constraints in the content of the document entity and any other parsed entities that they read.

[Definition: Validating processors must, at user option, report violations of the constraints expressed by the declarations in the DTD, and failures to fulfill the validity constraints given in this specification.] To accomplish this, validating XML processors must read and process the entire DTD and all external parsed entities referenced in the document.

Non-validating processors are required to check only the document entity, including the entire internal DTD subset, for well-formedness. [Definition: While they are not required to check the document for validity, they are required to process all the declarations they read in the internal DTD subset and in any parameter entity that they read, up to the first reference to a parameter entity that they do not read; that is to say, they must use the information in those declarations to normalize attribute values, include the replacement text of internal entities, and supply default attribute values.] Except when standalone="yes", they must not process entity declarations or attribute-list declarations encountered after a reference to a parameter entity that is not read, since the entity may have contained overriding declarations.

5.2 Using XML Processors

The behavior of a validating XML processor is highly predictable; it must read every piece of a document and report all well-formedness and validity violations. Less is required of a non-validating processor; it need not read any part of the document other than the document entity. This has two effects that may be important to users of XML processors:

- Certain well-formedness errors, specifically those that require reading external entities, may not be detected by a non-validating processor. Examples include the constraints entitled Entity Declared, Parsed Entity, and No Recursion, as well as some of the cases described as forbidden in 4.4 XML Processor Treatment of Entities and References.
- The information passed from the processor to the application may vary, depending on whether the processor reads parameter and external entities. For example, a non-validating processor may not normalize attribute values, include the replacement text of internal entities, or supply default attribute values, where doing so depends on having read declarations in external or parameter entities.
- For maximum reliability in interoperating between different XML processors, applications which use non-validating processors should not rely on any behaviors not required of such processors. Applications which require facilities such as

the use of default attributes or internal entities which are declared in external entities should use validating XML processors.

◆ 6 Notation

The formal grammar of XML is given in this specification using a simple Extended Backus-Naur Form (EBNF) notation. Each rule in the grammar defines one symbol, in the form

symbol ::= expression

Symbols are written with an initial capital letter if they are the start symbol of a regular language, otherwise with an initial lower case letter. Literal strings are quoted.

Within the expression on the right-hand side of a rule, the following expressions are used to match strings of one or more characters:

#xN

where N is a hexadecimal integer, the expression matches the character in ISO/IEC 10646 whose canonical (UCS-4) code value, when interpreted as an unsigned binary number, has the value indicated. The number of leading zeros in the #xN form is insignificant; the number of leading zeros in the corresponding code value is governed by the character encoding in use and is not significant for XML.

[a-zA-Z], [#xN-#xN]

matches any Char with a value in the range(s) indicated (inclusive).

[abc], [#xN#xN#xN]

matches any Char with a value among the characters enumerated. Enumerations and ranges can be mixed in one set of brackets.

[^a-z], [^#xN-#xN]

matches any Char with a value outside the range indicated.

[^abc], [^#xN#xN#xN]

matches any Char with a value not among the characters given. Enumerations and ranges of forbidden values can be mixed in one set of brackets.

"string"

matches a literal string matching that given inside the double quotes.

'string'

matches a literal string matching that given inside the single quotes.

These symbols may be combined to match more complex patterns as follows, where A and B represent simple expressions:

(expression)

expression is treated as a unit and may be combined as described in this list.

A?

matches A or nothing; optional A.

A B

matches A followed by B. This operator has higher precedence than alternation; thus A B | C D is identical to (A B) | (C D).

A | B

matches A or B but not both.

A - B

matches any string that matches A but does not match B.

A+

matches one or more occurrences of A.Concatenation has higher precedence than alternation; thus A+ | B+ is identical to (A+) | (B+).

A*

matches zero or more occurrences of A. Concatenation has higher precedence than alternation; thus A* | B* is identical to (A*) | (B*).

Other notations used in the productions are:

/* ... */

comment.

[wfc: ...]

well-formedness constraint; this identifies by name a constraint on well-formed documents associated with a production.

[vc: ...]

validity constraint; this identifies by name a constraint on valid documents associated with a production.

◆ A References

A.1 Normative References

IANA-CHARSETS
(Internet Assigned Numbers Authority) Official Names for Character Sets, ed. Keld Simonsen et al. See ftp://ftp.isi.edu/in-notes/iana/assignments/character-sets.

IETF RFC 1766
> IETF (Internet Engineering Task Force). RFC 1766: Tags for the Identification of Languages, ed. H. Alvestrand. 1995. (See "http://www.ietf.org/rfc/rfc1766.txt".)

ISO/IEC 10646
> ISO (International Organization for Standardization). ISO/IEC 10646-1993 (E). Information technology—Universal Multiple-Octet Coded Character Set (UCS)—Part 1: Architecture and Basic Multilingual Plane. [Geneva]: International Organization for Standardization, 1993 (plus amendments AM 1 through AM 7).

ISO/IEC 10646-2000
> ISO (International Organization for Standardization). ISO/IEC 10646-1:2000. Information technology—Universal Multiple-Octet Coded Character Set (UCS)—Part 1:

Architecture and Basic Multilingual Plane. [Geneva]: International Organization for Standardization, 2000.

Unicode
> The Unicode Consortium. The Unicode Standard, Version 2.0. Reading, Mass.: Addison-Wesley Developers Press, 1996.

Unicode3
> The Unicode Consortium. The Unicode Standard, Version 3.0. Reading, Mass.: Addison-Wesley Developers Press, 2000. ISBN 0-201-61633-5.

A.2 Other References

Aho/Ullman
> Aho, Alfred V., Ravi Sethi, and Jeffrey D. Ullman. Compilers: Principles, Techniques, and Tools. Reading: Addison-Wesley, 1986, rpt. corr. 1988.

Berners-Lee et al.
> Berners-Lee, T., R. Fielding, and L. Masinter. Uniform Resource Identifiers (URI): Generic Syntax and Semantics. 1997. (Work in progress; see updates to RFC1738.)

Brüggemann-Klein
> Brüggemann-Klein, Anne. Formal Models in Document Processing. Habilitationsschrift. Faculty of Mathematics at the University of Freiburg, 1993. (See ftp://ftp.informatik.uni-freiburg.de/documents/papers/brueggem/habil.ps.)

Brüggemann-Klein and Wood
> Brüggemann-Klein, Anne, and Derick Wood. Deterministic Regular Languages. Universität Freiburg, Institut für Informatik, Bericht 38, Oktober 1991. Extended abstract in A. Finkel, M. Jantzen, Hrsg., STACS 1992, S. 173-184. Springer-Verlag, Berlin 1992. Lecture Notes in Computer Science 577. Full version titled One-Unambiguous Regular Languages in Information and Computation 140 (2): 229-253, February 1998.

Clark
> James Clark. Comparison of SGML and XML. See http://www.w3.org/TR/NOTE-sgml-xml-971215.

IANA-LANGCODES
> (Internet Assigned Numbers Authority) Registry of Language Tags, ed. Keld Simonsen et al. (See http://www.isi.edu/in-notes/iana/assignments/languages/.)

IETF RFC2141

IETF (Internet Engineering Task Force). RFC 2141: URN Syntax, ed. R. Moats. 1997. (See http://www.ietf.org/rfc/rfc2141.txt.)

IETF RFC 2279

IETF (Internet Engineering Task Force). RFC 2279: UTF-8, a transformation format of ISO 10646, ed. F. Yergeau, 1998. (See http://www.ietf.org/rfc/rfc2279.txt.)

IETF RFC 2376

IETF (Internet Engineering Task Force). RFC 2376: XML Media Types. ed. E. Whitehead, M. Murata. 1998. (See http://www.ietf.org/rfc/rfc2376.txt.)

IETF RFC 2396

IETF (Internet Engineering Task Force). RFC 2396: Uniform Resource Identifiers (URI): Generic Syntax. T. Berners-Lee, R. Fielding, L. Masinter. 1998. (See http://www.ietf.org/rfc/rfc2396.txt.)

IETF RFC 2732

IETF (Internet Engineering Task Force). RFC 2732: Format for Literal IPv6 Addresses in URL's. R. Hinden, B. Carpenter, L. Masinter. 1999. (See http://www.ietf.org/rfc/rfc2732.txt.)

IETF RFC 2781

IETF (Internet Engineering Task Force). RFC 2781: UTF-16, an encoding of ISO 10646, ed. P. Hoffman, F. Yergeau. 2000. (See http://www.ietf.org/rfc/rfc2781.txt.)

ISO 639

(International Organization for Standardization). ISO 639:1988 (E). Code for the representation of names of languages. [Geneva]: International Organization for Standardization, 1988.

ISO 3166

(International Organization for Standardization). ISO 3166-1:1997 (E). Codes for the representation of names of countries and their subdivisions—Part 1: Country codes [Geneva]: International Organization for Standardization, 1997.

ISO 8879

ISO (International Organization for Standardization). ISO 8879: 1986(E). Information processing—Text and Office Systems—Standard Generalized Markup Language

(SGML). First edition—1986-10-15. [Geneva]: International Organization for Standardization, 1986.

ISO/IEC 10744

ISO (International Organization for Standardization). ISO/IEC 10744-1992 (E). Information technology—Hypermedia/Time-based Structuring Language (HyTime). [Geneva]: International Organization for Standardization, 1992. Extended Facilities Annexe. [Geneva]: International Organization for Standardization, 1996.

WEBSGML

ISO (International Organization for Standardization). ISO 8879:1986 TC2. Information technology—Document Description and Processing Languages. [Geneva]: International Organization for Standardization, 1998. (See http://www.sgmlsource .com/8879rev/n0029.htm.)

XML Names

Tim Bray, Dave Hollander, and Andrew Layman, editors. Namespaces in XML. Textuality, Hewlett-Packard, and Microsoft. World Wide Web Consortium, 1999. (See http://www.w3.org/TR/REC-xml-names/.)

◆ B Character Classes

Following the characteristics defined in the Unicode standard, characters are classed as base characters (among others, these contain the alphabetic characters of the Latin alphabet), ideographic characters, and combining characters (among others, this class contains most diacritics) Digits and extenders are also distinguished.

Characters

```
[84]      Letter      ::=      BaseChar | Ideographic
[85]      BaseChar    ::=      [#x0041-#x005A] | [#x0061-
#x007A] | [#x00C0-#x00D6] | [#x00D8-#x00F6] | [#x00F8-
#x00FF] | [#x0100-#x0131] | [#x0134-#x013E]
| [#x0141-#x0148] | [#x014A-#x017E] | [#x0180-#x01C3]
| [#x01CD-#x01F0] | [#x01F4-#x01F5] | [#x01FA-#x0217]
| [#x0250-#x02A8] | [#x02BB-#x02C1] | #x0386 | [#x0388-
#x038A] | #x038C | [#x038E-#x03A1] | [#x03A3-#x03CE]
| [#x03D0-#x03D6] | #x03DA | #x03DC | #x03DE | #x03E0
| [#x03E2-#x03F3] | [#x0401-#x040C] | [#x040E-#x044F]
| [#x0451-#x045C] | [#x045E-#x0481] | [#x0490-#x04C4]
| [#x04C7-#x04C8] | [#x04CB-#x04CC] | [#x04D0-#x04EB]
```

```
| [#x04EE-#x04F5] | [#x04F8-#x04F9] | [#x0531-#x0556]
| #x0559 | [#x0561-#x0586] | [#x05D0-#x05EA] | [#x05F0-
#x05F2] | [#x0621-#x063A] | [#x0641-#x064A] | [#x0671-
#x06B7] | [#x06BA-#x06BE] | [#x06C0-#x06CE]
| [#x06D0-#x06D3] | #x06D5 | [#x06E5-#x06E6] | [#x0905-
#x0939] | #x093D | [#x0958-#x0961] | [#x0985-#x098C]
| [#x098F-#x0990] | [#x0993-#x09A8] | [#x09AA-#x09B0]
| #x09B2 | [#x09B6-#x09B9] | [#x09DC-#x09DD] | [#x09DF-
#x09E1] | [#x09F0-#x09F1] | [#x0A05-#x0A0A] | [#x0A0F-
#x0A10] | [#x0A13-#x0A28] | [#x0A2A-#x0A30]
| [#x0A32-#x0A33] | [#x0A35-#x0A36] | [#x0A38-#x0A39]
| [#x0A59-#x0A5C] | #x0A5E | [#x0A72-#x0A74] | [#x0A85-
#x0A8B] | #x0A8D | [#x0A8F-#x0A91] | [#x0A93-#x0AA8]
| [#x0AAA-#x0AB0] | [#x0AB2-#x0AB3] | [#x0AB5-#x0AB9]
| #x0ABD | #x0AE0 | [#x0B05-#x0B0C] | [#x0B0F-#x0B10]
| [#x0B13-#x0B28] | [#x0B2A-#x0B30] | [#x0B32-#x0B33]
| [#x0B36-#x0B39] | #x0B3D | [#x0B5C-#x0B5D] | [#x0B5F-
#x0B61] | [#x0B85-#x0B8A] | [#x0B8E-#x0B90] | [#x0B92-
#x0B95] | [#x0B99-#x0B9A] | #x0B9C | [#x0B9E-#x0B9F]
| [#x0BA3-#x0BA4] | [#x0BA8-#x0BAA] | [#x0BAE-#x0BB5]
| [#x0BB7-#x0BB9] | [#x0C05-#x0C0C] | [#x0C0E-#x0C10]
| [#x0C12-#x0C28] | [#x0C2A-#x0C33] | [#x0C35-#x0C39]
| [#x0C60-#x0C61] | [#x0C85-#x0C8C] | [#x0C8E-#x0C90]
| [#x0C92-#x0CA8] | [#x0CAA-#x0CB3] | [#x0CB5-#x0CB9]
| #x0CDE | [#x0CE0-#x0CE1] | [#x0D05-#x0D0C] | [#x0D0E-
#x0D10] | [#x0D12-#x0D28] | [#x0D2A-#x0D39] | [#x0D60-
#x0D61] | [#x0E01-#x0E2E] | #x0E30 | [#x0E32-#x0E33]
| [#x0E40-#x0E45] | [#x0E81-#x0E82] | #x0E84 | [#x0E87-
#x0E88] | #x0E8A | #x0E8D | [#x0E94-#x0E97] | [#x0E99-
#x0E9F] | [#x0EA1-#x0EA3] | #x0EA5 | #x0EA7
| [#x0EAA-#x0EAB] | [#x0EAD-#x0EAE] | #x0EB0 | [#x0EB2-
#x0EB3] | #x0EBD | [#x0EC0-#x0EC4] | [#x0F40-#x0F47]
| [#x0F49-#x0F69] | [#x10A0-#x10C5] | [#x10D0-#x10F6]
| #x1100 | [#x1102-#x1103] | [#x1105-#x1107] | #x1109
| [#x110B-#x110C] | [#x110E-#x1112] | #x113C | #x113E
| #x1140 | #x114C | #x114E | #x1150 | [#x1154-#x1155]
| #x1159 | [#x115F-#x1161] | #x1163 | #x1165 | #x1167
| #x1169 | [#x116D-#x116E] | [#x1172-#x1173] | #x1175
| #x119E | #x11A8 | #x11AB | [#x11AE-#x11AF] | [#x11B7-
#x11B8] | #x11BA | [#x11BC-#x11C2] | #x11EB | #x11F0
| #x11F9 | [#x1E00-#x1E9B] | [#x1EA0-#x1EF9] | [#x1F00-
#x1F15] | [#x1F18-#x1F1D] | [#x1F20-#x1F45] | [#x1F48-
#x1F4D] | [#x1F50-#x1F57] | #x1F59 | #x1F5B | #x1F5D
| [#x1F5F-#x1F7D] | [#x1F80-#x1FB4] | [#x1FB6-#x1FBC]
| #x1FBE | [#x1FC2-#x1FC4] | [#x1FC6-#x1FCC] | [#x1FD0-
#x1FD3] | [#x1FD6-#x1FDB] | [#x1FE0-#x1FEC] | [#x1FF2-
#x1FF4] | [#x1FF6-#x1FFC] | #x2126 | [#x212A-#x212B]
| #x212E | [#x2180-#x2182] | [#x3041-#x3094] | [#x30A1-
#x30FA] | [#x3105-#x312C] | [#xAC00-#xD7A3]
[86]        Ideographic        ::=        [#x4E00-#x9FA5]
| #x3007 | [#x3021-#x3029]
```

```
[87]    CombiningChar   ::=         [#x0300-#x0345]
| [#x0360-#x0361] | [#x0483-#x0486] | [#x0591-#x05A1]
| [#x05A3-#x05B9] | [#x05BB-#x05BD] | #x05BF | [#x05C1-
#x05C2] | #x05C4 | [#x064B-#x0652] | #x0670 | [#x06D6-
#x06DC] | [#x06DD-#x06DF] | [#x06E0-#x06E4]
| [#x06E7-#x06E8] | [#x06EA-#x06ED] | [#x0901-#x0903]
| #x093C | [#x093E-#x094C] | #x094D | [#x0951-#x0954]
| [#x0962-#x0963] | [#x0981-#x0983] | #x09BC | #x09BE
| #x09BF | [#x09C0-#x09C4] | [#x09C7-#x09C8] | [#x09CB-
#x09CD] | #x09D7 | [#x09E2-#x09E3] | #x0A02 | #x0A3C
| #x0A3E | #x0A3F | [#x0A40-#x0A42] | [#x0A47-#x0A48]
| [#x0A4B-#x0A4D] | [#x0A70-#x0A71] | [#x0A81-#x0A83]
| #x0ABC | [#x0ABE-#x0AC5] | [#x0AC7-#x0AC9] | [#x0ACB-
#x0ACD] | [#x0B01-#x0B03] | #x0B3C | [#x0B3E-#x0B43]
| [#x0B47-#x0B48] | [#x0B4B-#x0B4D] | [#x0B56-#x0B57]
| [#x0B82-#x0B83] | [#x0BBE-#x0BC2] | [#x0BC6-#x0BC8]
| [#x0BCA-#x0BCD] | #x0BD7 | [#x0C01-#x0C03] | [#x0C3E-
#x0C44] | [#x0C46-#x0C48] | [#x0C4A-#x0C4D] | [#x0C55-
#x0C56] | [#x0C82-#x0C83] | [#x0CBE-#x0CC4]
| [#x0CC6-#x0CC8] | [#x0CCA-#x0CCD] | [#x0CD5-#x0CD6]
| [#x0D02-#x0D03] | [#x0D3E-#x0D43] | [#x0D46-#x0D48]
| [#x0D4A-#x0D4D] | #x0D57 | #x0E31 | [#x0E34-#x0E3A]
| [#x0E47-#x0E4E] | #x0EB1 | [#x0EB4-#x0EB9] | [#x0EBB-
#x0EBC] | [#x0EC8-#x0ECD] | [#x0F18-#x0F19] | #x0F35
| #x0F37 | #x0F39 | #x0F3E | #x0F3F | [#x0F71-#x0F84]
| [#x0F86-#x0F8B] | [#x0F90-#x0F95] | #x0F97 | [#x0F99-
#x0FAD] | [#x0FB1-#x0FB7] | #x0FB9 | [#x20D0-#x20DC]
| #x20E1 | [#x302A-#x302F] | #x3099 | #x309A
[88]        Digit       ::=         [#x0030-#x0039] | [#x0660-
#x0669] | [#x06F0-#x06F9] | [#x0966-#x096F] | [#x09E6-
#x09EF] | [#x0A66-#x0A6F] | [#x0AE6-#x0AEF]
| [#x0B66-#x0B6F] | [#x0BE7-#x0BEF] | [#x0C66-#x0C6F]
| [#x0CE6-#x0CEF] | [#x0D66-#x0D6F] | [#x0E50-#x0E59]
| [#x0ED0-#x0ED9] | [#x0F20-#x0F29]
[89]        Extender    ::=         #x00B7 | #x02D0 | #x02D1
| #x0387 | #x0640 | #x0E46 | #x0EC6 | #x3005 | [#x3031-
#x3035] | [#x309D-#x309E] | [#x30FC-#x30FE]
```

The character classes defined here can be derived from the Unicode 2.0 character database as follows:

- Name start characters must have one of the categories Ll, Lu, Lo, Lt, Nl.
- Name characters other than Name-start characters must have one of the categories Mc, Me, Mn, Lm, or Nd.
- Characters in the compatibility area (i.e. with character code greater than #xF900 and less than #xFFFE) are not allowed in XML names.
- Characters which have a font or compatibility decomposition (i.e. those with a "compatibility formatting tag" in

field 5 of the database — marked by field 5 beginning with a "<") are not allowed.

- The following characters are treated as name-start characters rather than name characters, because the property file classifies them as Alphabetic: [#x02BB-#x02C1], #x0559, #x06E5, #x06E6.
- Characters #x20DD-#x20E0 are excluded (in accordance with Unicode 2.0, section 5.14).
- Character #x00B7 is classified as an extender, because the property list so identifies it.
- Character #x0387 is added as a name character, because #x00B7 is its canonical equivalent.
- Characters ':' and '_' are allowed as name-start characters.
- Characters '-' and '.' are allowed as name characters.

◆ C XML and SGML (Non-Normative)

XML is designed to be a subset of SGML, in that every XML document should also be a conforming SGML document. For a detailed comparison of the additional restrictions that XML places on documents beyond those of SGML, see [Clark].

◆ D Expansion of Entity and Character References (Non-Normative)

This appendix contains some examples illustrating the sequence of entity- and character-reference recognition and expansion, as specified in 4.4 XML Processor Treatment of Entities and References.

If the DTD contains the declaration

```
<!ENTITY example "<p>An ampersand (&#38;#38;) may be escaped
numerically (&#38;#38;#38;) or with a general entity
(&amp;amp;).</p>" >
```

then the XML processor will recognize the character references when it parses the entity declaration, and resolve them before storing the following string as the value of the entity "example":

```
<p>An ampersand (&#38;) may be escaped
numerically (&#38;#38;) or with a general entity
(&amp;amp;).</p>
```

A reference in the document to "&example;" will cause the text to be reparsed, at which time the start- and end-tags of the p element will be recognized and the three references will be recognized and expanded, resulting in a p element with the following content (all data, no delimiters or markup):

An ampersand (&) may be escaped numerically (&) or with a general entity (&).

A more complex example will illustrate the rules and their effects fully. In the following example, the line numbers are solely for reference.

```
1 <?xml version='1.0'?>
2 <!DOCTYPE test [
3 <!ELEMENT test (#PCDATA) >
4 <!ENTITY % xx '&#37;zz;'>
5 <!ENTITY % zz '&#60;!ENTITY tricky "error-prone" >' >
6 %xx;
7 ]>
8 <test>This sample shows a &tricky; method.</test>
```

This produces the following:

- in line 4, the reference to character 37 is expanded immediately, and the parameter entity "xx" is stored in the symbol table with the value "%zz;". Since the replacement text is not rescanned, the reference to parameter entity "zz" is not recognized. (And it would be an error if it were, since "zz" is not yet declared.)

- in line 5, the character reference "<" is expanded immediately and the parameter entity "zz" is stored with the replacement text "<!ENTITY tricky "error-prone" >", which is a well-formed entity declaration.

- in line 6, the reference to "xx" is recognized, and the replacement text of "xx" (namely "%zz;") is parsed. The reference to "zz" is recognized in its turn, and its replacement text ("<!ENTITY tricky "error-prone" >") is parsed. The general entity "tricky" has now been declared, with the replacement text "error-prone".

- in line 8, the reference to the general entity "tricky" is recognized, and it is expanded, so the full content of the test element is the self-describing (and ungrammatical) string. This sample shows a error-prone method.

◆ E Deterministic Content Models (Non-Normative)

As noted in 3.2.1 Element Content, it is required that content models in element type declarations be deterministic. This requirement is for compatibility with SGML (which calls deterministic content models "unambiguous"); XML processors built using SGML systems may flag non-deterministic content models as errors.

For example, the content model ((b, c) | (b, d)) is non-deterministic, because given an initial b the XML processor cannot know which b in the model is being matched without looking ahead to see which element follows the b. In this case, the two references to b can be collapsed into a single reference, making the model read (b, (c | d)). An initial b now clearly matches only a single name in the content model. The processor doesn't need to look ahead to see what follows; either c or d would be accepted.

More formally: a finite state automaton may be constructed from the content model using the standard algorithms, e.g. algorithm 3.5 in section 3.9 of Aho, Sethi, and Ullman [Aho/Ullman]. In many such algorithms, a follow set is constructed for each position in the regular expression (i.e., each leaf node in the syntax tree for the regular expression); if any position has a follow set in which more than one following position is labeled with the same element type name, then the content model is in error and may be reported as an error.

Algorithms exist which allow many but not all non-deterministic content models to be reduced automatically to equivalent deterministic models; see Brüggemann-Klein 1991 [Brüggemann-Klein].

◆ F Autodetection of Character Encodings (Non-Normative)

The XML encoding declaration functions as an internal label on each entity, indicating which character encoding is in use. Before an XML processor can read the internal label, however, it apparently has to know what character encoding is in use—which is what the internal label is trying to indicate. In the general case, this is a hopeless situation. It is not entirely hopeless in XML, however, because XML limits the general case in two ways: each implementation is assumed to support only a finite set of character encodings, and the XML encoding declaration is restricted in position and content in order to make it feasible to autodetect the character encoding in use in each entity in normal cases. Also, in many cases other sources of information are available in addition to the XML data stream itself. Two cases may be distinguished, depending on whether the XML entity is presented to the processor without, or with, any accompanying (external) information. We consider the first case first.

F.1 Detection Without External Encoding Information

Because each XML entity not accompanied by external encoding information and not in UTF-8 or UTF-16 encoding must begin with an XML encoding declaration, in which the first characters must be '<?xml', any conforming processor can detect, after two to four octets of input, which of the following cases apply. In reading this list, it may help to know that in UCS-4, '<' is"#x0000003C" and '?' is "#x0000003F", and the Byte Order Mark required of UTF-16 data streams is "#xFEFF". The notation ## is used to denote any byte value except that two consecutive ##s cannot be both 00.

With a Byte Order Mark:

```
00 00 FE FF      UCS-4, big-endian machine (1234 order)
FF FE 00 00      UCS-4, little-endian machine (4321 order)
00 00 FF FE      UCS-4, unusual octet order (2143)
FE FF 00 00      UCS-4, unusual octet order (3412)
FE FF ## ##      UTF-16, big-endian
FF FE ## ##      UTF-16, little-endian
EF BB BF         UTF-8
```

Without a Byte Order Mark:

```
00 00 00 3C      UCS-4 or other encoding with a 32-bit code unit and ASCII
3C 00 00 00      characters encoded as ASCII values, in respectively big-
00 00 3C 00      endian (1234), little-endian (4321) and two unusual byte
00 3C 00 00      orders (2143 and 3412). The encoding declaration must be
                 read to determine which of UCS-4 or other supported 32-bit
                 encodings applies.

00 3C 00 3F      UTF-16BE or big-endian ISO-10646-UCS-2 or other encoding
                 with a 16-bit code unit in big-endian order and ASCII char-
                 acters encoded as ASCII values (the encoding declaration
                 must be read to determine which)
```

3C 00 3F 00	UTF-16LE or little-endian ISO-10646-UCS-2 or other encoding with a 16-bit code unit in little-endian order and ASCII characters encoded as ASCII values (the encoding declaration must be read to determine which)
3C 3F 78 6D	UTF-8, ISO 646, ASCII, some part of ISO 8859, Shift-JIS, EUC, or any other 7-bit, 8-bit, or mixed-width encoding which ensures that the characters of ASCII have their normal positions, width, and values; the actual encoding declaration must be read to detect which of these applies, but since all of these encodings use the same bit patterns for the relevant ASCII characters, the encoding declaration itself may be read reliably
4C 6F A7 94	EBCDIC (in some flavor; the full encoding declaration must be read to tell which code page is in use)
Other	UTF-8 without an encoding declaration, or else the data stream is mislabeled (lacking a required encoding declaration), corrupt, fragmentary, or enclosed in a wrapper of some kind

Note:

In cases above which do not require reading the encoding declaration to determine the encoding, section 4.3.3 still requires that the encoding declaration, if present, be read and that the encoding name be checked to match the actual encoding of the entity. Also, it is possible that new character encodings will be invented that will make it necessary to use the encoding declaration to determine the encoding, in cases where this is not required at present.

This level of autodetection is enough to read the XML encoding declaration and parse the character-encoding identifier, which is still necessary to distinguish the individual members of each family of encodings (e.g. to tell UTF-8 from 8859, and the parts of 8859 from each other, or to distinguish the specific EBCDIC code page in use, and so on).

Because the contents of the encoding declaration are restricted to characters from the ASCII repertoire (however encoded), a processor can reliably read the entire encoding declaration as soon as it has detected which family of encodings is in use. Since in practice, all widely used character encodings fall into one of the categories above, the XML encoding declaration allows reasonably reliable in-band labeling of character encodings, even when external sources of information at the operating-system or transport-protocol level are unreliable.

Character encodings such as UTF-7 that make overloaded usage of ASCII-valued bytes may fail to be reliably detected.

Once the processor has detected the character encoding in use, it can act appropriately, whether by invoking a separate input routine for each case, or by calling the proper conversion function on each character of input.

Like any self-labeling system, the XML encoding declaration will not work if any software changes the entity's character set or encoding without updating the encoding declaration. Implementors of character-encoding routines should be careful to ensure the accuracy of the internal and external information used to label the entity.

F.2 Priorities in the Presence of External Encoding Information

The second possible case occurs when the XML entity is accompanied by encoding information, as in some file systems and some network protocols. When multiple sources of information are available, their relative priority and the preferred method of handling conflict should be specified as part of the higher-level protocol used to deliver XML. In particular, please refer to [IETF RFC 2376] or its successor, which defines the text/xml and application/xml MIME types and provides some useful guidance. In the interests of interoperability, however, the following rule is recommended.

- If an XML entity is in a file, the Byte-Order Mark and encoding declaration are used (if present) to determine the character encoding.

◆ G W3C XML Working Group (Non-Normative)

This specification was prepared and approved for publication by the W3C XML Working Group (WG). WG approval of this specification does not necessarily imply that all WG members voted for its approval. The current and former members of the XML WG are:

- Jon Bosak, Sun (Chair)
- James Clark (Technical Lead)
- Tim Bray, Textuality and Netscape (XML Co-editor)
- Jean Paoli, Microsoft (XML Co-editor)
- C. M. Sperberg-McQueen, U. of Ill. (XML Co-editor)

- Dan Connolly, W3C (W3C Liaison)
- Paula Angerstein, Texcel
- Steve DeRose, INSO
- Dave Hollander, HP
- Eliot Kimber, ISOGEN
- Eve Maler, ArborText
- Tom Magliery, NCSA
- Murray Maloney, SoftQuad, Grif SA, Muzmo and Veo Systems
- MURATA Makoto (FAMILY Given), Fuji Xerox Information Systems
- Joel Nava, Adobe
- Conleth O'Connell, Vignette
- Peter Sharpe, SoftQuad
- John Tigue, DataChannel

◆ H W3C XML Core Group (Non-Normative)

The second edition of this specification was prepared by the W3C XML Core Working Group (WG). The members of the WG at the time of publication of this edition were:

- Paula Angerstein, Vignette
- Daniel Austin, Ask Jeeves
- Tim Boland
- Allen Brown, Microsoft
- Dan Connolly, W3C (Staff Contact)
- John Cowan, Reuters Limited
- John Evdemon, XMLSolutions Corporation
- Paul Grosso, Arbortext (Co-Chair)
- Arnaud Le Hors, IBM (Co-Chair)
- Eve Maler, Sun Microsystems (Second Edition Editor)
- Jonathan Marsh, Microsoft
- MURATA Makoto (FAMILY Given), IBM
- Mark Needleman, Data Research Associates
- David Orchard, Jamcracker
- Lew Shannon, NCR
- Richard Tobin, University of Edinburgh
- Daniel Veillard, W3C
- Dan Vint, Lexica
- Norman Walsh, Sun Microsystems
- François Yergeau, Alis Technologies (Errata List Editor)
- Kongyi Zhou, Oracle

◆ I Production Notes (Non-Normative)

This Second Edition was encoded in the XMLspec DTD (which has documentation available). The HTML versions were produced with a combination of the xmlspec.xsl, diffspec.xsl, and REC-xml-2e.xsl XSLT stylesheets. The PDF version was produced with the html2ps facility and a distiller program.

B XHTML DTD: Frameset

IN THIS CHAPTER

• Frameset DTD

XHTML has three DTDs: Strict, Transitional, and Frameset. The Strict DTD only contains elements that appear in HTML 4—no deprecated tags are included. The Transition DTD is the same as the Strict DTD, but it includes some deprecated tags. The Frameset DTD includes everything in the Transitional DTD, including `<frame>` *and* `<frameset>`.

◆ Frameset DTD

```
<!--
    Extensible HTML version 1.0 Frameset DTD

    This is the same as HTML 4.0 Frameset except for
    changes due to the differences between XML and SGML.

    Namespace = http://www.w3.org/1999/xhtml

    For further information, see: http://www.w3.org/TR/xhtml1

    Copyright (c) 1998-2000 W3C (MIT, INRIA, Keio),
    All Rights Reserved.

    This DTD module is identified by the PUBLIC and SYSTEM
identifiers:

    PUBLIC "-//W3C//DTD XHTML 1.0 Frameset//EN"
    SYSTEM "http://www.w3.org/TR/xhtml1/DTD/xhtml1-
frameset.dtd"
```

```
     $Revision: 1.1 $
     $Date: 2000/01/26 14:08:56 $

-->

<!--================= Character mnemonic entities
=========================-->

<!ENTITY % HTMLlat1 PUBLIC
   "-//W3C//ENTITIES Latin 1 for XHTML//EN"
   "xhtml-lat1.ent">
%HTMLlat1;

<!ENTITY % HTMLsymbol PUBLIC
   "-//W3C//ENTITIES Symbols for XHTML//EN"
   "xhtml-symbol.ent">
%HTMLsymbol;

<!ENTITY % HTMLspecial PUBLIC
   "-//W3C//ENTITIES Special for XHTML//EN"
   "xhtml-special.ent">
%HTMLspecial;

<!--================== Imported Names
====================================-->

<!ENTITY % ContentType "CDATA">
   <!-- media type, as per [RFC2045] -->

<!ENTITY % ContentTypes "CDATA">
   <!-- comma-separated list of media types, as per
[RFC2045] -->

<!ENTITY % Charset "CDATA">
   <!-- a character encoding, as per [RFC2045] -->

<!ENTITY % Charsets "CDATA">
   <!-- a space separated list of character encodings, as
per [RFC2045] -->

<!ENTITY % LanguageCode "NMTOKEN">
   <!-- a language code, as per [RFC1766] -->

<!ENTITY % Character "CDATA">
   <!-- a single character from [ISO10646] -->

<!ENTITY % Number "CDATA">
   <!-- one or more digits -->

<!ENTITY % LinkTypes "CDATA">
```

```
    <!-- space-separated list of link types -->

<!ENTITY % MediaDesc "CDATA">
    <!-- single or comma-separated list of media descriptors
-->

<!ENTITY % URI "CDATA">
    <!-- a Uniform Resource Identifier, see [RFC2396] -->

<!ENTITY % UriList "CDATA">
    <!-- a space separated list of Uniform Resource Identi-
fiers -->

<!ENTITY % Datetime "CDATA">
    <!-- date and time information. ISO date format -->

<!ENTITY % Script "CDATA">
    <!-- script expression -->

<!ENTITY % StyleSheet "CDATA">
    <!-- style sheet data -->

<!ENTITY % Text "CDATA">
    <!-- used for titles etc. -->

<!ENTITY % FrameTarget "NMTOKEN">
    <!-- render in this frame -->

<!ENTITY % Length "CDATA">
    <!-- nn for pixels or nn% for percentage length -->

<!ENTITY % MultiLength "CDATA">
    <!-- pixel, percentage, or relative -->

<!ENTITY % MultiLengths "CDATA">
    <!-- comma-separated list of MultiLength -->

<!ENTITY % Pixels "CDATA">
    <!-- integer representing length in pixels -->

<!-- these are used for image maps -->

<!ENTITY % Shape "(rect|circle|poly|default)">

<!ENTITY % Coords "CDATA">
    <!-- comma separated list of lengths -->

<!-- used for object, applet, img, input and iframe -->
<!ENTITY % ImgAlign "(top|middle|bottom|left|right)">

<!-- a color using sRGB: #RRGGBB as Hex values -->
```

```
<!ENTITY % Color "CDATA">

<!-- There are also 16 widely known color names with their
sRGB values:

    Black  = #000000    Green  = #008000
    Silver = #C0C0C0    Lime   = #00FF00
    Gray   = #808080    Olive  = #808000
    White  = #FFFFFF    Yellow = #FFFF00
    Maroon = #800000    Navy   = #000080
    Red    = #FF0000    Blue   = #0000FF
    Purple = #800080    Teal   = #008080
    Fuchsia= #FF00FF    Aqua   = #00FFFF
-->

<!--==================== Generic Attributes
================================-->

<!-- core attributes common to most elements
  id        document-wide unique id
  class     space separated list of classes
  style     associated style info
  title     advisory title/amplification
-->
<!ENTITY % coreattrs
 "id           ID              #IMPLIED
  class        CDATA           #IMPLIED
  style        %StyleSheet;    #IMPLIED
  title        %Text;          #IMPLIED"
  >

<!-- internationalization attributes
  lang          language code (backwards compatible)
  xml:lang      language code (as per XML 1.0 spec)
  dir           direction for weak/neutral text
-->
<!ENTITY % i18n
 "lang         %LanguageCode; #IMPLIED
  xml:lang     %LanguageCode; #IMPLIED
  dir          (ltr|rtl)       #IMPLIED"
  >

<!-- attributes for common UI events
  onclick      a pointer button was clicked
  ondblclick   a pointer button was double clicked
  onmousedown  a pointer button was pressed down
  onmouseup    a pointer button was released
  onmousemove  a pointer was moved onto the element
  onmouseout   a pointer was moved away from the element
  onkeypress   a key was pressed and released
  onkeydown    a key was pressed down
```

```
   onkeyup     a key was released
-->
<!ENTITY % events
 "onclick       %Script;       #IMPLIED
  ondblclick    %Script;       #IMPLIED
  onmousedown   %Script;       #IMPLIED
  onmouseup     %Script;       #IMPLIED
  onmouseover   %Script;       #IMPLIED
  onmousemove   %Script;       #IMPLIED
  onmouseout    %Script;       #IMPLIED
  onkeypress    %Script;       #IMPLIED
  onkeydown     %Script;       #IMPLIED
  onkeyup       %Script;       #IMPLIED"
  >


<!-- attributes for elements that can get the focus
  accesskey     accessibility key character
  tabindex      position in tabbing order
  onfocus       the element got the focus
  onblur        the element lost the focus
-->
<!ENTITY % focus
 "accesskey     %Character;    #IMPLIED
  tabindex      %Number;       #IMPLIED
  onfocus       %Script;       #IMPLIED
  onblur        %Script;       #IMPLIED"
  >


<!ENTITY % attrs "%coreattrs; %i18n; %events;">

<!-- text alignment for p, div, h1-h6. The default is
     align="left" for ltr headings, "right" for rtl -->

<!ENTITY % TextAlign "align (left|center|right) #IMPLIED">

<!--==================== Text Elements
=======================================-->

<!ENTITY % special
   "br | span | bdo |object | applet | img | map | iframe">

<!ENTITY % fontstyle "tt | i | b | big | small | u
                      | s | strike |font | basefont">

<!ENTITY % phrase "em | strong | dfn | code | q | sub | sup
|
                  samp | kbd | var | cite | abbr |
acronym">

<!ENTITY % inline.forms "input | select | textarea | label |
button">
```

```
<!-- these can occur at block or inline level -->
<!ENTITY % misc "ins | del | script | noscript">

<!ENTITY % inline "a | %special; | %fontstyle; | %phrase; |
%inline.forms;">

<!-- %Inline; covers inline or "text-level" elements -->
<!ENTITY % Inline "(#PCDATA | %inline; | %misc;)*">

<!--==================== Block level elements
================================-->

<!ENTITY % heading "h1|h2|h3|h4|h5|h6">
<!ENTITY % lists "ul | ol | dl | menu | dir">
<!ENTITY % blocktext "pre | hr | blockquote | address | cen-
ter">

<!ENTITY % block
    "p | %heading; | div | %lists; | %blocktext; | isindex |
fieldset | table">

<!ENTITY % Block "(%block; | form | %misc;)*">

<!-- %Flow; mixes Block and Inline and is used for list
items etc. -->
<!ENTITY % Flow "(#PCDATA | %block; | form | %inline; |
%misc;)*">

<!--==================== Content models for exclusions
======================-->

<!-- a elements use %Inline; excluding a -->

<!ENTITY % a.content
   "(#PCDATA | %special; | %fontstyle; | %phrase; |
%inline.forms; | %misc;)*">

<!-- pre uses %Inline excluding img, object, applet, big,
small,
     sub, sup, font, or basefont -->

<!ENTITY % pre.content
   "(#PCDATA | a | br | span | bdo | map | tt | i | b | u |
s |
      %phrase; | %inline.forms;)*">

<!-- form uses %Flow; excluding form -->

<!ENTITY % form.content "(#PCDATA | %block; | %inline; |
%misc;)*">
```

```
<!-- button uses %Flow; but excludes a, form, form controls,
iframe -->

<!ENTITY % button.content
   "(#PCDATA | p | %heading; | div | %lists; | %blocktext; |
      table | br | span | bdo | object | applet | img | map
|
      %fontstyle; | %phrase; | %misc;)*">

<!--================= Document Structure
===================================-->

<!-- the namespace URI designates the document profile -->

<!ELEMENT html (head, frameset)>
<!ATTLIST html
  %i18n;
  xmlns        %URI;          #FIXED
'http://www.w3.org/1999/xhtml'
  >

<!--================= Document Head
==========================================-->

<!ENTITY % head.misc
"(script|style|meta|link|object|isindex)*">

<!-- content model is %head.misc; combined with a single
     title and an optional base element in any order -->

<!ELEMENT head (%head.misc;,
     ((title, %head.misc;, (base, %head.misc;)?) |
      (base, %head.misc;, (title, %head.misc;))))>

<!ATTLIST head
  %i18n;
  profile      %URI;          #IMPLIED
  >

<!-- The title element is not considered part of the flow of
text.
      It should be displayed, for example as the page
header or
      window title. Exactly one title is required per docu-
ment.
    -->
<!ELEMENT title (#PCDATA)>
<!ATTLIST title %i18n;>

<!-- document base URI -->
```

```
<!ELEMENT base EMPTY>
<!ATTLIST base
  href        %URI;         #IMPLIED
  target      %FrameTarget; #IMPLIED
  >

<!-- generic metainformation -->
<!ELEMENT meta EMPTY>
<!ATTLIST meta
  %i18n;   ·
  http-equiv  CDATA         #IMPLIED
  name        CDATA         #IMPLIED
  content     CDATA         #REQUIRED
  scheme      CDATA         #IMPLIED
  >

<!--
  Relationship values can be used in principle:

    a) for document specific toolbars/menus when used
       with the link element in document head e.g.
         start, contents, previous, next, index, end, help
    b) to link to a separate style sheet (rel="stylesheet")
    c) to make a link to a script (rel="script")
    d) by stylesheets to control how collections of
       html nodes are rendered into printed documents
    e) to make a link to a printable version of this document
       e.g. a PostScript or PDF version (rel="alternate"
media="print")
-->

<!ELEMENT link EMPTY>
<!ATTLIST link
  %attrs;
  charset     %Charset;      #IMPLIED
  href        %URI;          #IMPLIED
  hreflang    %LanguageCode; #IMPLIED
  type        %ContentType;  #IMPLIED
  rel         %LinkTypes;    #IMPLIED
  rev         %LinkTypes;    #IMPLIED
  media       %MediaDesc;    #IMPLIED
  target      %FrameTarget;  #IMPLIED
  >

<!-- style info, which may include CDATA sections -->
<!ELEMENT style (#PCDATA)>
<!ATTLIST style
  %i18n;
  type        %ContentType;  #REQUIRED
  media       %MediaDesc;    #IMPLIED
```

```
  title       %Text;          #IMPLIED
  xml:space   (preserve)      #FIXED 'preserve'
  >

<!-- script statements, which may include CDATA sections -->
<!ELEMENT script (#PCDATA)>
<!ATTLIST script
  charset     %Charset;       #IMPLIED
  type        %ContentType;   #REQUIRED
  language    CDATA           #IMPLIED
  src         %URI;           #IMPLIED
  defer       (defer)         #IMPLIED
  xml:space   (preserve)      #FIXED 'preserve'
  >

<!-- alternate content container for non script-based ren-
dering -->

<!ELEMENT noscript %Flow;>
<!ATTLIST noscript
  %attrs;
  >


<!--======================= Frames
=======================================-->

<!-- only one noframes element permitted per document -->

<!ELEMENT frameset (frameset|frame|noframes)*>
<!ATTLIST frameset
  %coreattrs;
  rows        %MultiLengths; #IMPLIED
  cols        %MultiLengths; #IMPLIED
  onload      %Script;        #IMPLIED
  onunload    %Script;        #IMPLIED
  >

<!-- reserved frame names start with "_" otherwise starts
with letter -->

<!-- tiled window within frameset -->

<!ELEMENT frame EMPTY>
<!ATTLIST frame
  %coreattrs;
  longdesc      %URI;         #IMPLIED
  name          NMTOKEN       #IMPLIED
  src           %URI;         #IMPLIED
  frameborder (1|0)           "1"
  marginwidth  %Pixels;       #IMPLIED
  marginheight %Pixels;       #IMPLIED
```

```
    noresize     (noresize)        #IMPLIED
    scrolling    (yes|no|auto)     "auto"
    >


<!-- inline subwindow -->

<!ELEMENT iframe %Flow;>
<!ATTLIST iframe
  %coreattrs;
  longdesc     %URI;             #IMPLIED
  name         NMTOKEN           #IMPLIED
  src          %URI;             #IMPLIED
  frameborder (1|0)              "1"
  marginwidth %Pixels;           #IMPLIED
  marginheight %Pixels;          #IMPLIED
  scrolling    (yes|no|auto)     "auto"
  align        %ImgAlign;        #IMPLIED
  height       %Length;          #IMPLIED
  width        %Length;          #IMPLIED
  >


<!-- alternate content container for non frame-based render-
ing -->

<!ELEMENT noframes (body)>
<!ATTLIST noframes
  %attrs;
  >


<!--==================== Document Body
====================================-->

<!ELEMENT body %Flow;>
<!ATTLIST body
  %attrs;
  onload       %Script;          #IMPLIED
  onunload     %Script;          #IMPLIED
  background   %URI;             #IMPLIED
  bgcolor      %Color;           #IMPLIED
  text         %Color;           #IMPLIED
  link         %Color;           #IMPLIED
  vlink        %Color;           #IMPLIED
  alink        %Color;           #IMPLIED
  >


<!ELEMENT div %Flow;>  <!-- generic language/style container
-->
<!ATTLIST div
  %attrs;
  %TextAlign;
  >
```

```
<!--==================== Paragraphs
============================================-->

<!ELEMENT p %Inline;>
<!ATTLIST p
  %attrs;
  %TextAlign;
  >


<!--=================== Headings
============================================-->

<!--
  There are six levels of headings from h1 (the most impor-
tant)
  to h6 (the least important).
-->

<!ELEMENT h1  %Inline;>
<!ATTLIST h1
  %attrs;
  %TextAlign;
  >

<!ELEMENT h2 %Inline;>
<!ATTLIST h2
  %attrs;
  %TextAlign;
  >

<!ELEMENT h3 %Inline;>
<!ATTLIST h3
  %attrs;
  %TextAlign;
  >

<!ELEMENT h4 %Inline;>
<!ATTLIST h4
  %attrs;
  %TextAlign;
  >

<!ELEMENT h5 %Inline;>
<!ATTLIST h5
  %attrs;
  %TextAlign;
  >

<!ELEMENT h6 %Inline;>
<!ATTLIST h6
```

```
%attrs;
%TextAlign;
>


<!--==================== Lists
=============================================-->


<!-- Unordered list bullet styles -->

<!ENTITY % ULStyle "(disc|square|circle)">

<!-- Unordered list -->

<!ELEMENT ul (li)+>
<!ATTLIST ul
  %attrs;
  type        %ULStyle;      #IMPLIED
  compact     (compact)      #IMPLIED
  >


<!-- Ordered list numbering style

    1    arabic numbers      1, 2, 3, ...
    a    lower alpha         a, b, c, ...
    A    upper alpha         A, B, C, ...
    i    lower roman         i, ii, iii, ...
    I    upper roman         I, II, III, ...

    The style is applied to the sequence number which by de-
fault
    is reset to 1 for the first list item in an ordered
list.
-->
<!ENTITY % OLStyle "CDATA">

<!-- Ordered (numbered) list -->

<!ELEMENT ol (li)+>
<!ATTLIST ol
  %attrs;
  type        %OLStyle;      #IMPLIED
  compact     (compact)      #IMPLIED
  start       %Number;       #IMPLIED
  >


<!-- single column list (DEPRECATED) -->
<!ELEMENT menu (li)+>
<!ATTLIST menu
  %attrs;
  compact     (compact)      #IMPLIED
  >
```

```
<!-- multiple column list (DEPRECATED) -->
<!ELEMENT dir (li)+>
<!ATTLIST dir
  %attrs;
  compact      (compact)       #IMPLIED
  >


<!-- LIStyle is constrained to: "(%ULStyle;|%OLStyle;)" -->
<!ENTITY % LIStyle "CDATA">


<!-- list item -->

<!ELEMENT li %Flow;>
<!ATTLIST li
  %attrs;
  type         %LIStyle;       #IMPLIED
  value        %Number;        #IMPLIED
  >


<!-- definition lists - dt for term, dd for its definition -->

<!ELEMENT dl (dt|dd)+>
<!ATTLIST dl
  %attrs;
  compact      (compact)       #IMPLIED
  >


<!ELEMENT dt %Inline;>
<!ATTLIST dt
  %attrs;
  >


<!ELEMENT dd %Flow;>
<!ATTLIST dd
  %attrs;
  >


<!--==================== Address
========================================-->


<!-- information on author -->

<!ELEMENT address %Inline;>
<!ATTLIST address
  %attrs;
  >


<!--==================== Horizontal Rule
=================================-->
```

```
<!ELEMENT hr EMPTY>
<!ATTLIST hr
  %attrs;
  align         (left|center|right) #IMPLIED
  noshade       (noshade)        #IMPLIED
  size          %Pixels;         #IMPLIED
  width         %Length;         #IMPLIED
  >


<!--==================== Preformatted Text
================================-->

<!-- content is %Inline; excluding
        "img|object|applet|big|small|sub|sup|font|basefont"
-->

<!ELEMENT pre %pre.content;>
<!ATTLIST pre
  %attrs;
  width         %Number;         #IMPLIED
  xml:space     (preserve)       #FIXED 'preserve'
  >


<!--==================== Block-like Quotes
================================-->

<!ELEMENT blockquote %Flow;>
<!ATTLIST blockquote
  %attrs;
  cite          %URI;            #IMPLIED
  >


<!--==================== Text alignment
====================================-->

<!-- center content -->
<!ELEMENT center %Flow;>
<!ATTLIST center
  %attrs;
  >


<!--==================== Inserted/Deleted Text
=============================-->


<!--
  ins/del are allowed in block and inline content, but its
  inappropriate to include block content within an ins ele-
ment
  occurring in inline content.
```

```
-->
<!ELEMENT ins %Flow;>
<!ATTLIST ins
  %attrs;
  cite          %URI;           #IMPLIED
  datetime      %Datetime;      #IMPLIED
  >


<!ELEMENT del %Flow;>
<!ATTLIST del
  %attrs;
  cite          %URI;           #IMPLIED
  datetime      %Datetime;      #IMPLIED
  >


<!--=================== The Anchor Element
===================================-->

<!-- content is %Inline; except that anchors shouldn't be
nested -->

<!ELEMENT a %a.content;>
<!ATTLIST a
  %attrs;
  charset       %Charset;       #IMPLIED
  type          %ContentType;   #IMPLIED
  name          NMTOKEN         #IMPLIED
  href          %URI;           #IMPLIED
  hreflang      %LanguageCode;  #IMPLIED
  rel           %LinkTypes;     #IMPLIED
  rev           %LinkTypes;     #IMPLIED
  accesskey     %Character;     #IMPLIED
  shape         %Shape;         "rect"
  coords        %Coords;        #IMPLIED
  tabindex      %Number;        #IMPLIED
  onfocus       %Script;        #IMPLIED
  onblur        %Script;        #IMPLIED
  target        %FrameTarget;   #IMPLIED
  >


<!--===================== Inline Elements
===================================-->

<!ELEMENT span %Inline;> <!-- generic language/style con-
tainer -->
<!ATTLIST span
  %attrs;
  >


<!ELEMENT bdo %Inline;>  <!-- I18N BiDi over-ride -->
<!ATTLIST bdo
```

```
   %coreattrs;
   %events;
   lang          %LanguageCode; #IMPLIED
   xml:lang      %LanguageCode; #IMPLIED
   dir           (ltr|rtl)        #REQUIRED
   >

<!ELEMENT br EMPTY>    <!-- forced line break -->
<!ATTLIST br
  %coreattrs;
  clear          (left|all|right|none) "none"
  >

<!ELEMENT em %Inline;>    <!-- emphasis -->
<!ATTLIST em %attrs;>

<!ELEMENT strong %Inline;>    <!-- strong emphasis -->
<!ATTLIST strong %attrs;>

<!ELEMENT dfn %Inline;>    <!-- definitional -->
<!ATTLIST dfn %attrs;>

<!ELEMENT code %Inline;>    <!-- program code -->
<!ATTLIST code %attrs;>

<!ELEMENT samp %Inline;>    <!-- sample -->
<!ATTLIST samp %attrs;>

<!ELEMENT kbd %Inline;>   <!-- something user would type -->
<!ATTLIST kbd %attrs;>

<!ELEMENT var %Inline;>    <!-- variable -->
<!ATTLIST var %attrs;>

<!ELEMENT cite %Inline;>    <!-- citation -->
<!ATTLIST cite %attrs;>

<!ELEMENT abbr %Inline;>    <!-- abbreviation -->
<!ATTLIST abbr %attrs;>

<!ELEMENT acronym %Inline;>    <!-- acronym -->
<!ATTLIST acronym %attrs;>

<!ELEMENT q %Inline;>    <!-- inlined quote -->
<!ATTLIST q
   %attrs;
   cite          %URI;            #IMPLIED
   >

<!ELEMENT sub %Inline;> <!-- subscript -->
<!ATTLIST sub %attrs;>
```

```
<!ELEMENT sup %Inline;> <!-- superscript -->
<!ATTLIST sup %attrs;>

<!ELEMENT tt %Inline;>   <!-- fixed pitch font -->
<!ATTLIST tt %attrs;>

<!ELEMENT i %Inline;>   <!-- italic font -->
<!ATTLIST i %attrs;>

<!ELEMENT b %Inline;>   <!-- bold font -->
<!ATTLIST b %attrs;>

<!ELEMENT big %Inline;>   <!-- bigger font -->
<!ATTLIST big %attrs;>

<!ELEMENT small %Inline;>   <!-- smaller font -->
<!ATTLIST small %attrs;>

<!ELEMENT u %Inline;>   <!-- underline -->
<!ATTLIST u %attrs;>

<!ELEMENT s %Inline;>   <!-- strike-through -->
<!ATTLIST s %attrs;>

<!ELEMENT strike %Inline;>   <!-- strike-through -->
<!ATTLIST strike %attrs;>

<!ELEMENT basefont EMPTY>   <!-- base font size -->
<!ATTLIST basefont
  id          ID            #IMPLIED
  size        CDATA         #REQUIRED
  color       %Color;       #IMPLIED
  face        CDATA         #IMPLIED
  >

<!ELEMENT font %Inline;> <!-- local change to font -->
<!ATTLIST font
  %coreattrs;
  %i18n;
  size        CDATA         #IMPLIED
  color       %Color;       #IMPLIED
  face        CDATA         #IMPLIED
  >

<!--==================== Object
=====================================-->
<!--
   object is used to embed objects as part of HTML pages.
   param elements should precede other content. Parameters
   can also be expressed as attribute/value pairs on the
```

```
      object element itself when brevity is desired.
   -->

<!ELEMENT object (#PCDATA | param | %block; | form |%inline;
| %misc;)*>
<!ATTLIST object
  %attrs;
  declare     (declare)      #IMPLIED
  classid     %URI;          #IMPLIED
  codebase    %URI;          #IMPLIED
  data        %URI;          #IMPLIED
  type        %ContentType;  #IMPLIED
  codetype    %ContentType;  #IMPLIED
  archive     %UriList;      #IMPLIED
  standby     %Text;         #IMPLIED
  height      %Length;       #IMPLIED
  width       %Length;       #IMPLIED
  usemap      %URI;          #IMPLIED
  name        NMTOKEN        #IMPLIED
  tabindex    %Number;       #IMPLIED
  align       %ImgAlign;     #IMPLIED
  border      %Pixels;       #IMPLIED
  hspace      %Pixels;       #IMPLIED
  vspace      %Pixels;       #IMPLIED
  >

<!--
   param is used to supply a named property value.
   In XML it would seem natural to follow RDF and support an
   abbreviated syntax where the param elements are replaced
   by attribute value pairs on the object start tag.
   -->
<!ELEMENT param EMPTY>
<!ATTLIST param
  id          ID             #IMPLIED
  name        CDATA          #REQUIRED
  value       CDATA          #IMPLIED
  valuetype   (data|ref|object) "data"
  type        %ContentType;  #IMPLIED
  >

<!--=================== Java applet
====================================-->
<!--
  One of code or object attributes must be present.
  Place param elements before other content.
  -->
<!ELEMENT applet (#PCDATA | param | %block; | form |
%inline; | %misc;)*>
<!ATTLIST applet
  %coreattrs;
```

```
     codebase    %URI;            #IMPLIED
     archive     CDATA            #IMPLIED
     code        CDATA            #IMPLIED
     object      CDATA            #IMPLIED
     alt         %Text;           #IMPLIED
     name        NMTOKEN          #IMPLIED
     width       %Length;         #REQUIRED
     height      %Length;         #REQUIRED
     align       %ImgAlign;       #IMPLIED
     hspace      %Pixels;         #IMPLIED
     vspace      %Pixels;         #IMPLIED
     >

<!--=================== Images
============================================-->

<!--
    To avoid accessibility problems for people who aren't
    able to see the image, you should provide a text
    description using the alt and longdesc attributes.
    In addition, avoid the use of server-side image maps.
-->

<!ELEMENT img EMPTY>
<!ATTLIST img
  %attrs;
  src         %URI;            #REQUIRED
  alt         %Text;           #REQUIRED
  name        NMTOKEN          #IMPLIED
  longdesc    %URI;            #IMPLIED
  height      %Length;         #IMPLIED
  width       %Length;         #IMPLIED
  usemap      %URI;            #IMPLIED
  ismap       (ismap)          #IMPLIED
  align       %ImgAlign;       #IMPLIED
  border      %Pixels;         #IMPLIED
  hspace      %Pixels;         #IMPLIED
  vspace      %Pixels;         #IMPLIED
  >

<!-- usemap points to a map element which may be in this
document
  or an external document, although the latter is not widely
supported -->

<!--=================== Client-side image maps
=============================-->

<!-- These can be placed in the same document or grouped in
a
```

separate document although this isn't yet widely sup-
ported -->

```
<!ELEMENT map ((%block; | form | %misc;)+ | area+)>
<!ATTLIST map
  %i18n;
  %events;
  id          ID              #REQUIRED
  class       CDATA           #IMPLIED
  style       %StyleSheet;    #IMPLIED
  title       %Text;          #IMPLIED
  name        NMTOKEN         #IMPLIED
  >

<!ELEMENT area EMPTY>
<!ATTLIST area
  %attrs;
  shape       %Shape;         "rect"
  coords      %Coords;        #IMPLIED
  href        %URI;           #IMPLIED
  nohref      (nohref)        #IMPLIED
  alt         %Text;          #REQUIRED
  tabindex    %Number;        #IMPLIED
  accesskey   %Character;     #IMPLIED
  onfocus     %Script;        #IMPLIED
  onblur      %Script;        #IMPLIED
  target      %FrameTarget;   #IMPLIED
  >

<!--================= Forms
==================================================-->

<!ELEMENT form %form.content;>   <!-- forms shouldn't be
nested -->

<!ATTLIST form
  %attrs;
  action      %URI;           #REQUIRED
  method      (get|post)      "get"
  name        NMTOKEN         #IMPLIED
  enctype     %ContentType;   "application/x-www-form-
urlencoded"
  onsubmit    %Script;        #IMPLIED
  onreset     %Script;        #IMPLIED
  accept      %ContentTypes;  #IMPLIED
  accept-charset %Charsets;   #IMPLIED
  target      %FrameTarget;   #IMPLIED
  >

<!--
  Each label must not contain more than ONE field
```

```
      Label elements shouldn't be nested.
-->
<!ELEMENT label %Inline;>
<!ATTLIST label
  %attrs;
  for          IDREF          #IMPLIED
  accesskey    %Character;    #IMPLIED
  onfocus      %Script;       #IMPLIED
  onblur       %Script;       #IMPLIED
  >

<!ENTITY % InputType
  "(text | password | checkbox |
    radio | submit | reset |
    file | hidden | image | button)"
  >

<!-- the name attribute is required for all but submit & re-
set -->

<!ELEMENT input EMPTY>     <!-- form control -->
<!ATTLIST input
  %attrs;
  type         %InputType;    "text"
  name         CDATA          #IMPLIED
  value        CDATA          #IMPLIED
  checked      (checked)      #IMPLIED
  disabled     (disabled)     #IMPLIED
  readonly     (readonly)     #IMPLIED
  size         CDATA          #IMPLIED
  maxlength    %Number;       #IMPLIED
  src          %URI;          #IMPLIED
  alt          CDATA          #IMPLIED
  usemap       %URI;          #IMPLIED
  tabindex     %Number;       #IMPLIED
  accesskey    %Character;    #IMPLIED
  onfocus      %Script;       #IMPLIED
  onblur       %Script;       #IMPLIED
  onselect     %Script;       #IMPLIED
  onchange     %Script;       #IMPLIED
  accept       %ContentTypes; #IMPLIED
  align        %ImgAlign;     #IMPLIED
  >

<!ELEMENT select (optgroup|option)+> <!-- option selector -->
<!ATTLIST select
  %attrs;
  name         CDATA          #IMPLIED
  size         %Number;       #IMPLIED
  multiple     (multiple)     #IMPLIED
  disabled     (disabled)     #IMPLIED
```

```
    tabindex     %Number;        #IMPLIED
    onfocus      %Script;        #IMPLIED
    onblur       %Script;        #IMPLIED
    onchange     %Script;        #IMPLIED
    >

<!ELEMENT optgroup (option)+>   <!-- option group -->
<!ATTLIST optgroup
    %attrs;
    disabled     (disabled)      #IMPLIED
    label        %Text;          #REQUIRED
    >

<!ELEMENT option (#PCDATA)>       <!-- selectable choice -->
<!ATTLIST option
    %attrs;
    selected     (selected)      #IMPLIED
    disabled     (disabled)      #IMPLIED
    label        %Text;          #IMPLIED
    value        CDATA           #IMPLIED
    >

<!ELEMENT textarea (#PCDATA)>      <!-- multi-line text field
-->
<!ATTLIST textarea
    %attrs;
    name         CDATA           #IMPLIED
    rows         %Number;        #REQUIRED
    cols         %Number;        #REQUIRED
    disabled     (disabled)      #IMPLIED
    readonly     (readonly)      #IMPLIED
    tabindex     %Number;        #IMPLIED
    accesskey    %Character;     #IMPLIED
    onfocus      %Script;        #IMPLIED
    onblur       %Script;        #IMPLIED
    onselect     %Script;        #IMPLIED
    onchange     %Script;        #IMPLIED
    >

<!--
   The fieldset element is used to group form fields.
   Only one legend element should occur in the content
   and if present should only be preceded by whitespace.
-->
<!ELEMENT fieldset (#PCDATA | legend | %block; | form |
%inline; | %misc;)*>
<!ATTLIST fieldset
    %attrs;
    >
```

```
<!ENTITY % LAlign "(top|bottom|left|right)">

<!ELEMENT legend %Inline;>      <!-- fieldset label -->
<!ATTLIST legend
  %attrs;
  accesskey    %Character;    #IMPLIED
  align        %LAlign;       #IMPLIED
  >

<!--
 Content is %Flow; excluding a, form, form controls, iframe
-->
<!ELEMENT button %button.content;>  <!-- push button -->
<!ATTLIST button
  %attrs;
  name         CDATA          #IMPLIED
  value        CDATA          #IMPLIED
  type         (button|submit|reset) "submit"
  disabled     (disabled)     #IMPLIED
  tabindex     %Number;       #IMPLIED
  accesskey    %Character;    #IMPLIED
  onfocus      %Script;       #IMPLIED
  onblur       %Script;       #IMPLIED
  >

<!-- single-line text input control (DEPRECATED) -->
<!ELEMENT isindex EMPTY>
<!ATTLIST isindex
  %coreattrs;
  %i18n;
  prompt       %Text;         #IMPLIED
  >

<!--======================= Tables
=======================================-->

<!-- Derived from IETF HTML table standard, see [RFC1942] -->

<!--
 The border attribute sets the thickness of the frame around
the
 table. The default units are screen pixels.

 The frame attribute specifies which parts of the frame
around
 the table should be rendered. The values are not the same
as
 CALS to avoid a name clash with the valign attribute.
-->
```

```
<!ENTITY % TFrame
 "(void|above|below|hsides|lhs|rhs|vsides|box|border)">

<!--
 The rules attribute defines which rules to draw between
cells:

 If rules is absent then assume:
     "none" if border is absent or border="0" otherwise
"all"
-->

<!ENTITY % TRules "(none | groups | rows | cols | all)">

<!-- horizontal placement of table relative to document -->
<!ENTITY % TAlign "(left|center|right)">

<!-- horizontal alignment attributes for cell contents

  char         alignment char, e.g. char=":"
  charoff      offset for alignment char
-->
<!ENTITY % cellhalign
   "align         (left|center|right|justify|char) #IMPLIED
    char          %Character;     #IMPLIED
    charoff       %Length;        #IMPLIED"
   >

<!-- vertical alignment attributes for cell contents -->
<!ENTITY % cellvalign
   "valign        (top|middle|bottom|baseline) #IMPLIED"
   >

<!ELEMENT table
     (caption?, (col*|colgroup*), thead?, tfoot?,
(tbody+|tr+))>
<!ELEMENT caption  %Inline;>
<!ELEMENT thead    (tr)+>
<!ELEMENT tfoot    (tr)+>
<!ELEMENT tbody    (tr)+>
<!ELEMENT colgroup (col)*>
<!ELEMENT col      EMPTY>
<!ELEMENT tr       (th|td)+>
<!ELEMENT th       %Flow;>
<!ELEMENT td       %Flow;>

<!ATTLIST table
   %attrs;
   summary       %Text;          #IMPLIED
   width         %Length;        #IMPLIED
   border        %Pixels;        #IMPLIED
```

```
frame       %TFrame;        #IMPLIED
rules       %TRules;        #IMPLIED
cellspacing %Length;        #IMPLIED
cellpadding %Length;        #IMPLIED
align       %TAlign;        #IMPLIED
bgcolor     %Color;         #IMPLIED
  >

<!ENTITY % CAlign "(top|bottom|left|right)">

<!ATTLIST caption
  %attrs;
  align       %CAlign;        #IMPLIED
  >


<!--
colgroup groups a set of col elements. It allows you to
group
several semantically related columns together.
-->
<!ATTLIST colgroup
  %attrs;
  span        %Number;        "1"
  width       %MultiLength;   #IMPLIED
  %cellhalign;
  %cellvalign;
  >


<!--
 col elements define the alignment properties for cells in
 one or more columns.

 The width attribute specifies the width of the columns,
e.g.

    width=64        width in screen pixels
    width=0.5*      relative width of 0.5

 The span attribute causes the attributes of one
 col element to apply to more than one column.
-->
<!ATTLIST col
  %attrs;
  span        %Number;        "1"
  width       %MultiLength;   #IMPLIED
  %cellhalign;
  %cellvalign;
  >


<!--
    Use thead to duplicate headers when breaking table
```

```
        across page boundaries, or for static headers when
        tbody sections are rendered in scrolling panel.

        Use tfoot to duplicate footers when breaking table
        across page boundaries, or for static footers when
        tbody sections are rendered in scrolling panel.

        Use multiple tbody sections when rules are needed
        between groups of table rows.
-->
<!ATTLIST thead
    %attrs;
    %cellhalign;
    %cellvalign;
    >

<!ATTLIST tfoot
    %attrs;
    %cellhalign;
    %cellvalign;
    >

<!ATTLIST tbody
    %attrs;
    %cellhalign;
    %cellvalign;
    >

<!ATTLIST tr
    %attrs;
    %cellhalign;
    %cellvalign;
    bgcolor       %Color;          #IMPLIED
    >

<!-- Scope is simpler than headers attribute for common ta-
bles -->
<!ENTITY % Scope "(row|col|rowgroup|colgroup)">

<!-- th is for headers, td for data and for cells acting as
both -->

<!ATTLIST th
    %attrs;
    abbr          %Text;           #IMPLIED
    axis          CDATA            #IMPLIED
    headers       IDREFS           #IMPLIED
    scope         %Scope;          #IMPLIED
    rowspan       %Number;         "1"
    colspan       %Number;         "1"
    %cellhalign;
```

```
    %cellvalign;
    nowrap      (nowrap)        #IMPLIED
    bgcolor     %Color;         #IMPLIED
    width       %Pixels;        #IMPLIED
    height      %Pixels;        #IMPLIED
    >

<!ATTLIST td
    %attrs;
    abbr        %Text;          #IMPLIED
    axis        CDATA           #IMPLIED
    headers     IDREFS          #IMPLIED
    scope       %Scope;         #IMPLIED
    rowspan     %Number;        "1"
    colspan     %Number;        "1"
    %cellhalign;
    %cellvalign;
    nowrap      (nowrap)        #IMPLIED
    bgcolor     %Color;         #IMPLIED
    width       %Pixels;        #IMPLIED
    height      %Pixels;        #IMPLIED
    >
```

C XHTML DTDs: Entities

IN THIS CHAPTER

- Special Characters DTD
- Latin characters DTD
- Symbols DTD

Here are all of the DTDs for all of the entities that you can use in XHTML.

◆ Special Characters DTD

```
<!-- Special characters for HTML -->

<!-- Character entity set. Typical invocation:
     <!ENTITY % HTMLspecial PUBLIC
       "-//W3C//ENTITIES Special for XHTML//EN"
       "http://www.w3.org/TR/xhtml1/DTD/xhtml-special.ent">
     %HTMLspecial;
-->

<!-- Portions (C) International Organization for Standard-
ization 1986:
     Permission to copy in any form is granted for use with
     conforming SGML systems and applications as defined in
     ISO 8879, provided this notice is included in all cop-
ies.
-->

<!-- Relevant ISO entity set is given unless names are newly
introduced.
```

New names (i.e., not in ISO 8879 list) do not clash
with any
    existing ISO 8879 entity names. ISO 10646 character
numbers
    are given for each character, in hex. values are deci-
mal
    conversions of the ISO 10646 values and refer to the
document
    character set. Names are Unicode names.
-->

```
<!-- C0 Controls and Basic Latin -->
<!ENTITY quot    "&#34;"> <!-- quotation mark = APL quote,
                                     U+0022 ISOnum -->
<!ENTITY amp     "&#38;#38;"> <!-- ampersand, U+0026 ISOnum
-->
<!ENTITY lt      "&#38;#60;"> <!-- less-than sign, U+003C
ISOnum -->
<!ENTITY gt      "&#62;"> <!-- greater-than sign, U+003E
ISOnum -->
<!ENTITY apos  "&#39;"> <!-- apostrophe mark, U+0027
ISOnum -->


<!-- Latin Extended-A -->
<!ENTITY OElig   "&#338;"> <!-- latin capital ligature OE,
                                     U+0152 ISOlat2 -->
<!ENTITY oelig   "&#339;"> <!-- latin small ligature oe,
U+0153 ISOlat2 -->
<!-- ligature is a misnomer, this is a separate character in
some languages -->
<!ENTITY Scaron  "&#352;"> <!-- latin capital letter S with
caron,
                                    U+0160 ISOlat2 -->
<!ENTITY scaron  "&#353;"> <!-- latin small letter s with
caron,
                                    U+0161 ISOlat2 -->
<!ENTITY Yuml    "&#376;"> <!-- latin capital letter Y with
diaeresis,
                                    U+0178 ISOlat2 -->


<!-- Spacing Modifier Letters -->
<!ENTITY circ    "&#710;"> <!-- modifier letter circumflex
accent,
                                    U+02C6 ISOpub -->
<!ENTITY tilde   "&#732;"> <!-- small tilde, U+02DC ISOdia
-->


<!-- General Punctuation -->
<!ENTITY ensp    " "> <!-- en space, U+2002 ISOpub -->
<!ENTITY emsp    " "> <!-- em space, U+2003 ISOpub -->
```

```
<!ENTITY thinsp   " "> <!-- thin space, U+2009 ISOpub
-->
<!ENTITY zwnj     "&#8204;"> <!-- zero width non-joiner,
                                  U+200C NEW RFC 2070 -->
<!ENTITY zwj      "&#8205;"> <!-- zero width joiner, U+200D
NEW RFC 2070 -->
<!ENTITY lrm      "&#8206;"> <!-- left-to-right mark, U+200E
NEW RFC 2070 -->
<!ENTITY rlm      "&#8207;"> <!-- right-to-left mark, U+200F
NEW RFC 2070 -->
<!ENTITY ndash    "&#8211;"> <!-- en dash, U+2013 ISOpub -->
<!ENTITY mdash    "&#8212;"> <!-- em dash, U+2014 ISOpub -->
<!ENTITY lsquo    "&#8216;"> <!-- left single quotation mark,
                                  U+2018 ISOnum -->
<!ENTITY rsquo    "&#8217;"> <!-- right single quotation mark,
                                  U+2019 ISOnum -->
<!ENTITY sbquo    "&#8218;"> <!-- single low-9 quotation
mark, U+201A NEW -->
<!ENTITY ldquo    "&#8220;"> <!-- left double quotation mark,
                                  U+201C ISOnum -->
<!ENTITY rdquo    "&#8221;"> <!-- right double quotation mark,
                                  U+201D ISOnum -->
<!ENTITY bdquo    "&#8222;"> <!-- double low-9 quotation
mark, U+201E NEW -->
<!ENTITY dagger   "&#8224;"> <!-- dagger, U+2020 ISOpub -->
<!ENTITY Dagger   "&#8225;"> <!-- double dagger, U+2021
ISOpub -->
<!ENTITY permil   "&#8240;"> <!-- per mille sign, U+2030
ISOtech -->
<!ENTITY lsaquo   "&#8249;"> <!-- single left-pointing angle
quotation mark,
                                  U+2039 ISO proposed -->
<!-- lsaquo is proposed but not yet ISO standardized -->
<!ENTITY rsaquo   "&#8250;"> <!-- single right-pointing angle
quotation mark,
                                  U+203A ISO proposed -->
<!-- rsaquo is proposed but not yet ISO standardized -->
<!ENTITY euro     "&#8364;"> <!-- euro sign, U+20AC NEW -->
```

◆ Latin Characters DTD

```
<!-- Portions (C) International Organization for Standard-
ization 1986
      Permission to copy in any form is granted for use with
      conforming SGML systems and applications as defined in
      ISO 8879, provided this notice is included in all cop-
ies.
-->
<!-- Character entity set. Typical invocation:
    <!ENTITY % HTMLlat1 PUBLIC
```

```
     "-//W3C//ENTITIES Latin 1 for XHTML//EN"
     "http://www.w3.org/TR/xhtml1/DTD/xhtml-lat1.ent">
     %HTMLlat1;
-->


<!ENTITY nbsp    " "> <!-- no-break space = non-breaking
space,
                                U+00A0 ISOnum -->
<!ENTITY iexcl   "&#161;"> <!-- inverted exclamation mark,
U+00A1 ISOnum -->
<!ENTITY cent    "&#162;"> <!-- cent sign, U+00A2 ISOnum -->
<!ENTITY pound   "&#163;"> <!-- pound sign, U+00A3 ISOnum -->
<!ENTITY curren  "&#164;"> <!-- currency sign, U+00A4 ISOnum
-->
<!ENTITY yen     "&#165;"> <!-- yen sign = yuan sign, U+00A5
ISOnum -->
<!ENTITY brvbar  "&#166;"> <!-- broken bar = broken vertical
bar,
                                U+00A6 ISOnum -->
<!ENTITY sect    "&#167;"> <!-- section sign, U+00A7 ISOnum
-->
<!ENTITY uml     "&#168;"> <!-- diaeresis = spacing diaere-
sis,
                                U+00A8 ISOdia -->
<!ENTITY copy    "&#169;"> <!-- copyright sign, U+00A9 ISOnum
-->
<!ENTITY ordf    "&#170;"> <!-- feminine ordinal indicator,
U+00AA ISOnum -->
<!ENTITY laquo   "&#171;"> <!-- left-pointing double angle
quotation mark
                                = left pointing guillemet,
U+00AB ISOnum -->
<!ENTITY not     "&#172;"> <!-- not sign = discretionary hy-
phen,
                                U+00AC ISOnum -->
<!ENTITY shy     "&#173;"> <!-- soft hyphen = discretionary
hyphen,
                                U+00AD ISOnum -->
<!ENTITY reg     "&#174;"> <!-- registered sign = registered
trade mark sign,
                                U+00AE ISOnum -->
<!ENTITY macr    "&#175;"> <!-- macron = spacing macron =
overline
                                = APL overbar, U+00AF ISO-
dia -->
<!ENTITY deg     "&#176;"> <!-- degree sign, U+00B0 ISOnum
-->
<!ENTITY plusmn  "&#177;"> <!-- plus-minus sign = plus-or-
minus sign,
                                U+00B1 ISOnum -->
```

```
<!ENTITY sup2   "&#178;"> <!-- superscript two = superscript
digit two
                              = squared, U+00B2 ISOnum
-->
<!ENTITY sup3   "&#179;"> <!-- superscript three = super-
script digit three
                              = cubed, U+00B3 ISOnum -->
<!ENTITY acute  "&#180;"> <!-- acute accent = spacing acute,
                          U+00B4 ISOdia -->
<!ENTITY micro  "&#181;"> <!-- micro sign, U+00B5 ISOnum -->
<!ENTITY para   "&#182;"> <!-- pilcrow sign = paragraph
sign,
                          U+00B6 ISOnum -->
<!ENTITY middot "&#183;"> <!-- middle dot = Georgian comma
                              = Greek middle dot, U+00B7
ISOnum -->
<!ENTITY cedil  "&#184;"> <!-- cedilla = spacing cedilla,
U+00B8 ISOdia -->
<!ENTITY sup1   "&#185;"> <!-- superscript one = superscript
digit one,
                          U+00B9 ISOnum -->
<!ENTITY ordm   "&#186;"> <!-- masculine ordinal indicator,
                          U+00BA ISOnum -->
<!ENTITY raquo  "&#187;"> <!-- right-pointing double angle
quotation mark
                              = right pointing
guillemet, U+00BB ISOnum -->
<!ENTITY frac14 "&#188;"> <!-- vulgar fraction one quarter
                              = fraction one quarter,
U+00BC ISOnum -->
<!ENTITY frac12 "&#189;"> <!-- vulgar fraction one half
                              = fraction one half,
U+00BD ISOnum -->
<!ENTITY frac34 "&#190;"> <!-- vulgar fraction three quar-
ters
                              = fraction three quarters,
U+00BE ISOnum -->
<!ENTITY iquest "&#191;"> <!-- inverted question mark
                              = turned question mark,
U+00BF ISOnum -->
<!ENTITY Agrave "&#192;"> <!-- latin capital letter A with
grave
                              = latin capital letter A
grave,
                          U+00C0 ISOlat1 -->
<!ENTITY Aacute "&#193;"> <!-- latin capital letter A with
acute,
                          U+00C1 ISOlat1 -->
<!ENTITY Acirc  "&#194;"> <!-- latin capital letter A with
circumflex,
                          U+00C2 ISOlat1 -->
```

```
<!ENTITY Atilde "&#195;"> <!-- latin capital letter A with
tilde,
                                  U+00C3 ISOlat1 -->
<!ENTITY Auml   "&#196;"> <!-- latin capital letter A with
diaeresis,
                                  U+00C4 ISOlat1 -->
<!ENTITY Aring  "&#197;"> <!-- latin capital letter A with
ring above
                          = latin capital letter A
ring,
                                  U+00C5 ISOlat1 -->
<!ENTITY AElig  "&#198;"> <!-- latin capital letter AE
                          = latin capital ligature
AE,
                                  U+00C6 ISOlat1 -->
<!ENTITY Ccedil "&#199;"> <!-- latin capital letter C with
cedilla,
                                  U+00C7 ISOlat1 -->
<!ENTITY Egrave "&#200;"> <!-- latin capital letter E with
grave,
                                  U+00C8 ISOlat1 -->
<!ENTITY Eacute "&#201;"> <!-- latin capital letter E with
acute,
                                  U+00C9 ISOlat1 -->
<!ENTITY Ecirc  "&#202;"> <!-- latin capital letter E with
circumflex,
                                  U+00CA ISOlat1 -->
<!ENTITY Euml   "&#203;"> <!-- latin capital letter E with
diaeresis,
                                  U+00CB ISOlat1 -->
<!ENTITY Igrave "&#204;"> <!-- latin capital letter I with
grave,
                                  U+00CC ISOlat1 -->
<!ENTITY Iacute "&#205;"> <!-- latin capital letter I with
acute,
                                  U+00CD ISOlat1 -->
<!ENTITY Icirc  "&#206;"> <!-- latin capital letter I with
circumflex,
                                  U+00CE ISOlat1 -->
<!ENTITY Iuml   "&#207;"> <!-- latin capital letter I with
diaeresis,
                                  U+00CF ISOlat1 -->
<!ENTITY ETH    "&#208;"> <!-- latin capital letter ETH,
U+00D0 ISOlat1 -->
<!ENTITY Ntilde "&#209;"> <!-- latin capital letter N with
tilde,
                                  U+00D1 ISOlat1 -->
<!ENTITY Ograve "&#210;"> <!-- latin capital letter O with
grave,
                                  U+00D2 ISOlat1 -->
<!ENTITY Oacute "&#211;"> <!-- latin capital letter O with
acute,
```

```
                                        U+00D3 ISOlat1 -->
<!ENTITY Ocirc  "&#212;"> <!-- latin capital letter O with
circumflex,
                                        U+00D4 ISOlat1 -->
<!ENTITY Otilde "&#213;"> <!-- latin capital letter O with
tilde,
                                        U+00D5 ISOlat1 -->
<!ENTITY Ouml   "&#214;"> <!-- latin capital letter O with
diaeresis,
                                        U+00D6 ISOlat1 -->
<!ENTITY times  "&#215;"> <!-- multiplication sign, U+00D7
ISOnum -->
<!ENTITY Oslash "&#216;"> <!-- latin capital letter O with
stroke
                              = latin capital letter O
slash,
                                        U+00D8 ISOlat1 -->
<!ENTITY Ugrave "&#217;"> <!-- latin capital letter U with
grave,
                                        U+00D9 ISOlat1 -->
<!ENTITY Uacute "&#218;"> <!-- latin capital letter U with
acute,
                                        U+00DA ISOlat1 -->
<!ENTITY Ucirc  "&#219;"> <!-- latin capital letter U with
circumflex,
                                        U+00DB ISOlat1 -->
<!ENTITY Uuml   "&#220;"> <!-- latin capital letter U with
diaeresis,
                                        U+00DC ISOlat1 -->
<!ENTITY Yacute "&#221;"> <!-- latin capital letter Y with
acute,
                                        U+00DD ISOlat1 -->
<!ENTITY THORN  "&#222;"> <!-- latin capital letter THORN,
                                        U+00DE ISOlat1 -->
<!ENTITY szlig  "&#223;"> <!-- latin small letter sharp s =
ess-zed,
                                        U+00DF ISOlat1 -->
<!ENTITY agrave "&#224;"> <!-- latin small letter a with
grave
                              = latin small letter a
grave,
                                        U+00E0 ISOlat1 -->
<!ENTITY aacute "&#225;"> <!-- latin small letter a with
acute,
                                        U+00E1 ISOlat1 -->
<!ENTITY acirc  "&#226;"> <!-- latin small letter a with
circumflex,
                                        U+00E2 ISOlat1 -->
<!ENTITY atilde "&#227;"> <!-- latin small letter a with
tilde,
                                        U+00E3 ISOlat1 -->
```

```
<!ENTITY auml    "&#228;"> <!-- latin small letter a with di-
aeresis,
                                  U+00E4 ISOlat1 -->
<!ENTITY aring   "&#229;"> <!-- latin small letter a with
ring above
                                  = latin small letter a
ring,
                                  U+00E5 ISOlat1 -->
<!ENTITY aelig   "&#230;"> <!-- latin small letter ae
                                  = latin small ligature ae,
U+00E6 ISOlat1 -->
<!ENTITY ccedil "&#231;"> <!-- latin small letter c with
cedilla,
                                  U+00E7 ISOlat1 -->
<!ENTITY egrave "&#232;"> <!-- latin small letter e with
grave,
                                  U+00E8 ISOlat1 -->
<!ENTITY eacute "&#233;"> <!-- latin small letter e with
acute,
                                  U+00E9 ISOlat1 -->
<!ENTITY ecirc   "&#234;"> <!-- latin small letter e with
circumflex,
                                  U+00EA ISOlat1 -->
<!ENTITY euml    "&#235;"> <!-- latin small letter e with di-
aeresis,
                                  U+00EB ISOlat1 -->
<!ENTITY igrave "&#236;"> <!-- latin small letter i with
grave,
                                  U+00EC ISOlat1 -->
<!ENTITY iacute "&#237;"> <!-- latin small letter i with
acute,
                                  U+00ED ISOlat1 -->
<!ENTITY icirc   "&#238;"> <!-- latin small letter i with
circumflex,
                                  U+00EE ISOlat1 -->
<!ENTITY iuml    "&#239;"> <!-- latin small letter i with di-
aeresis,
                                  U+00EF ISOlat1 -->
<!ENTITY eth     "&#240;"> <!-- latin small letter eth,
U+00F0 ISOlat1 -->
<!ENTITY ntilde "&#241;"> <!-- latin small letter n with
tilde,
                                  U+00F1 ISOlat1 -->
<!ENTITY ograve "&#242;"> <!-- latin small letter o with
grave,
                                  U+00F2 ISOlat1 -->
<!ENTITY oacute "&#243;"> <!-- latin small letter o with
acute,
                                  U+00F3 ISOlat1 -->
<!ENTITY ocirc   "&#244;"> <!-- latin small letter o with
circumflex,
```

```
                                    U+00F4 ISOlat1 -->
<!ENTITY otilde "&#245;"> <!-- latin small letter o with
tilde,
                                    U+00F5 ISOlat1 -->
<!ENTITY ouml    "&#246;"> <!-- latin small letter o with di-
aeresis,
                                    U+00F6 ISOlat1 -->
<!ENTITY divide "&#247;"> <!-- division sign, U+00F7 ISOnum
-->
<!ENTITY oslash "&#248;"> <!-- latin small letter o with
stroke,
                                    = latin small letter o
slash,
                                    U+00F8 ISOlat1 -->
<!ENTITY ugrave "&#249;"> <!-- latin small letter u with
grave,
                                    U+00F9 ISOlat1 -->
<!ENTITY uacute "&#250;"> <!-- latin small letter u with
acute,
                                    U+00FA ISOlat1 -->
<!ENTITY ucirc  "&#251;"> <!-- latin small letter u with
circumflex,
                                    U+00FB ISOlat1 -->
<!ENTITY uuml    "&#252;"> <!-- latin small letter u with di-
aeresis,
                                    U+00FC ISOlat1 -->
<!ENTITY yacute "&#253;"> <!-- latin small letter y with
acute,
                                    U+00FD ISOlat1 -->
<!ENTITY thorn  "&#254;"> <!-- latin small letter thorn
with,
                                    U+00FE ISOlat1 -->
<!ENTITY yuml    "&#255;"> <!-- latin small letter y with di-
aeresis,
                                    U+00FF ISOlat1 -->
```

◆ Symbols DTD

```
<!-- Mathematical, Greek and Symbolic characters for HTML
-->

<!-- Character entity set. Typical invocation:
    <!ENTITY % HTMLsymbol PUBLIC
       "-//W3C//ENTITIES Symbols for XHTML//EN"
       "http://www.w3.org/TR/xhtml1/DTD/xhtml-symbol.ent">
    %HTMLsymbol;
-->

<!-- Portions (C) International Organization for Standard-
ization 1986:
```

```
            Permission to copy in any form is granted for use with
            conforming SGML systems and applications as defined in
            ISO 8879, provided this notice is included in all
copies.
-->

<!-- Relevant ISO entity set is given unless names are newly
introduced.
            New names (i.e., not in ISO 8879 list) do not clash
with any
            existing ISO 8879 entity names. ISO 10646 character
numbers
            are given for each character, in hex. values are deci-
mal
            conversions of the ISO 10646 values and refer to the
document
            character set. Names are Unicode names.
-->

<!-- Latin Extended-B -->
<!ENTITY fnof       "&#402;"> <!-- latin small f with hook =
function
                                        = florin, U+0192 ISOtech
-->

<!-- Greek -->
<!ENTITY Alpha      "&#913;"> <!-- greek capital letter alpha,
U+0391 -->
<!ENTITY Beta       "&#914;"> <!-- greek capital letter beta,
U+0392 -->
<!ENTITY Gamma      "&#915;"> <!-- greek capital letter gamma,
                                        U+0393 ISOgrk3 -->
<!ENTITY Delta      "&#916;"> <!-- greek capital letter delta,
                                        U+0394 ISOgrk3 -->
<!ENTITY Epsilon    "&#917;"> <!-- greek capital letter ep-
silon, U+0395 -->
<!ENTITY Zeta       "&#918;"> <!-- greek capital letter zeta,
U+0396 -->
<!ENTITY Eta        "&#919;"> <!-- greek capital letter eta,
U+0397 -->
<!ENTITY Theta      "&#920;"> <!-- greek capital letter theta,
                                        U+0398 ISOgrk3 -->
<!ENTITY Iota       "&#921;"> <!-- greek capital letter iota,
U+0399 -->
<!ENTITY Kappa      "&#922;"> <!-- greek capital letter kappa,
U+039A -->
<!ENTITY Lambda     "&#923;"> <!-- greek capital letter
lambda,
                                        U+039B ISOgrk3 -->
<!ENTITY Mu         "&#924;"> <!-- greek capital letter mu,
U+039C -->
```

```
<!ENTITY Nu        "&#925;"> <!-- greek capital letter nu,
U+039D -->
<!ENTITY Xi        "&#926;"> <!-- greek capital letter xi,
U+039E ISOgrk3 -->
<!ENTITY Omicron   "&#927;"> <!-- greek capital letter omi-
cron, U+039F -->
<!ENTITY Pi        "&#928;"> <!-- greek capital letter pi,
U+03A0 ISOgrk3 -->
<!ENTITY Rho       "&#929;"> <!-- greek capital letter rho,
U+03A1 -->
<!-- there is no Sigmaf, and no U+03A2 character either -->
<!ENTITY Sigma     "&#931;"> <!-- greek capital letter sigma,
                                  U+03A3 ISOgrk3 -->
<!ENTITY Tau       "&#932;"> <!-- greek capital letter tau,
U+03A4 -->
<!ENTITY Upsilon   "&#933;"> <!-- greek capital letter up-
silon,
                                  U+03A5 ISOgrk3 -->
<!ENTITY Phi       "&#934;"> <!-- greek capital letter phi,
                                  U+03A6 ISOgrk3 -->
<!ENTITY Chi       "&#935;"> <!-- greek capital letter chi,
U+03A7 -->
<!ENTITY Psi       "&#936;"> <!-- greek capital letter psi,
                                  U+03A8 ISOgrk3 -->
<!ENTITY Omega     "&#937;"> <!-- greek capital letter omega,
                                  U+03A9 ISOgrk3 -->

<!ENTITY alpha     "&#945;"> <!-- greek small letter alpha,
                                  U+03B1 ISOgrk3 -->
<!ENTITY beta      "&#946;"> <!-- greek small letter beta,
U+03B2 ISOgrk3 -->
<!ENTITY gamma     "&#947;"> <!-- greek small letter gamma,
                                  U+03B3 ISOgrk3 -->
<!ENTITY delta     "&#948;"> <!-- greek small letter delta,
                                  U+03B4 ISOgrk3 -->
<!ENTITY epsilon   "&#949;"> <!-- greek small letter epsilon,
                                  U+03B5 ISOgrk3 -->
<!ENTITY zeta      "&#950;"> <!-- greek small letter zeta,
U+03B6 ISOgrk3 -->
<!ENTITY eta       "&#951;"> <!-- greek small letter eta,
U+03B7 ISOgrk3 -->
<!ENTITY theta     "&#952;"> <!-- greek small letter theta,
                                  U+03B8 ISOgrk3 -->
<!ENTITY iota      "&#953;"> <!-- greek small letter iota,
U+03B9 ISOgrk3 -->
<!ENTITY kappa     "&#954;"> <!-- greek small letter kappa,
                                  U+03BA ISOgrk3 -->
<!ENTITY lambda    "&#955;"> <!-- greek small letter lambda,
                                  U+03BB ISOgrk3 -->
<!ENTITY mu        "&#956;"> <!-- greek small letter mu,
U+03BC ISOgrk3 -->
```

```
<!ENTITY nu        "&#957;"> <!-- greek small letter nu,
U+03BD ISOgrk3 -->
<!ENTITY xi        "&#958;"> <!-- greek small letter xi,
U+03BE ISOgrk3 -->
<!ENTITY omicron   "&#959;"> <!-- greek small letter omicron,
U+03BF NEW -->
<!ENTITY pi        "&#960;"> <!-- greek small letter pi,
U+03C0 ISOgrk3 -->
<!ENTITY rho       "&#961;"> <!-- greek small letter rho,
U+03C1 ISOgrk3 -->
<!ENTITY sigmaf    "&#962;"> <!-- greek small letter final
sigma,
                                    U+03C2 ISOgrk3 -->
<!ENTITY sigma     "&#963;"> <!-- greek small letter sigma,
                                    U+03C3 ISOgrk3 -->
<!ENTITY tau       "&#964;"> <!-- greek small letter tau,
U+03C4 ISOgrk3 -->
<!ENTITY upsilon   "&#965;"> <!-- greek small letter upsilon,
                                    U+03C5 ISOgrk3 -->
<!ENTITY phi       "&#966;"> <!-- greek small letter phi,
U+03C6 ISOgrk3 -->
<!ENTITY chi       "&#967;"> <!-- greek small letter chi,
U+03C7 ISOgrk3 -->
<!ENTITY psi       "&#968;"> <!-- greek small letter psi,
U+03C8 ISOgrk3 -->
<!ENTITY omega     "&#969;"> <!-- greek small letter omega,
                                    U+03C9 ISOgrk3 -->
<!ENTITY thetasym "&#977;"> <!-- greek small letter theta
symbol,
                                    U+03D1 NEW -->
<!ENTITY upsih     "&#978;"> <!-- greek upsilon with hook
symbol,
                                    U+03D2 NEW -->
<!ENTITY piv       "&#982;"> <!-- greek pi symbol, U+03D6
ISOgrk3 -->

<!-- General Punctuation -->
<!ENTITY bull      "&#8226;"> <!-- bullet = black small cir-
cle,
                                    U+2022 ISOpub  -->
<!-- bullet is NOT the same as bullet operator, U+2219 -->
<!ENTITY hellip    "&#8230;"> <!-- horizontal ellipsis =
three dot leader,
                                    U+2026 ISOpub  -->
<!ENTITY prime     "&#8242;"> <!-- prime = minutes = feet,
U+2032 ISOtech -->
<!ENTITY Prime     "&#8243;"> <!-- double prime = seconds =
inches,
                                    U+2033 ISOtech -->
<!ENTITY oline     "&#8254;"> <!-- overline = spacing over-
score,
```

```
                                        U+203E NEW -->
<!ENTITY frasl    "&#8260;"> <!-- fraction slash, U+2044 NEW
-->


<!-- Letterlike Symbols -->
<!ENTITY weierp   "&#8472;"> <!-- script capital P = power
set
                                = Weierstrass p, U+2118
ISOamso -->
<!ENTITY image    "&#8465;"> <!-- blackletter capital I =
imaginary part,
                                U+2111 ISOamso -->
<!ENTITY real     "&#8476;"> <!-- blackletter capital R =
real part symbol,
                                U+211C ISOamso -->
<!ENTITY trade    "&#8482;"> <!-- trade mark sign, U+2122
ISOnum -->
<!ENTITY alefsym  "&#8501;"> <!-- alef symbol = first trans-
finite cardinal,
                                U+2135 NEW -->
<!-- alef symbol is NOT the same as hebrew letter alef,
    U+05D0 although the same glyph could be used to depict
both characters -->


<!-- Arrows -->
<!ENTITY larr     "&#8592;"> <!-- leftwards arrow, U+2190
ISOnum -->
<!ENTITY uarr     "&#8593;"> <!-- upwards arrow, U+2191
ISOnum-->
<!ENTITY rarr     "&#8594;"> <!-- rightwards arrow, U+2192
ISOnum -->
<!ENTITY darr     "&#8595;"> <!-- downwards arrow, U+2193
ISOnum -->
<!ENTITY harr     "&#8596;"> <!-- left right arrow, U+2194
ISOamsa -->
<!ENTITY crarr    "&#8629;"> <!-- downwards arrow with cor-
ner leftwards
                                = carriage return,
U+21B5 NEW -->
<!ENTITY lArr     "&#8656;"> <!-- leftwards double arrow,
U+21D0 ISOtech -->
<!-- Unicode does not say that lArr is the same as the 'is
implied by' arrow
    but also does not have any other character for that
function. So ? lArr can
    be used for 'is implied by' as ISOtech suggests -->
<!ENTITY uArr     "&#8657;"> <!-- upwards double arrow,
U+21D1 ISOamsa -->
<!ENTITY rArr     "&#8658;"> <!-- rightwards double arrow,
                                U+21D2 ISOtech -->
```

```
<!-- Unicode does not say this is the 'implies' character
but does not have
     another character with this function so ?
     rArr can be used for 'implies' as ISOtech suggests -->
<!ENTITY dArr     "&#8659;"> <!-- downwards double arrow,
U+21D3 ISOamsa -->
<!ENTITY hArr     "&#8660;"> <!-- left right double arrow,
                                 U+21D4 ISOamsa -->


<!-- Mathematical Operators -->
<!ENTITY forall   "&#8704;"> <!-- for all, U+2200 ISOtech
-->
<!ENTITY part     "&#8706;"> <!-- partial differential,
U+2202 ISOtech   -->
<!ENTITY exist    "&#8707;"> <!-- there exists, U+2203
ISOtech -->
<!ENTITY empty    "&#8709;"> <!-- empty set = null set = di-
ameter,
                                 U+2205 ISOamso -->
<!ENTITY nabla    "&#8711;"> <!-- nabla = backward differ-
ence,
                                 U+2207 ISOtech -->
<!ENTITY isin     "&#8712;"> <!-- element of, U+2208 ISOtech
-->
<!ENTITY notin    "&#8713;"> <!-- not an element of, U+2209
ISOtech -->
<!ENTITY ni       "&#8715;"> <!-- contains as member, U+220B
ISOtech -->
<!-- should there be a more memorable name than 'ni'? -->
<!ENTITY prod     "&#8719;"> <!-- n-ary product = product
sign,
                                 U+220F ISOamsb -->
<!-- prod is NOT the same character as U+03A0 'greek capital
letter pi' though
     the same glyph might be used for both -->
<!ENTITY sum      "&#8721;"> <!-- n-ary sumation, U+2211
ISOamsb -->
<!-- sum is NOT the same character as U+03A3 'greek capital
letter sigma'
     though the same glyph might be used for both -->
<!ENTITY minus    "&#8722;"> <!-- minus sign, U+2212 ISOtech
-->
<!ENTITY lowast   "&#8727;"> <!-- asterisk operator, U+2217
ISOtech -->
<!ENTITY radic    "&#8730;"> <!-- square root = radical
sign,
                                 U+221A ISOtech -->
<!ENTITY prop     "&#8733;"> <!-- proportional to, U+221D
ISOtech -->
<!ENTITY infin    "&#8734;"> <!-- infinity, U+221E ISOtech
-->
```

```
<!ENTITY ang        "&#8736;"> <!-- angle, U+2220 ISOamso -->
<!ENTITY and        "&#8743;"> <!-- logical and = wedge,
U+2227 ISOtech -->
<!ENTITY or         "&#8744;"> <!-- logical or = vee, U+2228
ISOtech -->
<!ENTITY cap        "&#8745;"> <!-- intersection = cap, U+2229
ISOtech -->
<!ENTITY cup        "&#8746;"> <!-- union = cup, U+222A
ISOtech -->
<!ENTITY int        "&#8747;"> <!-- integral, U+222B ISOtech
-->
<!ENTITY there4     "&#8756;"> <!-- therefore, U+2234 ISOtech
-->
<!ENTITY sim        "&#8764;"> <!-- tilde operator = varies
with = similar to,
                                 U+223C ISOtech -->
<!-- tilde operator is NOT the same character as the tilde,
U+007E,
     although the same glyph might be used to represent both
-->
<!ENTITY cong       "&#8773;"> <!-- approximately equal to,
U+2245 ISOtech -->
<!ENTITY asymp      "&#8776;"> <!-- almost equal to = asymp-
totic to,
                                 U+2248 ISOamsr -->
<!ENTITY ne         "&#8800;"> <!-- not equal to, U+2260
ISOtech -->
<!ENTITY equiv      "&#8801;"> <!-- identical to, U+2261
ISOtech -->
<!ENTITY le         "&#8804;"> <!-- less-than or equal to,
U+2264 ISOtech -->
<!ENTITY ge         "&#8805;"> <!-- greater-than or equal to,
                                 U+2265 ISOtech -->
<!ENTITY sub        "&#8834;"> <!-- subset of, U+2282 ISOtech
-->
<!ENTITY sup        "&#8835;"> <!-- superset of, U+2283
ISOtech -->
<!-- note that nsup, 'not a superset of, U+2283' is not cov-
ered by the Symbol
     font encoding and is not included. Should it be, for
symmetry?
     It is in ISOamsn  -->
<!ENTITY nsub       "&#8836;"> <!-- not a subset of, U+2284
ISOamsn -->
<!ENTITY sube       "&#8838;"> <!-- subset of or equal to,
U+2286 ISOtech -->
<!ENTITY supe       "&#8839;"> <!-- superset of or equal to,
                                 U+2287 ISOtech -->
<!ENTITY oplus      "&#8853;"> <!-- circled plus = direct sum,
                                 U+2295 ISOamsb -->
```

```
<!ENTITY otimes   "&#8855;"> <!-- circled times = vector
product,
                              U+2297 ISOamsb -->
<!ENTITY perp     "&#8869;"> <!-- up tack = orthogonal to =
perpendicular,
                              U+22A5 ISOtech -->
<!ENTITY sdot     "&#8901;"> <!-- dot operator, U+22C5
ISOamsb -->
<!-- dot operator is NOT the same character as U+00B7 middle
dot -->

<!-- Miscellaneous Technical -->
<!ENTITY lceil    "&#8968;"> <!-- left ceiling = apl up-
stile,
                              U+2308 ISOamsc  -->
<!ENTITY rceil    "&#8969;"> <!-- right ceiling, U+2309
ISOamsc  -->
<!ENTITY lfloor   "&#8970;"> <!-- left floor = apl down-
stile,
                              U+230A ISOamsc  -->
<!ENTITY rfloor   "&#8971;"> <!-- right floor, U+230B
ISOamsc  -->
<!ENTITY lang     "&#9001;"> <!-- left-pointing angle
bracket = bra,
                              U+2329 ISOtech -->
<!-- lang is NOT the same character as U+003C 'less than'
    or U+2039 'single left-pointing angle quotation mark'
-->
<!ENTITY rang     "&#9002;"> <!-- right-pointing angle
bracket = ket,
                              U+232A ISOtech -->
<!-- rang is NOT the same character as U+003E 'greater than'
    or U+203A 'single right-pointing angle quotation mark'
-->

<!-- Geometric Shapes -->
<!ENTITY loz      "&#9674;"> <!-- lozenge, U+25CA ISOpub -->

<!-- Miscellaneous Symbols -->
<!ENTITY spades   "&#9824;"> <!-- black spade suit, U+2660
ISOpub -->
<!-- black here seems to mean filled as opposed to hollow
-->
<!ENTITY clubs    "&#9827;"> <!-- black club suit = sham-
rock,
                              U+2663 ISOpub -->
<!ENTITY hearts   "&#9829;"> <!-- black heart suit = valen-
tine,
                              U+2665 ISOpub -->
<!ENTITY diams    "&#9830;"> <!-- black diamond suit, U+2666
ISOpub -->
```

D XML Tools and Software

IN THIS CHAPTER

- XML Editors
- DTD Software
- XML Parsers

The number of tools available to work with XML is increasing daily. Here's a partial list of what you can start using immediately.

◆ XML Editors

- XML Spy (*www.xmlspy.com*)—The front-runner of XML editors.
- EditML Pro (*www.editml.com*)
- Morphon XML-Editor (*www.morphon.com*)
- Merlot XML Editor (*www.merlotxml.org*)

For Macs

- BBEdit (*www.barebones.com*)—My personal favorite.
- ElfData XML Editor (*www.elfdata.com/xmleditor/*)
- Emile XML Editor for Macs (*www.in-progress.com/emile/*)

◆ DTD Software

- 4Suite (*www.4suite.org*)—A collection of Python tools for XML processing and object database management.

- DTD Editor for COBOL (*XML4cobol.com/*)—An XML solution for you hardcore mainframers.
- DTDExplorer (*www.mathweb.org/~paul/DTDexplorer/*)—A little Java applet that loads a DTD and visually displays all the parent-child relationships.

◆ XML Parsers

- Electric XML (*www.themindelectric.com/products/xml/xml.html*)—Open-source and Java-based, this parser is designed to have a small memory footprint as part of the GLUE distributed computing platform.
- Expat (*www.jclark.com/xml/expat.html*)—XML Parser Toolkit that's fully conformant, but doesn't validate yet (future versions likely will).
- IBM's XML for Java EA2 (*www.alphaworks.ibm.com/formula/xml*)—A Java-based validating parser that is currently supports SAX 2, DOM Level 2, and XML Schema.
- Microsoft XML Parser Version 3.0 Release (MSXML) (*msdn.microsoft.com/xml/general/xmlparser.asp*)—Implements XSLT, XPath, SAX2, and better DOM and namespace support.
- Mac OS X XML Parser (*developer.apple.com/techpubs/macosx/CoreFoundation/XMLServices/XML_Services/index.html*)—Part of the Apple Developer Connection's XML Services.
- XML::Twig (*www.xmltwig.cx/*)—A Perl module that provides a tree interface and allows very large documents to be processed without requiring the use of an event-based based parser —also known as push-pull processing.
- Ælfred XML Parser for Palm (*www.opentext.com/services/content_management_services/xml_sgml_solutions.html*)—An XML parser for the Palm.

E Keeping Up to Date on XML

There are new developments in the XML world every day, and it can take some work to find out what's going on.

- *xml.com*—Solid general XML info.
- *xml101.com*—Solid general XML info.
- *xmlhack*.com—News for the XML developer community.
- CNET Builder.com (*www.builder.com*)—Click on the XML link. More for beginners than advanced folk.
- *slashdot.org*—Great general tech info. I check this site at least once every day.
- *scripting.com*—Dave Winer's howl to the developer community. Love him or hate him, he often has some interesting things here.

Index

A

abbreviated location paths,
132–133
abbreviated predicates, 134–135
`actuate` attribute, 101, 115–116
advanced element definition, 25–28
ambiguous code, 28
&amp, 17
animation modules, 189–191
annotation, 81
`ANY`, 28
&apos, 17
arc, 96
arc-type elements, 104, 109–113
arcrole, 112–113
`arcrole` attribute, 102, 115
Attr interface, 218
attribute defaults in XML 1.0 specification, 251–252
attribute-list declarations in XML
1.0 specification, 248
attribute nodes, 129
attribute types in XML 1.0 specification, 249–251
attribute-value normalization in
XML 1.0 specification, 252–253
attributes
`CDATA` attribute, 30
complex type elements, 70–74
defining, 29–30, 70–74
and elements, 70–72

`ENTITIES` attribute, 43–44
`ENTITY` attribute, 43
`Enumerated` attribute, 32–33
`ID` attribute, 33–34
`IDREF` attribute, 34–35
`IDREFS` attribute, 35
namespaces, 88
naming, 14
`NMTOKEN` attribute, 35
`NMTOKENS` attribute, 36
`NOTATION` attribute, 44
overview, 14
rules for, 14
and text, 72–73
text, nested elements and attributes combined, 73–74
text nodes compared, 15
uses of, 70
XHTML, 98–99, 114–116
`xsd:extension`, 73
`xsd:restriction`, 72–73
AudioLayout Module, 193
autodetection of character encodings (non-normative) in XML
1.0 specification, 279–282
axis, 131–132

B

BasicAnimation Module, 189–191
BasicContentControl Module,
191–192

DATE DUE

Demco, Inc. 38-293